Michael Rush is the author of *Video Art* (Thames & Hudson, 2003), the first comprehensive survey of this medium in twenty years. A widely published writer and essayist, he has been a frequent contributor to several publications, including the *New York Times*, *Art in America*, and *Bookforum*. He is also an award-winning curator of numerous contemporary visual art exhibitions and a former writer/director for the experimental theater. He holds a doctorate from Harvard University.

D0981311

# Thames & Hudson world of art

This famous series provides the widest available range of illustrated books on art in all its aspects. If you would like to receive a complete list of titles in print please write to:

THAMES & HUDSON
181A High Holborn
London WC1V 7QX

In the United States please write to:

THAMES & HUDSON INC.
500 Fifth Avenue
New York, New York 10110

Printed in Singapore

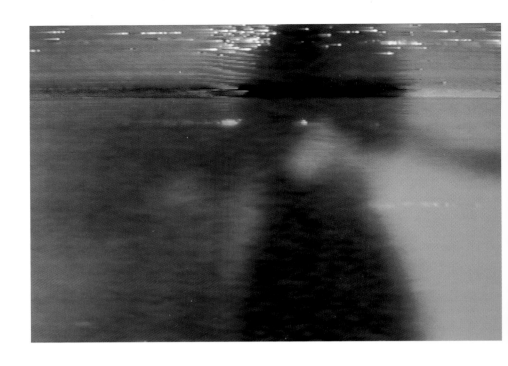

Michael Rush

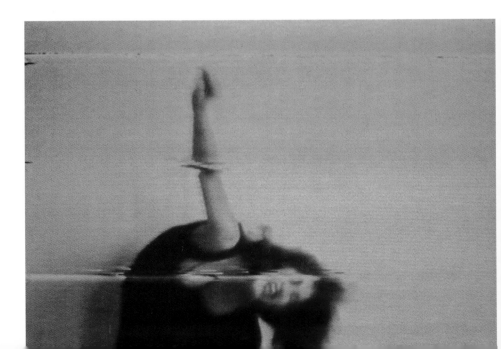

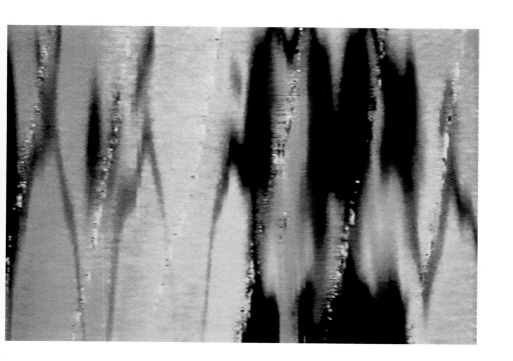

# New Media in Art

Second edition

267 illustrations, 124 in color

Thames & Hudson world of art

To Nikos Stangos, in memoriam

## Acknowledgments

*I wish to thank numerous colleagues who have shared their breadth of knowledge with me over several years, including Chrissie Iles, Christine van Assche, Lori Zippay, Galen Joseph-Hunter, Berta Sichel, John Hanhardt, Magda Sawon, Dominique Nahas, Barbara London and so many artists, to name a few, Vito Acconci, Carolee Schneemann, Martha Rosler, Michal Rovner, Douglas Gordon, Gary Hill, Thomas Hirschhorn, Grahame Weinbren. Special thanks to my editors at the* New York Times, *Annette Grant, and* Art in America, *Betsy Baker; to Electronic Arts Intermix, to Julia MacKenzie and the staff at Thames & Hudson, especially editor Andrew Brown. Thanks as well to Al Sabatini, Bill Castellino, and Lily.*

1–3. (title page) **Pipilotti Rist**,
three stills from *I'm not the Girl Who Misses Much*, 1986.

First published in 1999 in paperback in the United States of America by Thames & Hudson Inc., 500 Fifth Avenue, New York, New York 10110

thamesandhudsonusa.com

Second edition 2005

Library of Congress Catalog Card Number 2003108927

ISBN-13:  978-0-500-20378-1
ISBN-10:  0-500-20378-4

The first edition of this book was published under the title *New Media in Late 20th-Century Art*.

Designed by John Morgan
Typeset by Omnific
Printed and bound in Singapore by C.S. Graphics

# Contents

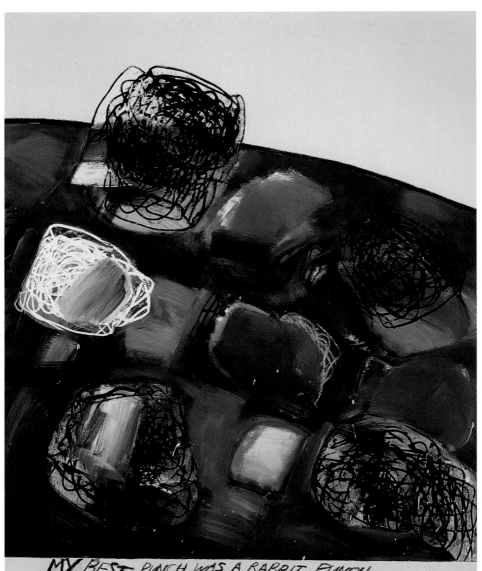

MY BEST PUNCH WAS A RABBIT PUNCH, BUT THEY WOULDN'T LET ME FIGHT A RABBIT.

# Introduction

One of the characteristic perceptions of twentieth-century art was its persistent tendency to question the long tradition of painting as the privileged medium of representation. Early in the century Braque's and Picasso's determination to incorporate everyday material in their paintings, such as newsprint, tablecloth fringe, or rope, was expressive of their struggle to extend the content of the canvas beyond paint. This 'struggle with the canvas' pointed the way for scores of twentieth-century artists, from the Russians Malevich and Tatlin, to Pollock at mid-century, to a painter such as Richard Prince (b. 1949) whose abstractions take shape in a computer before they are painted onto the canvas. Abstraction, Surrealism, and Conceptualism, to name but a few twentieth-century forms, all participated in a profound questioning of traditional painting.

This perception, while apt in some ways, is too generalized and does not tell us enough about the breadth of practices introduced in the last century. Another characterization of the period focuses on the 'experimental' nature of its art: artists bursting from the shells of painting and sculpture in a huge variety of ways and incorporating new materials into their work; paintings affixed with readymade objects or fragments of objects representing everyday life; shifts in focus away from 'objective' representation to personal expression; uses of new technological media to render meaning and new ideas of time and space. 'All art is experimental,' US film and video critic Gene Youngblood wrote, 'or it isn't art.'

The speed with which the twentieth century created an electronically linked planet is reflected in the swift expansion of art practices beyond traditional painting and sculpture to an almost frantic inclusion of everyday things into the arena of art. Anything that can be parsed as a subject or a noun has probably been included in a work of art somewhere by someone. This inclusiveness bespeaks a central preoccupation of the contemporary artist, which is to find the best possible means of making a personal statement in art. Following a complex psychological path laid down by Nietzsche and Freud that places the subject at the center of history, art, too has become entwined with 'the personal'. This view, championed by, among others, Marcel Duchamp, put the artist at the very core of the artistic enterprise in a new way. No longer under the

4. **Richard Prince**, *My Best*, 1996. Words and paint have appeared on canvases since the early part of the twentieth century, but what is not immediately apparent in this painting by Richard Prince is that the bundles of intertwining lines took shape in his computer and were then silk-screened onto the canvas.

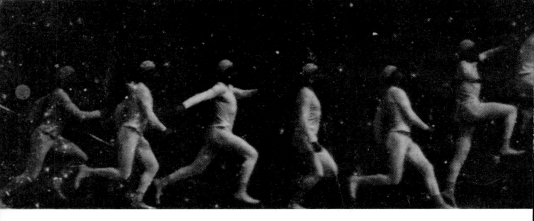

gravitational pull of the canvas, the artist was free to express any concept through whatever means possible. This concept can relate to the history of art, to the politics of the day, or to the politics of the self. The manner in which expression is conveyed and the means used to achieve it have led to such a proliferation of materials that one critic, Arthur Danto, has declared 'the end of art' as we have known it. 'It came to an end,' he writes, 'when art, as it were, recognized that there was no special way a work of art had to be.'

The final avant-garde of the twentieth century was that art that engaged the most enduring revolution of a century of revolutions: the technological revolution. Initiated by inventions outside the world of art, technology-based art (encompassing a range of practices from photography to film to video to virtual reality, and much else in between) has directed art into areas once dominated by engineers and technicians.

Curiously, while new technology itself involves a plenitude of machines, wires, and dense mathematical and physical components, the art that has been born from the art-and-technology marriage is perhaps the most ephemeral art of all: the art of time. A photograph is said to capture and preserve a moment of time; an image created inside a computer resides in no place or time at all. Images, scanned into a computer, then edited, montaged, erased, or scrambled, can seem to collapse the normal barriers of past, present, and future.

Of all the new materials introduced into art since the mid-twentieth century, this book will explore the dominant trends in media and performance, video art, video installation and digital art, including photographic manipulations, virtual reality and other interactive forms. Not daunted by technological change, artists who employ these new media see themselves as part of the change and want to participate in it. They are excited by the possi-

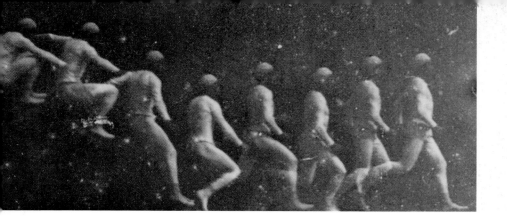

5. **Etienne-Jules Marey**, *Gymnast Jumping over a Chair*, 1883.

bilities of technology, not alienated by them. Film and television have informed their everyday experience, but unlike those who pursue commercialized uses of technologies, these artists seek to make personal statements without regard for the commodity value of what they do. Like other artists who work in paint or wood or steel, these artists explore, and often subvert, both the critical and technological potentials of the new media. That technological advances have come from some of the artists who have probed the uses of media in their work is itself an interesting by-product.

While the use of new media in art does have a history, it is not easily delineated. This history has yet to be written, largely because it is always developing. This does not mean that we cannot attempt a history, or at least a synthesis of different approaches to this history; for it is art history's duty to suggest links and point the way toward historical understanding, even within the confines of what must be a limited overview.

The simplest way to trace a history of new media in art would be through the development of the technology itself (from, say, Marey and Muybridge in photography, to Edison and the Lumière brothers in film, and so on) but then all we would have is a timeline similar to the one devoted to the development of aviation. While certain key artists and movements in twentieth-century art present themselves as precursors to artists who work in technological media (what branch of contemporary art, for example, would not claim Marcel Duchamp as a predecessor?) with this art no straightforward linear narrative is possible. Not only are we still in the midst of the story, the story itself began and continues with simultaneous activities among different kinds of artists in separate parts of the world. For these reasons a thematic approach seems more appropriate than a strictly chronological one.

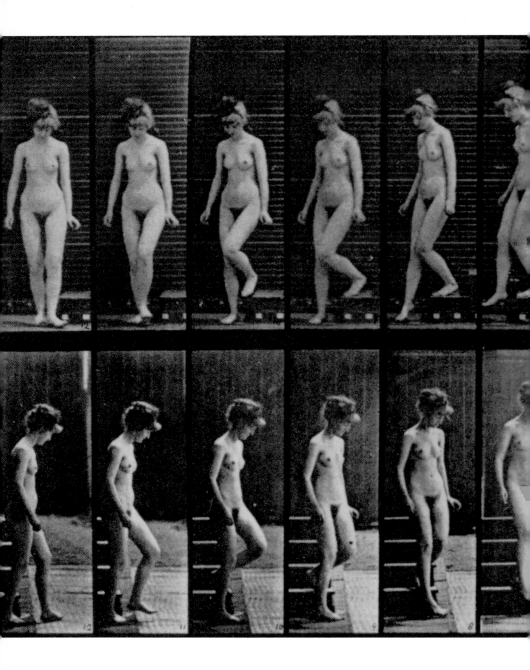

6. Eadweard Muybridge,
*Descending Stairs and Turning
Around* from the series *Animal
Locomotion*, 1884–85.

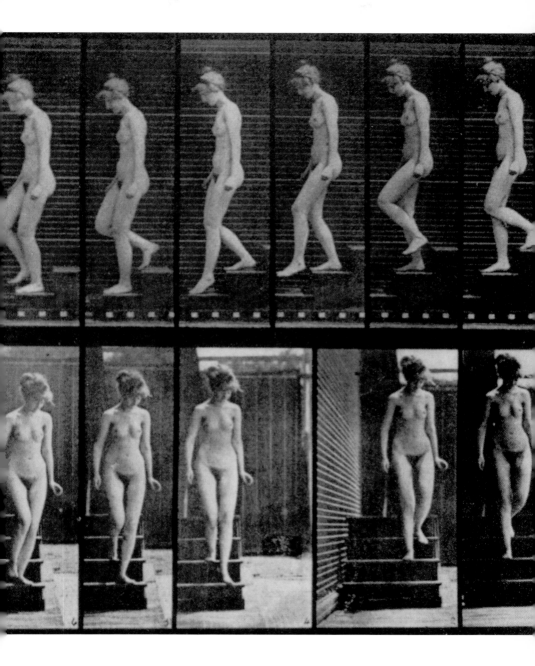

## Time Art

After the mid-1960s, as critic and curator Anne-Marie Duguet has said, 'Time emerged not only as a recurrent theme but also as a constituent parameter of the very nature of an art work.' With the emergence of performances, events, Happenings, installations, then videos, the temporality of the art form was central. Currently, computer-based interactive art supplies and requires a suspension of time as the viewer enters into a contract with the machine that inaugurates and sustains the art action.

The story of media art is inextricably linked to developments in photography throughout the century. Time and memory, both personal and historical, are the substance of photography, and with the still and moving image, artists and amateurs were introduced to a new way of visualizing time. Representation clearly involves space (the space occupied by the object represented and the space of the painting or sculpture itself; the placement of the image, etc.); but less clear is time, and this is where the revolution wrought by photography and its now bigger cousin, moving photography, film, assumes its place of importance. With photography, humans began to participate in the manipulation of time itself: capturing it, reconfiguring it, and creating variations on it with time lapses, fast forward, slow motion, and all those other time-related phrases which are proper to the art and science of photography.

The French philosopher Henri Bergson's (1859–1941) study of 'time' strongly influenced artists of all stripes: photographers, painters, writers, choreographers, videographers. Bergson placed time at the center of metaphysics; for him, reality consisted of flux, essentially the movement of time. 'The essence of time is that it goes by,' he wrote in his immensely influential book, *Matter and Memory* (1896). 'What I call "my present" has one foot in my past, and another in the future.' These notions were seized upon by artists and critics, and throughout the Western world even popular magazines would discuss Bergson's notions of time because they addressed a universal hunger for understanding. For artists, who had always been fascinated with the body in space and time, he became a muse who championed the interaction between intuition and perception. Ironically, potent as his ideas were for artists, Bergson disdained the introduction of technology into the arts, believing that the pure perception allowed by intuition, unaided by machines, was what mattered.

From the beginnings of photography, however, art and technology co-existed in an essential bond that has benefitted

7. **Eadweard Muybridge**, *La Nature: Studies in Animal Locomotion*, 1878.

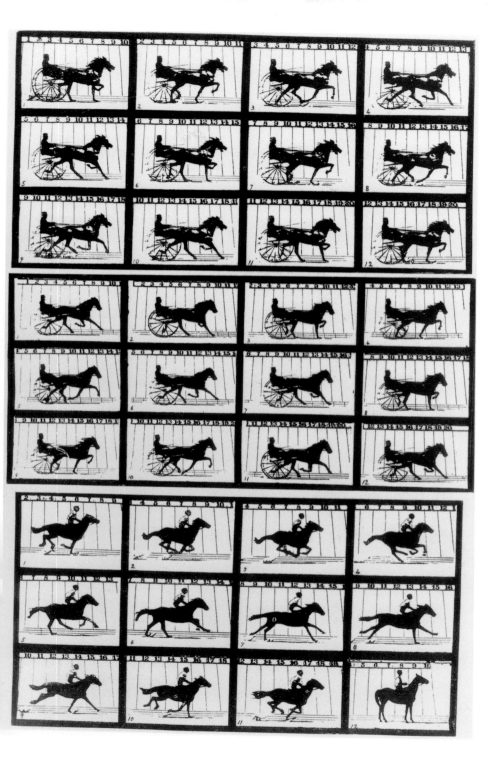

both for more than one hundred years. Etienne-Jules Marey (1830–1904), a scientist and physician whose tenure at the Collège de France overlapped with Bergson's in the early 1900s, and Eadweard Muybridge (1830–1904), an artist, were the pioneers of instantaneous photography, or 'chronophotography,' which had a profound effect on artists, from Futurists, especially Giacomo Balla, to Marcel Duchamp, Kurt Schwitters, and mid-century avant-garde filmmakers like Hollis Frampton and Stan Brakhage. Seurat, Degas and many other artists were also taken with the camera's ability to capture successive movement in still frames, but their interest was not directly obvious in their canvases. Artists like the Futurists who propounded a mechanistic aesthetic embraced photographic technology and applied it to their painting. Towards mid-century, as we shall see, it was the technological advances in film and video that were adopted by artists to create what we know now as multi-media art.

8. **Giacomo Balla**, *Dynamism of a Dog on a Leash*, 1912. Balla creates the illusion of motion through a series of minute, radiating diagonals.

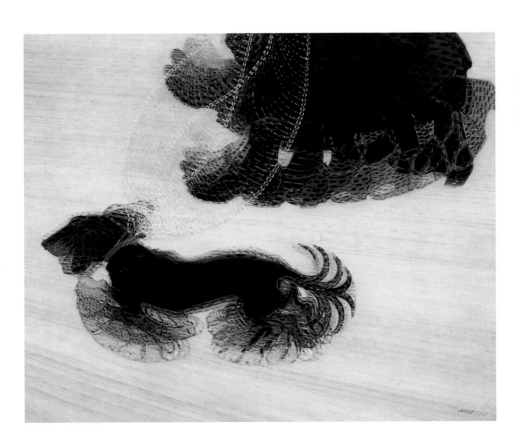

Muybridge's 1878 photographs of horses in motion were the first to capture what looked like the actual, discrete sequence of motion. Muybridge devised the means of portraying the speed of a horse's running by the action of several cameras (in this case, twelve) set up in a row and arranged to go off in sequence as the horse ran by. He attached a piece of string to the shutter and extended it across the horse's path. As the horse ran in front of Muybridge's cameras the shutters were released by the horse's movements over the string, each making an image at 1/200th of a second. The resulting images, when placed next to each other, showed the horse in what appeared to be continuous rapid movement. Muybridge went on to use as many as twenty-four cameras in his attempts to perfect the capturing of motion. The results of his efforts comprise the eleven-volume *Studies in Animal Locomotion* 7 (1888). Initially, his photographs were intended as adjuncts to scientific studies, but quickly they were adopted by artists in their studies of human and animal motion.

In 1911, the Futurist Carlo Carrà depicted motion in *Funeral of the Anarchist Galli* and in 1912 Giacomo Balla painted the extraordinary *Dynamism of a Dog on a Leash*. Umberto Boccioni, like them, turned to photographic studies to learn how the portrayal of movement is realized through repetition. His *Dynamism of a Cyclist* (1913) offers proof of the drama in dynamic sequencing of images.

Marcel Duchamp's *Nude Descending a Staircase, No. 2* (1912), 10 one of the most controversial paintings of its time, took direct inspiration from several of Muybridge's studies, perhaps especially *Ascending and Descending Stairs* (1884–85), in which a woman 9 can be seen carrying a water bucket up, then down, the stairs.

*Film and Avant-Garde Cinema I*

As revolutionary as these 'studies in time' may have appeared, another means of capturing movement was evolving across the Atlantic that would mark the emergence of one of the major artistic influences of the twentieth century: cinema. Both popular and avant-garde cinema of the early century were to have a profound impact on media art of the mid-century.

Cinema was developed in the laboratories of American inventor Thomas Edison (1847–1931) who assigned his assistant William Kennedy Laurie Dickson (1860–1935) to use the phonograph as a model for making moving images that could be watched through a viewer. In 1890, Dickson made a moving image camera called the Kinetograph, followed a year later by the Kinetoscope viewer. By 1895, several innovators, starting with the Lumière

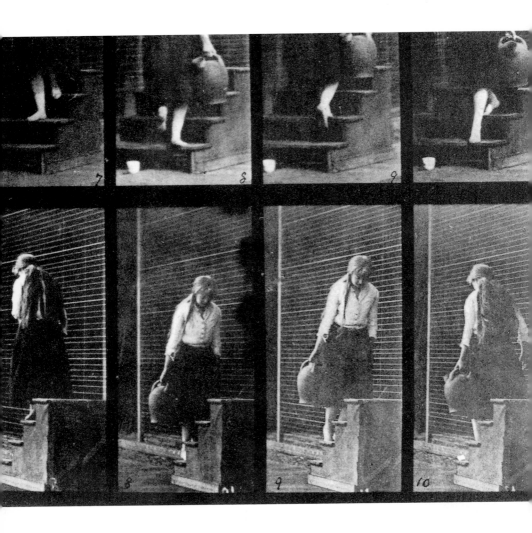

9. (above) **Eadweard Muybridge**,
*Ascending and Descending Stairs*
from the series *Animal
Locomotion*, 1884–85.

10. (right) **Marcel Duchamp**,
*Nude Descending a Staircase,
No. 2*, 1912.
Duchamp abstracted Muybridge's
studies in motion in his own exploratic
of time and the fourth dimension.

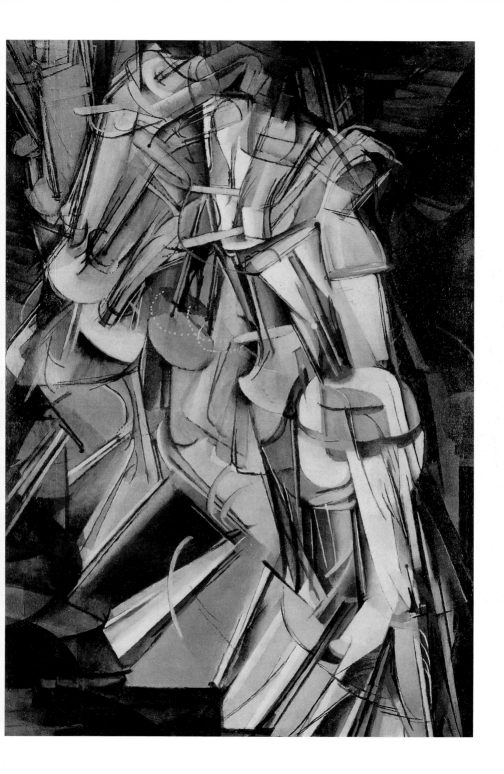

brothers, had projected filmed images onto screens for a paying public. In quick succession, Frenchman George Melies (1861–1938), often referred to as 'the first screen artist,' introduced dissolves, time-lapse photography, and artful lighting (the essence of cinematography) in films such as *Cinderella* (1899) and *The Dreyfus Affair* (1899). Looking very much like an out-take from a 1950s science fiction film, Melies's *A Trip to the Moon*, 1902, shows a 'rocket' landing in the eye of the 'man in the moon.' In 1903, Edwin S. Porter from Edison's lab made *The Great Train Robbery* in which editing techniques were used for the first time to establish continuity and to create narrative tension.

The art of film attracted several practitioners right away who made lasting contributions to the form. As early as 1915, the American D. W. Griffith (1875–1948) made his epic *The Birth of the Nation* followed only a year later by *Intolerance*, an interweaving of four narratives exposing the dangers of hypocrisy throughout history. Other early directors whose work is still referenced by artists in international cinema would include Frenchmen Louis Feuillade and Abel Gance (1889–1981), the Germans F. W. Murnau (1888–1931) and Fritz Lang (1890–1976), the Swede Victor Sjöström, the British-born Charlie Chaplin (1889–1977) and the Russian Sergei Eisenstein (1898–1948).

Eisenstein's work is a clear product of the dynamic interplay between art, technology and life during the Soviet avant-garde period (roughly from 1915 to 1932). He represented a new type of media artist who had training in mathematics, engineering and art, and was for several years in his youth a theater designer with Russian avant-garde director Vsevolod Meyerhold (1874–1940). Eisenstein, expressing his links to Constructivism and Cubism, perfected the techniques of cinematic montage (initiated by D. W. Griffith), which enabled him to manipulate emotional responses through the vibrant processes of film editing. Eisenstein sought new ways of seeing which would parallel the new world image under Marxism. His art has clearly outlived the political struggle that nurtured it. Film critic Stanley Kaufman, writing about *The Battleship Potemkin* (1925), noted that Eisentein 'felt that a new society meant a new kind of vision; that the way people saw things must be altered; that it was insufficient to put new material before old eyes.'

In a certain sense, given his background in the technology of engineering, Eisenstein is the perfect paradigm for the technological artist. He thought of his cinema as totally utilitarian, rational, and materialistic, claiming that he merely applied what he learned in mathematics and engineering to the making of his films. If the Russian avant-garde can be characterized by the tension between Vladimir Tatlin's view of art as an industrial process and Kazimir Malevich and Vasily Kandinsky's aesthetically based 'pure feeling' of art, Eisenstein would side with Tatlin. Nonetheless, long after its utility had passed (as a tool for exciting support among the masses for the Revolution) his film *The Battleship Potemkin*, for example, is heralded for the sheer energy of its emotional peaks and unflinching vision and artistry.

Eisenstein's dynamic images, accomplished by varied camera angles and sophisticated montage editing, owe much to the fragmented shapes of Cubism, in which multiple views of reality (seen simultaneously as if from above and from the side in repetitive layerings) allowed for multiple understandings of reality. This key aspect of modernism, enhancing perception by altering it, found a home in Russian photography and cinematography of the 1920s and 1930s. Russian filmmaker Dziga Vertov (1896–1954), though overshadowed in history by Eisenstein, was equally influential in his development of montage techniques for his politically charged films such as *The Man with the Movie Camera* (1929).

During the same period, the century-long tradition of avant-garde film in France was taking hold, strongly influenced by the writings of Louis Delluc (1890–1924) who called for a 'pure' cinema, equal to a 'symphonic poem based on images,' as distinct from the melodramas that were then dominating American, French, and German films. Abstract art, cubism, and collage all made an appearance in films by visual artists Man Ray (*Return to Reason*, 1923)

12

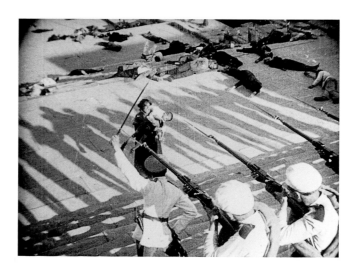

11. **Sergei Eisenstein**, still from *The Battleship Potemkin*, 1925. Artist and engineer Sergei Eisenstein joined the precision of science with the vision of art in films that he felt advanced the cause of the Bolshevik Revolution.

and Fernand Léger (*Le Ballet mécanique*, 1924), as well as filmmakers René Clair (*Entr'acte*, 1924) and Luis Buñuel (*L'Age d'or*, made with Salvador Dalí, 1930). Abel Gance perhaps best represented Dulac's 'cinematic poem' in films such as *Dr Tube's Mania* (1915), *J'accuse* (1919), *La Roue* (1922), and especially his magnum opus, *Napoleon* (1927). Other examples of early avant-garde cinema include the German Expressionist classic *The Cabinet of Dr Caligari* (1919), directed by Robert Wiene, and *A Page of Madness* (1926) by Japanese director Teinosuke Kinugasa.

Thus, by the beginning of the twentieth century, the photography of images of movement, first achieved by Muybridge in 1878, had evolved into the 'illusion' of mechanically produced movement which is cinema. Within a few short years an aesthetic of the poetic image developed and the captured (or filmed) image, aided by the still photography of László Moholy-Nagy and his peer Alfred Stieglitz, assumed an undeniable legitimacy as an art form. Art and technology, as represented by still photography and cinema, were becoming forever entwined as the thematic dichotomy between art and life gradually dissolved in the face of ubiquitous machines.

As cinema became more and more dominated by Hollywood from the late 1920s and into the 1940s the international avant-garde languished somewhat until its renewal in the US in the 1950s. Meanwhile, the visual arts were undergoing radical transformations under the influence of European Dada, especially as practised by Marcel Duchamp (1887–1968), whose importance to the issue of art and new media is central.

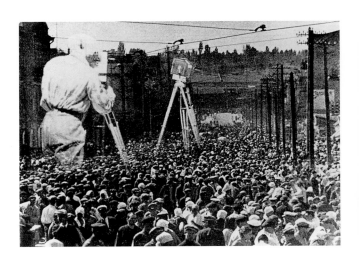

12. **Dziga Vertov**, still from *The Man with the Movie Camera*, 1929. Along with Eisenstein, Dziga Vertov created 'dialectical montage,' or a use of multiple images aimed at 'liberating the sight of the masses' in the new Russia.

13. **László Moholy-Nagy**, *Lightprop*, 1922, from the film *Ein Lichtspiel: Schwarz/Weiss/Grau* (Light Play: Black/White/Grey), 1922–30.

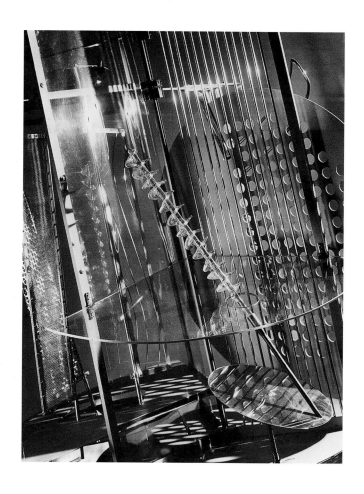

## Duchamp to Cage to Fluxus

How one feels about Marcel Duchamp is, essentially, how one feels about a great deal of contemporary art, so profound was his influence. He stepped outside any confining notion of art, and with his readymades (the wheels, shovels, coat racks he chose to exhibit as art), forced the question 'What is art?' to its deepest level. Duchamp produced a prodigious body of work extending from painting, to mixed media (*The Large Glass*, also known as *The Bride Stripped Bare by Her Bachelors, Even*, 1915–23), to installation (*Etant donnés*, 1946–66), to film (*Anemic Cinema*, 1926). Duchamp's radical shift of emphasis from object to concept allowed for multiple methods to be introduced to a redefined artistic enterprise. His importance to the present study rests not only in what he did but in what he allowed or initiated in art. The type of thinking he encouraged made explo-

15

14

rations into different media and artistic forms seem very natural, almost expected. Especially for those who found the 'business' of art so distasteful, Duchamp's liberal approach to materials and forms detached the object from commercial appeal, at least initially, because it was the *idea* that was important; and it was not yet clear how to sell an idea. (Later Conceptual artists, properly so called, like Sol LeWitt, Donald Judd and Joseph Kosuth, figured out a way.)

For artists of the late 1950s and 1960s who were in one way or another influenced by Duchamp in their thinking about what constituted art, no material seemed out of place as a means of personal expression. Joseph Beuys (1921–86) – who criticized Duchamp for his lack of political engagement – exhibited felt suits; Robert Rauschenberg affixed pillows and quilts to canvases.

By the late 1950s the time was right for an artistic iconoclast like Duchamp to exert wide influence, especially in America,

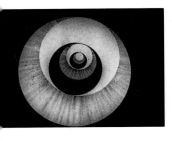

14. (above) **Marcel Duchamp**, *Optical disc No. 10* from *Anemic Cinema*, 1925–26.

15. (right) **Marcel Duchamp**, *The Large Glass (The Bride Stripped Bare by Her Bachelors Even)*, 1915–23.
For Duchamp, everyday objects like the chocolate grinder (visible in the lower portion of this work on glass), replete with its manufactured geometrical design, liberated him from 'the cubist straitjacket,' as he called it.

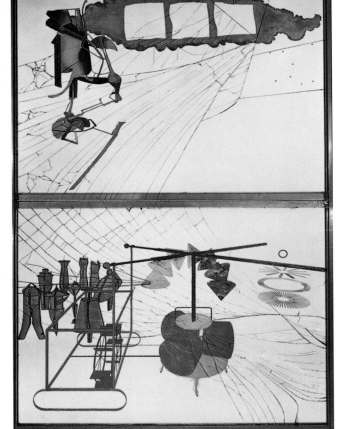

where he had settled permanently after the Second World War. Younger American artists had wearied of the hegemony of Abstract Expressionism whose rugged, gestural style had become synonymous with American art. There was a restlessness in the art world that was manifested in the emergence of Pop art and the multimedia experiments of John Cage (1912–92) and his Black Mountain College collaborators: Robert Rauschenberg, dancer/choreographer Merce Cunningham, and musician David Tudor. Furthermore, by 1950 the important writings of European and American Dadaists, including Duchamp, had been collected and published by Robert Motherwell and were becoming well known.

Cage, with his own synthesis of Eastern philosophy and experimental music (inherited from Arnold Schönberg, among others), began having a great influence on younger artists through

16. (below) **Joseph Beuys**, *Felt Suit*, 1970.

17. (below right) **Robert Rauschenberg**, *Bed*, 1955.

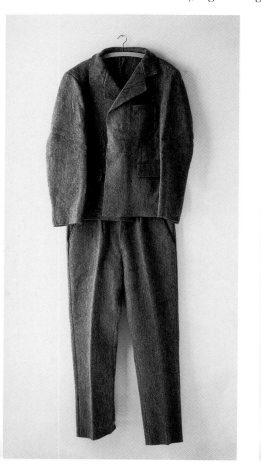

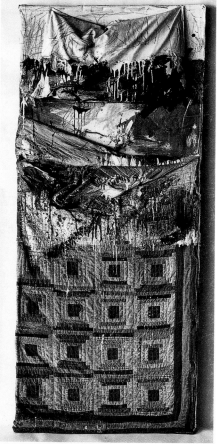

his teaching at Black Mountain, then at the New School for Social Research in New York, where his classes on new music attracted future performance artists like Allan Kaprow (b. 1927) and Richard Higgins (b. 1938). Based on his studies of the *I Ching (Book of Changes)* and Zen Buddhism, Cage emphasized the element of 'chance' in art as a valid way of making a work. His music compositions incorporated ambient noises from the street, sounds produced by pounding on the wood and strings of a piano, and, uniquely, silence (*4' 33"*, 1952). His notions became epitomized in the choroegraphy of his companion Merce Cunningham whose intricate dance steps reflect the essence of non-sequential movement exercizes.

Armed with notions of art as an idea and the role of chance in life and art, artists were ready for a new explosion of creativity as epitomized by Fluxus, an 'intermedia' movement that flourished in the 1960s and inaugurated several innovations in performance, film, and, eventually, video. Fluxus was an international movement of artists, writers, filmmakers, and musicians under the leadership of George Maciunas (1931–78), the Lithuanian-born provocateur who organized the early Fluxus events, first at AG Gallery in New York (1961) and then at festivals in Europe starting in 1962. Similar in spirit to Dada (Maciunas's manifesto described it as 'Neo-Dada in music, theater, poetry, art'), Fluxus, as an avant-garde, was anti-art, particularly art as the exclusive property of museums and collectors. It made jabs at the seriousness of high modernism and attempted, following Duchamp, to affirm what the Fluxists felt to be an essential link between everyday objects and events and art. They made this notion manifest in minimal, yet acessible performances. A Fluxus event, as defined by German-American artist George Brecht, was the smallest unit of a situation. One, devised by artist Mieko Shiomi, was described as 'an open event.' The event was simply 'an invitation to open something which is closed.' Participants were asked to write down exactly what happened during their 'event.' This simple charge became a statement against the loftiness of museum art as well as a participatory action as people gathered to perform it.

Similarly minimal music compositions, referred to as 'scores' by John Cage, stripped all artifice from the orchestral or performance setting and required only attention to a minute detail. LaMonte Young's (b. 1935) *Piano Piece for David Tudor #2* (1960) consisted of this direction: 'Open the keyboard cover without making, from the operation, any sound that is audible to you. Try as many times as you like.' These minimal instructions, present in all Fluxus performances, whether of a so-called musical nature or not, opened the event to multiple interpretations as well as accidents. Anything could happen during one of these events, resulting in chance occurrences and the desired multiple interpretations. Audience members became participants (or co-conspirators), no longer passive observers. Fluxus events thus became the perfect embodiments of Duchamp's dictum that the viewer completes the work of art. Indeed, with Fluxus, the viewer not only completes, but actually becomes the work of art in his or her direct participation in the event.

A minimal aesthetic began to develop, inherited from concrete poetry, Dada manifestos and experimental music, and extended to film as well, becoming an important element in the development of media art. Fluxfilms, as they are referred to, comprise approximately forty short films created by several of the artists (few of them filmmakers) associated with Fluxus. Nam June Paik's *Zen for Film* (1962–64), a prototypical Fluxus film, was presented at the Fluxhall (Maciunas's loft on New York's Canal Street). Actually an early installation (a tableau consisting of a home movie screen, an upright piano, and double bass), Paik's film turned its back to the entire mechanism of large scale moviemaking (from expensive film stock to lights, sets, optical effects editing, marketing, etc.). The film was nothing more than approximately one thousand feet of clear 16-millimetre leader projected, unprocessed, onto the screen with a running time of thirty minutes. Stripping film to its barest essential (the film stock itself), Paik's imageless projection became the minimalist example for all Fluxfilms to follow.

American film writer and curator Bruce Jenkins makes the cogent observation that Paik, in subverting the usual expectations of film viewing, 'instilled a performative aspect into the screening context and, in the process, liberated the viewer from the manipulations of both the commercial and the alternative cinema.' Without images or sound, Paik's film became a *tabula rasa* for the viewer's free associations. With each additional screening of the film, scratches, dust, and other chance events of film projection inevitably occurred, thus rendering the film new, in a certain way, each time.

Fluxus artist and photographer Peter Moore (b. 1932), using a high-speed, slow motion camera, made *Disappearing Music for Face* (1966). Based on another performance score by Mieko Shiomi (which, *in toto*, reads: 'Performers begin the piece with a smile and

19

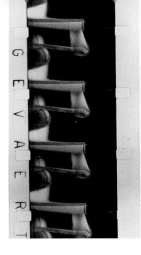

during the duration of the piece, change the smile very gradually to no-smile') the film featured Yoko Ono (b. 1933), another Fluxus artist. Ono's mouth, chin, and cheeks are seen in close-up, revealing the minute changes in expression that occur during the film. Shot in only eight seconds of film time, when projected in slow motion, it ran for eleven minutes.

Another fragment of Ono's face, this time her right eye, is featured in *Eyeblink* (*c.* 1961), which, as its title suggests, is the most minimal of all acts. Ono's own film, *No. 1* (*c.* 1964), recalling the still photographs of Harold Edgerton, features a slow-burning match, suggesting perhaps the dangerous underside of even the most minimal act.

By 1966, Fluxus had produced a body of films that, in their elemental nature (also referred to as essentialist), called into question all of the common associations viewers bring to the watching of a film, including being the one observed (as Ono stares into the camera at the end of *Disappearing Music for Face*). George Maciunas made his own film, *10 Feet* (1966), consisting entirely of ten feet of clear lead. Other Fluxfilms included George Brecht's *Entry-Exit* (1965), which consisted of a shot of the word 'Entrance' on a plain white wall which gradually fades to dark then lightens to reveal the word 'Exit,' and James Riddle's *Nine Minutes* (1966), in which stencilled numbers appear on the black screen every minute.

18. (above) **Yoko Ono**, *Filmstrip from Film No. 1 (Fluxfilm No.14) – Lighting Piece*, 1955/1966.

19. (below) **Nam June Paik**, *Zen for Film*, 1964.
The spare aesthetic of Minimalism was adopted even by the iconoclastic artists of Fluxus. Here Nam June Paik projected clear film leader inside a television set.

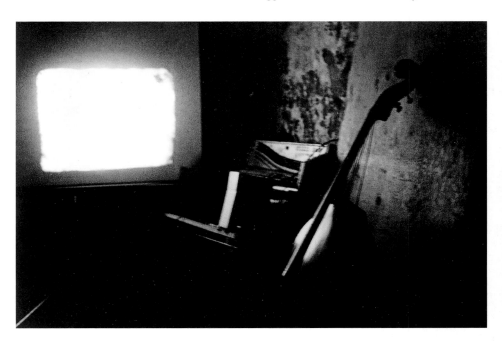

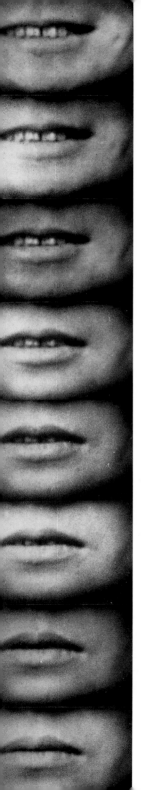

While Fluxfilms are generally considered critiques of mainstream and even avant-garde film, they also generated a new energy in filmmaking with their simplicity and playfulness. From our remove, it is clear that Fluxfilms like Paik's *Zen for Film* or Michael Snow's *Wavelength* (1969), though ostensibly concerned with the essentials of film and film technique, are, in themselves, highly poetic and meditative works. Though nothing in art or life seemed sacred to them, Fluxists found meaning in the everyday material of their art (whether it be their bodies, or the strings of their pianos, or the leader of their film).

Some of the targets of the Fluxists, in terms of film, were the tremendously influential new wave French filmmakers, especially Jean-Luc Godard (b. 1930), and the American Stan Brakhage (b. 1933). With Godard representing the political/poetic art film and Brakhage the personal/poetic, their films comprise what to the Fluxists were the elitist strategies of both poles of the avant-garde. Not everyone was Fluxist, however, and avant-garde cinema thrived in the middle of the twentieth century as it had earlier.

*Film and Avant-Garde Cinema II*
The fervor for cinematic experimentation reached a peak in the 1950s and 1960s, first in the United States, then in France. The Eastman Kodak Company had released 16-millimetre film for amateur use in 1923, but even it was too expensive for most independent artists. As its use became more commonplace by mid-century, artists, though still relatively few in number, began to make films. Among the most influential are the Americans Stan Brakhage, Kenneth Anger, Hollis Frampton, Maya Deren (born in Russia), Jack Smith, Bruce Conner, Marie Menken, Andy Warhol, Pat O'Neill, Jordan Belson, and John Whitney, the Canadian Michael Snow and the Greek-American Gregory Markopoulos.

In his *Allegories of Cinema* (1989), American film historian David James noted that most of these filmmakers, several of whom had migrated into filmmaking from other media, brought issues that preoccupied painters to film. Among these he included the representation of motion and duration; and the expression of 'extraordinary psychological states.' While the latter could be said of any art form (poetry, fiction, drama), the former resulted from the originating tactics of the technology of photography. The technology improved when artists adopted it but the

20. **Mieko (Chieko) Shiomi,**
*Disappearing Music for Face*, 1966.

technology came first. As we shall see in later chapters, James indicates that artists who came to technological media from other forms often transferred their painterly or sculptural concerns to the new medium, whether film, video, or digital art. Naturally, other artists have engaged new media from the start, not as a secondary practice.

Markopoulos and Warhol will serve as good examples of each approach. Gregory Markopoulos (1928–92), who as a teenager studied with Hollywood director Josef von Sternberg, represents the filmmaker as poet, a phrase one might also use to describe Stan Brakhage. By eighteen Markopoulos had begun shooting what is still considered a classic of avant-garde cinema, the trilogy, *Du Sang, De la Volupté, et De la Mort* (Of Blood, Pleasure, and Death, 1947–48). In subsequent films such as *Swain* (1950), *Twice a Man* (1963), and *The Mysteries* (1968), he made original use of color, composition, rhythm, and fractured temporal structures. Often inspired by classic works of Greek mythology, Markopoulos's films explored abstract narratives with an economy of means that incorporated his own inventions, including in-camera editing, a radical approach based on the single frame rather than the single shot. *The Illiac Passion* (1964–67), based on Aeschylus's *Prometheus Bound*, featured several well known underground personalities of the 1960s cast as mythical figures: Andy Warhol as Poseidon, Jack Smith as Orpheus, Taylor Meade as Sprite, Kenneth King as Adonis, and the Beauvais brothers, Richard and David, as Prometheus and his conscience. After he moved to Europe in 1967, Markopoulos made over one hundred films, many of which remain unprinted.

The use of 16-millimetre film continues among avant-garde filmmakers but to a much lesser extent, having been replaced by digital video which can be transferred to film. American-born Robert Beavers (b. 1949) explores abstract associations between the human form, visual art and architecture in films such as *The Painting* (1977–97) and *Efpsychi* (1997). American Lawrence 24, Brose (b. 1951) investigates Oscar Wilde's notions of aesthetics and desire in his abstract 16-millimetre film *De Profundis* (1997). American Ernie Gehr (b. 1941) has made two dozen experimental films in 16-millimetre since 1967. In *Serene Velocity* (1970) he focuses his camera on a corridor in an office building. Nothing ever moves in this twenty-three minute film except for Gehr's camera lens which he alternates between the zoom setting and normal every quarter of a second, thus giving the impression that the corridor is shaking.

Representative of artists coming to film from another medium, Andy Warhol (1928–87), intrigued by the 'underground' films of his acquaintances Jonas Meekas and Jack Smith, began making films in 1963. Obviously enamored of the reproducibility of art objects through his experience as a designer and print maker (e.g. *100 Campbell's Soup Cans*, 1962, or *35 Jackies*, 1963), as well as photographer, Warhol was naturally drawn to the moving camera. He was not immune to fame, to say the least, knowing full well 'movies' were the most alluring path to it. He made over sixty films between 1963 and 1968, many of them classics of the underground genre. In films such *Sleep* (1963), featuring actor John Giorno sleeping for six hours in front of a stationary camera; *Kiss* (1963), with its extended close-ups of couples kissing; and *Eat* (1964), in which artist Robert Indiana slowly eats one mushroom, Warhol confounded viewers with a mix of real and filmic time. With Warhol the underground surfaced for a while as his films found their way into legitimate theaters. He also translated to the canvas filmic techniques of editing, repetition of frames, and structural tension. In his famous portraits of actresses Marilyn Monroe and Elizabeth Taylor, he also joined the legends of Hollywood to avant-garde art, while aligning himself with both at the same time.

Occupying an uneasy place between commercial and avant-garde cinema is the Swiss-born Jean-Luc Godard. In his more than seventy films and full-length videos since the late 1950s, he has repeatedly questioned the nature of cinema itself. In his ongoing project *Histoire(s) du cinema* (History(ies) of Cinema, begun in 1989), a combination of film and video, he traces the entire history of worldwide film via many layers of images, interwoven with superimposed texts and loud music. For Godard, montage reveals rather than obfuscates deeper truths.

21. (below) **Andy Warhol**, *Kiss*, 1963.

22. (below right) **Andy Warhol**, *Eat*, 1964, with Robert Indiana. Warhol's early films represent the artist's manipulation of time. Repetition, freeze frames, extended stationary camera shots, and retarded projection speeds all conspired to alter the viewer's experience of time.

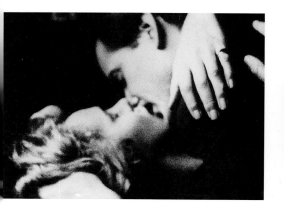

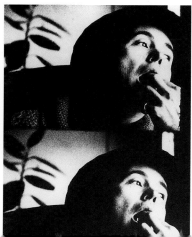

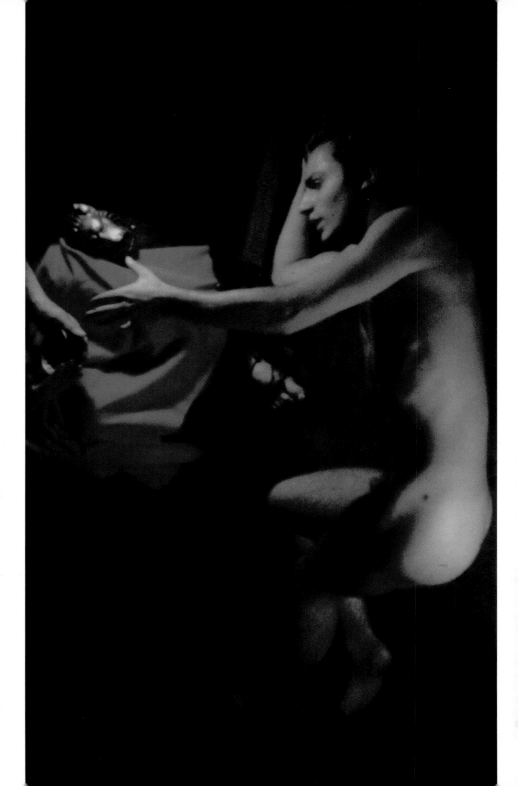

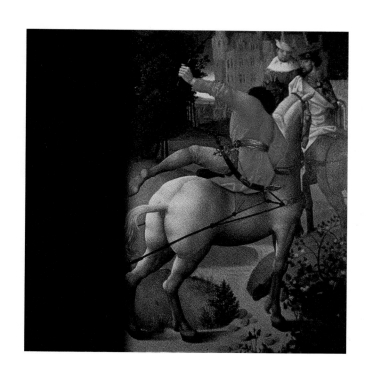

23. (left) **Gregory J. Markopolous**, *The Illiac Passion*, 1964–67. Gerard Malanga as Ganymede and Paul Swan as Zeus. Less 'cool' (or distant) than Warhol, Gregory Markopoulos filmed what he called 'emotional landscapes,' rich in color and composition, enhanced by his own in-camera editing device.

24, 25. (right and above) **Robert Beavers**, *The Painting*, 1977/1997. Detail shows a side panel of *The Martyrdom of St Hippolytus* in the Museum of Fine Arts, Boston. Continuing in the spirit of 1960s formal experimentation, Beavers juxtaposes images to create emotional tension. The figure on horseback is one of the executioners tearing the saint apart, while the young man below (Beavers himself) looks nervously through a window.

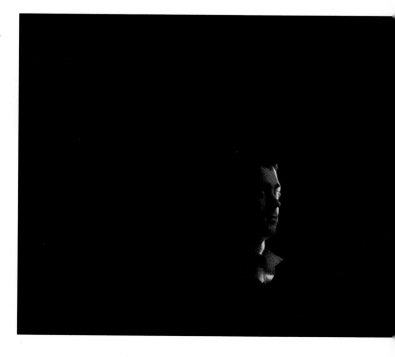

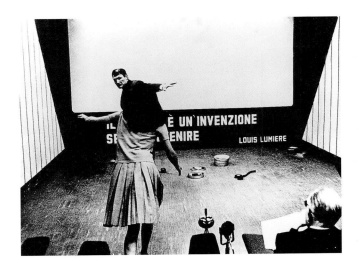

26, 27. **Jean-Luc Godard**, two stills from *Le Mépris* (Contempt), 1963. Strongly influenced by Russian revolutionary filmmakers, especially Dziga Vertov, Jean-Luc Godard has created a personal and political cinema constructed on what he calls 'sound, image, and text.'

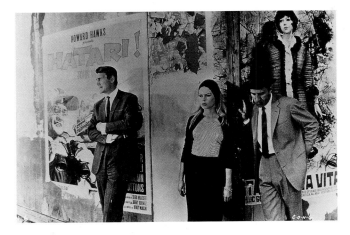

Often neglected by critics until recently, 8-millimetre films, introduced in 1932 and the cheapest alternative available, became quite popular among hobbyists as well as artists after the war. Following in the footsteps of 16-millimetre, the 8-millimetre film became even more of a protest against the excesses of Hollywood. Compact, cheap, and easy to hold, this camera became the means of personal expression for artists shut out of the commercial system. It also attracted artists who made careers out of the filmed media rather than practising it occasionally while engaged in their primary medium.

Artists such as Ken Jacobs, Saul Levine, George and Mike Kuchar, Joe Gibbons, Lewis Klahr, Robert C. Morgan, and Stan

Brakhage, among scores of others, made singular, intimate films with 8-millimetre stock. Ken Jacobs made quirky, diaristic films that use actors (*Winter Sky*, 1964) and family members (he and his wife on their honeymoon in *We Stole Away*, 1964). In *Window* (1964) the small camera becomes an extension of the artist's body. In a similar vein, Saul Levine's *Saul's Scarf* (1966–67) and *Note to Pati* (1969) are poetic, often fast-paced, personal narratives. Especially memorable for capturing innocence and youth are scenes shot in the snow in *Note to Pati*.

Use of 8-millimetre continued into the 1990s. Peggy Ahwesh's (b. 1954) *The Fragments Project* (1984–94) contains an intimate look at the characters who populate her personal life. More abstract is Scott Stark's *Acceleration* (1993) which captures the traces of a moving train from the perspective of a stationary camera.

The 16-millimetre and 8-millimetre cameras were portable and available for artists to own, rent or borrow. Many did, not only to make experimental films, but also to record the work they were doing in their studios or to use in performances. And soon, yet more portable, and eventually more affordable, the Sony Portapak video camera became available and a new chapter in media art began.

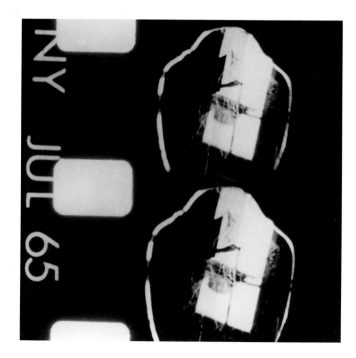

28. **Ken Jacobs**, *Window*, 1964. For Jacobs, 'There was a short period when Underground Film was a buzzword. There was the kind of glow of celebrity about some of the people making work. The celebrity made those people crazy and the lack of celebrity made the rest of us crazy.'

Following pages:
29. **Scott Stark**, *Acceleration*, 1993. For artists like Scott Stark, 8-millimetre film was a portable and affordable means to approximate the texture and rich color of more expensive film.

# Chapter 1:   Media and Performance

In 1949 the canvas was dripped and poured on by the American Jackson Pollock (*No. 1*), slashed by Argentinian-born Lucio Fontana (*Concetto Spaziale*) and punctured by Japanese Shozo Shimamoto (*Work [Holes]*). In each of these paintings, done within months of each other, the face of art was changed, contended American curator Paul Schimmel, as the painterly action took precedence over the painted subject. A worldwide contingent of artists including Allan Kaprow, Georges Mathieu, Yves Klein, Atsuko Tanaka, Otto Muehl, Gunther Brus, Joseph Beuys, Jean Tinguely, Niki de Saint Phalle, Robert Rauschenberg, and Piero Manzoni, soon extended the gestural art of Pollock into actual Performances, Happenings, and Events. The social and sexual revolutions of the 1960s found expression in art that was directed away from the canvas into actions that incorporated the viewer into the work of art. For American artists at this time it was a short step from action painting (Jackson Pollock's all-over and free application of paint) to action itself as a form of art. Disenchanted with the canonization of Abstract Expressionism by critic Clement Greenberg and seeking greater freedom of expression in the spirit of the times, artists from New York, and, soon after, from California, declared their repudiation of the canvas. Writing in *Art News* in 1958, Allan Kaprow stated 'Pollock's near destruction of this tradition [painting] may well be a return to the point where art was more actively involved in ritual, magic, and life.' Though Performance art has assumed many forms, from Kazuo Shiraga's crawling through mud in 1955 to Ion Grigorescu's screaming alone in a Romanian forest in 1977, this chapter will deal with the uses of film and video in a variety of performance contexts.

*1960s Multimedia Performances*
Performance was not exclusively related to the canvas: the cross-fertilization between theater, dance, film, video, and visual art was essential for the birth of Performance art. The dance and media experiments that flourished in New York in the 1960s among the Judson Church artists (an influential collective of choreographers and performance artists) extended to visual artists as well,

chief among them Robert Rauschenberg, who was an early proponent of the intermingling of art and technology. In 1960, Rauschenberg met Billy Klüver, an electronic engineer and sound wizard who had collaborated with several artists, most notably Jean Tinguely on his self-destroying machine, *Hommage à New York*. In 1965, Klüver worked with John Cage and Merce Cunningham in one of the earliest multimedia stage events, *Variations V*, for which Klüver devised a sound system that reacted to movements, sounds, and projections through a complicated system of photoelectric cells and microphones. The resultant sounds functioned as a kind of score for the dancers. Featured also were a film by Stan Vanderbeek and video images by Nam June Paik. Critic Söke Dinkla points out that this system anticipated the computer-controlled interaction between live performance and sound effects commonly seen in theater and dance since the early 1990s.

Rauschenberg, a close associate of Cage and Cunningham, was invited, along with them and other choreographers, including Lucinda Childs and Deborah Hay, to participate in the Stockholm Festival of Art and Technology in the summer of 1966. Although the Stockholm appearance did not take place, Rauschenberg and associates staged what they had developed in New York in October 1966, in *Nine Evenings: Theater and Engineering*, a seminal event in

30. Photograph of **Robert Rauschenberg**'s performance *Open Score (Bong)* from *Nine Evenings: Theater and Engineering* held at the Sixty-Ninth Regiment Armory, New York, 14 October, 1966. Rauschenberg's *Open Score (Bong)* involved a tennis match between painter Frank Stella and professional tennis player Mimi Kanarek using rackets wired for sound as well as a video projection of infrared images of performance volunteers.

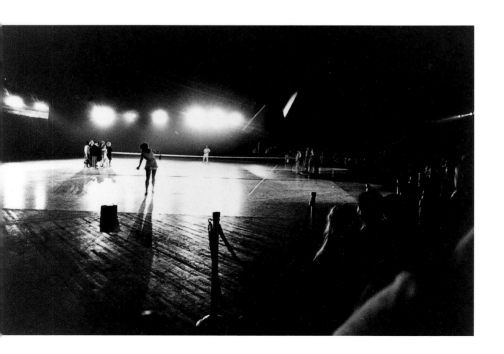

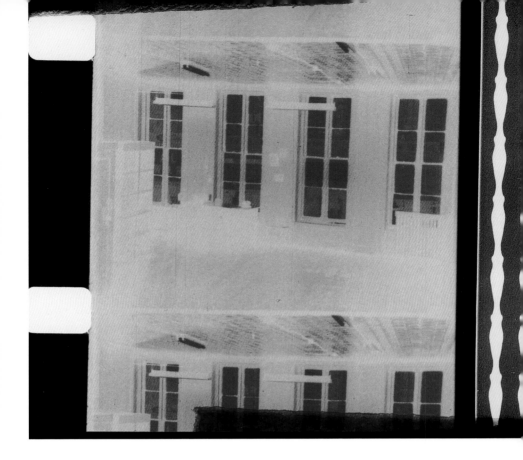

31. (above) **Michael Snow**, film still from *Wavelength*, 1967.

32. (above right) **Carolee Schneemann**, *Snows*, 1967. Schneemann used her own body as 'material' in her work. 'I wanted my actual body to be combined with the work as an integral material.' Though thinking of herself as a painter, she often uses photography, film and video in her work.

33. (below right) **Carolee Schneemann**, *Mortal Coils*, 1994–95.

performance and media held in the vast Sixty-Ninth Regiment Armory building on New York's East Side. For Rauschenberg's performance, *Open Score (Bong)*, approximately five hundred volunteers were gathered in a totally dark playing area performing simple gestures that were recorded by infrared cameras and projected onto three large screens. Also shown were projections of the darting movements of performers playing tennis with radio transmitting rackets. This is all the audience saw, for when the lights came on, the performers were gone. It was the artists' delight in the possibilities of the new technology that became the main event. In his performance work *Linoleum* (1966), Rauschenberg wore a plastic suit, wired for sound by Klüver, and projected a film he made from found footage of recreational water sports and military aircraft maneuvers. His collaborations with Klüver led to their founding EAT (Experiments in Art and Technology) in 1967, an enduring and influential collaboration between artists and engineers.

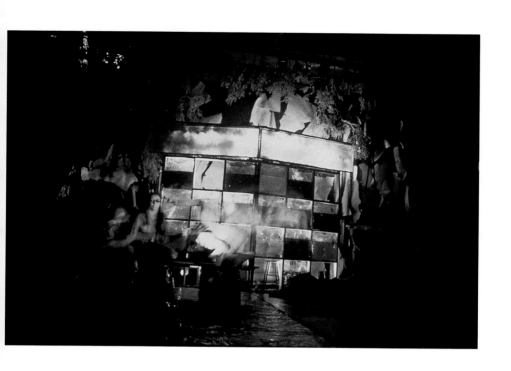

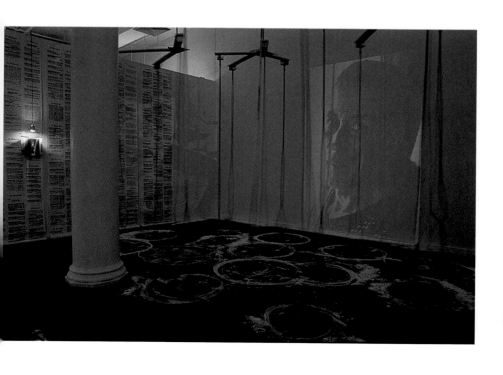

Rauschenberg and his collaborators, especially dancer-choreographers Trisha Brown, Deborah Hay, Steve Paxton, and Lucinda Childs, continued to stage their events in a variety of spaces, with the space itself often dictating the nature of the performance. The Filmmaker's Cinémathèque (whose name reflects the influence of the French *nouvelle vague* film directors, Jean-Luc Godard, François Truffaut, and others) was such a venue. Robert Whitman's (b. 1935) *Prune Flat* (1965) featured live performers interacting with filmed images (often of themselves) which were projected onto the performers and onto screens behind them. Whitman, who began as a painter, thus transposed the flatness of the canvas to the flatness of the screen on which he attempted to visualize temporal relationships (past, as represented by the film, present and future in the gestures of the performers) in a spatial context. The same year, Canadian artist Michael Snow (b. 1929) literally tackled the role of cinema in art with *Right Reader*, a video performance in which he stood behind a plexiglass frame as if he were in a movie. He moves his lips in time to a recording of his own voice in which he comments on the sometimes banal nature of films. We think he is speaking in real time,

34. **Robert Whitman**,
*Prune Flat*, 1965.
Performed at the Filmmaker's
Cinémathèque, New York.
The photograph shows a more
recent reconstruction of the same
event. Photograph: Copyright
© 1976, Babette Mangolte,
all rights of reproduction reserved.

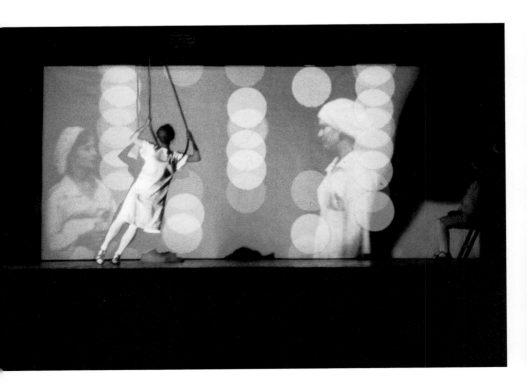

but soon we realize he is not: the whole experience, like film, is a contrived experience based on technology. Snow's innovative use of the camera in his films and video performances is also notable. He created a spherical machine for rotating the camera through 360 degrees; and, in *Wavelength* (1967) he made camera tricks ('panning,' 'trucking,' and 'dollying') the protagonists of the film.

In 1967 an important work in the history of media and performance was performed by Deborah Hay, one of the Judson Church choreographers. *Group One* consisted, in part, of a black and white film projected onto the corner of a gallery space. Men and women in dark suits and dresses were shown engaging in everyday walking patterns that, while choreographed, retained their naturalness. After the film, other performers enacted similar sequences live. The result, for American historian Michael Kirby, was a new form of art dance in which people and film 'were used as elements out of which an architectonic or sculptural human mass could be assembled in relationship to an actual architectural element, the corner of the room.' The film added another perceptual illusion: the use of black and white suggested figures from another time moving along its walls.

American painter Carolee Schneemann (b. 1939) created private actions she called *Eye Body* (1963) which she documented through photography. In these bodily 'still lifes,' which anticipated body and performance art, she re-created mythical goddess imagery, using her own body as sculpture. Her 1967 multimedia performance work *Snows* was an elaborate interaction of 16- millimetre and 8-millimetre film, slides, revolving light sculpture, strobe lights, and eight racially diverse performers. Underneath randomly chosen seats in New York's Martinique Theatre (a Broadway house) Schneemann and her engineers fixed microphones that transferred signals into a silicon-controlled rectifier switching system. Any motion by an audience member in these seats would set off the system, which, in turn, activated the media elements.

Like Schneemann, Joan Jonas (b. 1936) has worked with media and performance from the 1960s to the present day. While a graduate student in New York she participated in dance workshops with the Judson Church group, which included Trisha Brown, Deborah Hay, Steve Paxton, and Yvonne Rainer. Each of them shared a sensibility that embraced conceptual, cultural, psychological, as well as performative issues. Trained as a sculptor, Jonas was initially attracted by the sculptural elements of performance and film. 'I brought to performance,' she said in a 1995 interview,

*my experience of looking at the illusionistic space of painting and of walking around sculptures and architectural spaces. I was barely in my early performance pieces; I was in them like a piece of material, or an object that moved very stiffly, like a puppet or a figure in a medieval painting... I gave up making sculpture and I walked into the space... What attracted me to performance was the possibility of mixing sound, movement, image, all the different elements to make a complex statement. What I wasn't good at was making a single, simple statement — like a sculpture.*

35. (below) **Joan Jonas**, *Organic Honey's Visual Telepathy/Vertical Roll*, 1972/1994.

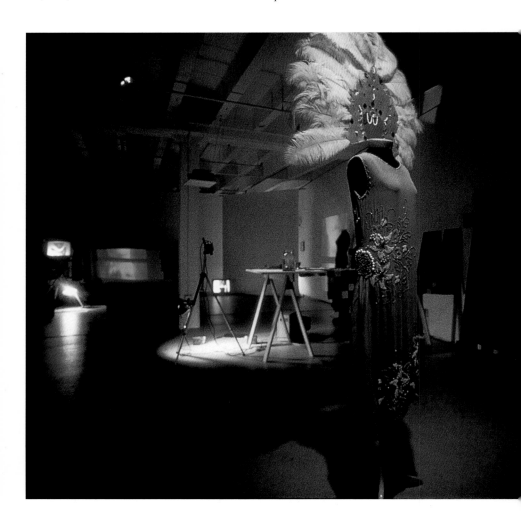

From the beginning, her performances have incorporated first film and then video. Her first public performance, *Oad Lau* (1968; the title is the name of a Moroccan village that translates as 'watering-place'), contained the film *Wind*, which dealt with wind and water as basic elements. Jonas used the camera and monitor both as theatrical props and as sculptural elements in her performances. Like Nam June Paik before her, she bought her own Sony Portapak camera in 1970. Finding video 'very magical' and imagining herself as 'an electronic sorceress conjuring the images,' she invented the name Organic Honey as an alter ego. *Organic Honey's Visual Telepathy* (1972) was a performative video featuring a 'set' or installation in which Jonas created a room out of Organic Honey's imagination. The video of Jonas's movements supplied a mirror-like reflection of the action that altered the audience's perception of what they were seeing. These performances would change often, displaying Jonas's versatility as a performer and 'conjurer,' a role she assumed by wearing long blue robes and carrying a magician's funnel hat.

*Funnel* (1974) incorporated three performance areas, separated by curtains, in which Jonas performed rituals based on her interest in magic and the traditions of the native Americans of the American Southwest. In one area a live video was projected on a monitor, providing a detailed view of her whole performance. Jonas returned to several of the images used in *Funnel* in her 1998 installation at New York's Pat Hearn Gallery. *My New Theater II (Big Mirror)* is a video theater mounted inside a large funnel-like structure supported by two saw-horses. Peering through the funnel, the viewer sees Jonas on a screen performing daily routines (such as sweeping the

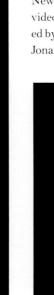

36. (right) **Joan Jonas**, *Organic Honey's Visual Telepathy*, 1972.

37

38

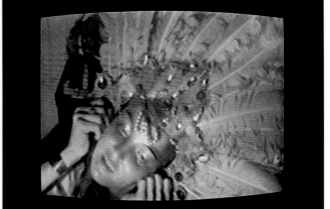

floor) that turn into frantic stomping dances, while songs and texts are heard on the soundtrack (including William Carlos Williams's poem 'Big Mirror', and folk songs that speak of friends who have died).

Jonas continues to break new ground decades after her early work caused such a stir, a rare achievement. After experiencing a 'slump,' as she calls it, in the mid-1980s, when the art world was changing radically and her old brand of formal experimentation

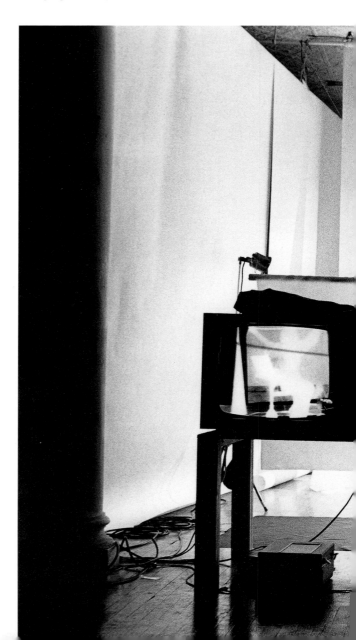

37. **Joan Jonas**, *Funnel*, 1972. Performance at The Kitchen, New York. Photograph: Copyright © 1974, Babette Mangolte, all rights of reproduction reserved.

was on the wane, Jonas re-emerged in 1987 with a sweeping media performance piece, *Volcano Saga*, based on a thirteenth-century Icelandic poem; in 1994, she created *Sweeney Astray*, based on a medieval Irish poem and commissioned by the Stedelijk Museum, Amsterdam, for their retrospective of Jonas's work. Reflecting her enduring interest in the various perceptions and misperceptions afforded by the video camera in a performance context, Jonas here

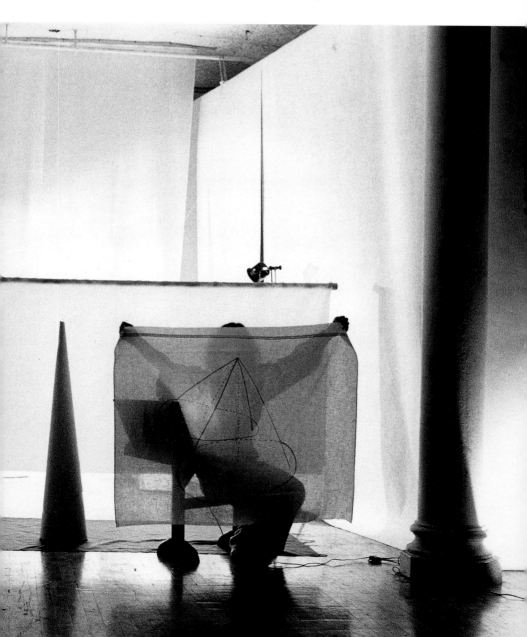

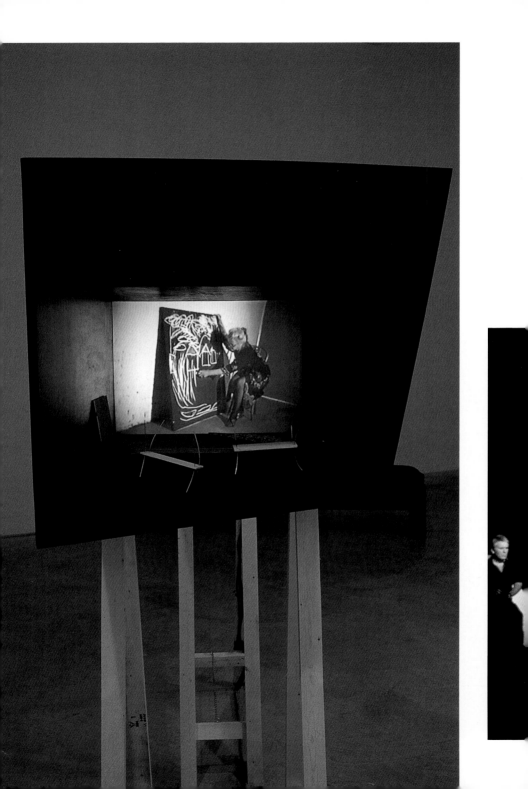

placed a camera under a glass table to record performers acting on top of the table. These shots were projected onto freestanding scrims, with camera operators, performers, and musicians all visible to the viewer.

### 'Studio' Performances

The video camera became a partner in the performances of several influential artists drawn to electronic media, recording intimate, often ritualized actions. Although there is, arguably, an historical continuum from Dada performance to Fluxus, Happenings and Performance art, 'media and performance art' does not fit neatly into it. Unlike their Dada predecessors, artists like Bruce Nauman (b. 1941) and Vito Acconci (b. 1940) did not set for themselves the goal of interactivity with an audience. Sometimes their performances were private affairs, exercizes performed in their studios, that were videotaped but not necessarily shown. Instead of marketable objects (such as paintings or sculptures), the physical

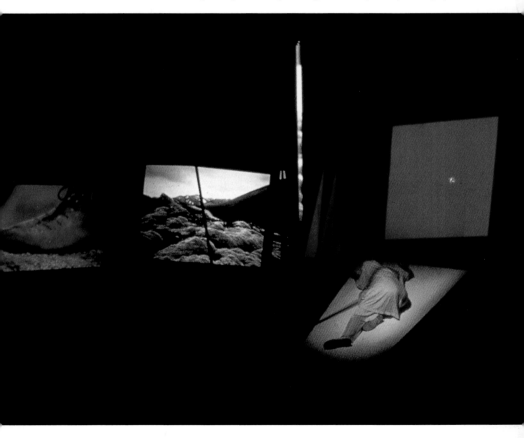

process of art-making became the work itself. The video camera represented 'the other,' or the audience. It was also instrumental in these artists' attempts to free themselves from the confines of traditional art-making.

The private media-based performances of Nauman and Acconci refer to the artist alone in his studio. Showing in isolation their bodies (hands, fingers) and their movements (hands painting or sculpting), they created works that made explicit the artist's fundamental gestures. According to Acconci, 'If Minimalism was so great, what could I do? What was missing was the source. I had to reveal the source;' by this he meant the body and movement of the maker of the art. In the iconoclastic spirit of the 1960s, Acconci and others sought to free themselves from the influence of art history by eliminating all but the process from their work. 'People did performance in order *not* to do painting and sculpture,' Acconci says. 'Painting and sculpture had the power of the One True God of Art; performance was a way to intrude, in the middle of a single belief system, the swarm of multiple gods.'

For Nauman, his private performances, or 'representations,' as he called them, explored the relationship between his sculpture (for example, *Neon Templates of the Left Hand of My Body Taken at Ten Inch Intervals*, 1966, or his wax over cloth *From Hand to Mouth*, 1967), and his own activities in the studio. In one of his performances, he assumed discrete positions (including sitting, bending, squatting), creating a 'living sculpture' with his body. Nauman, also a musician, was deeply influenced by the extended sense of time in serialist compositions by Philip Glass, Steve Reich, and Terry Riley. Reich's *Violin Phase* (1967) featured one basic pattern played repeatedly by several violins. Nauman incorporated this open-ended format (a seeming lack of beginning or end) into his video performances, which made use of a fixed camera recording gestures and movements that he considered art in themselves. The view that even ordinary movements could be considered art owed something to choreographer Meredith Monk whom he met in 1968. During the 1960s Nauman made about twenty-five videotapes consisting of repetitive, mundane actions. This was an approach to dance which had its origins in the pioneering work of San Francisco choreographer Anne Halprin (b. 1920) whose workshops were frequented by such future influential dancer/choreographers as Trisha Brown (b. 1936), dancer turned filmmaker Yvonne Rainer (b. 1934), and Simone Forti (b. 1935).

The interplay of performance and sculpture in Nauman's work was also influenced by the Viennese philosopher Ludwig

Wittgenstein and Irish dramatist and novelist Samuel Beckett. Wittgenstein exerted an influence on several Conceptual artists who were drawn to his exploration of the philosophical implications of ordinary language. It was the variety of language-games, as he called them, which revealed meaning, derived from the way words were used. 'The term language-game,' Wittgenstein wrote in *Philosophical Investigations*, 'is meant to bring into prominence the fact that the speaking of language is part of an activity, or of a form of life.' Language as an activity that can be at once revealing and secretive, a source of bonding as well as of separation, has occupied Nauman in many performative video installations. In *Anthro/Socio (Rinde Facing Camera)*, 1991, and *Anthro/Socio (Rinde Spinning)*, 1992, Nauman collaborated with performance artist/musician Rinde Eckert whose face he filmed in close-up engaging in the Wittgensteinian language games of play-acting and singing phrases ('Help me, hurt me sociology; feed me, eat me anthropology').

Nauman dealt with issues of identity in four silent 16 millimetre films from 1967 to 1968. Called *Art Make-Up*, they show him applying different colors to his skin to mask his identity. This motif surfaced later in his clown videos. Nauman frequently used the clown as an icon in performance videos that illustrate the artist's interest in language and the extremes of human behavior. The clown in *Clown Torture* (1987) was forced to stand on one leg, and at another time, to balance two fish bowls and a bucket of water, all the while shouting 'No, no, no,' and 'I'm sorry, I'm sorry,' over and over. This interest in extreme behavior reflects Nauman's keen interest in Beckett whose spare narratives often portray people in impossible situations: constrained in garbage cans or buried neck-deep in sand. Nauman's performative video, *Slow Angle Walk* (1968) which he subtitled *Beckett Walk*, shows the

41

-0. **Bruce Nauman**, *Anthro/Socio (Rinde Spinning)*, 1992.

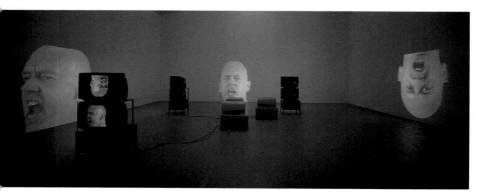

artist performing a strained walk around his studio. He lifts a stiff-ened leg high into the air, then swivels his body in a half turn before letting the leg land on the floor. One can imagine Buster Keaton, whom Beckett chose as the performer in his only film, entitled *Film* (1964), inventing such a move. Destructive actions, such as those by Italian Gina Pane who slashed her toes in her per-formance sculpture *Le corps pressenti* (1975), recur in the work of artist Pier Marton (b. 1950) whose series *Performance for Video* (1978–82) contained sequences where Marton would beat himself with a guitar until it disintegrated. Portrayals of extremes of lan-guage and gesture recall Bertolt Brecht's notion of alienation in theatre as a paradoxical means of drawing an audience closer to the play. By arousing their emotions, even in a negative way, the artist involves the audience with the action or narrative.

Acconci, whose involvement with media spans single-channel video (one tape on one monitor), installation, and performance, expressed the essentials of his performative art in a 1979 essay, *Steps Into Performance (And Out)*:

> *if I specialize in a medium, I would be fixing a ground for myself,*
> *a ground I would have to be digging myself out of, constantly, as one*
> *medium was substituted for another – so, then instead of turning*
> *toward 'ground' I would shift my attention and turn to 'instrument,'*
> *I would focus on myself as the instrument that acted on whatever*
> *ground was available.*

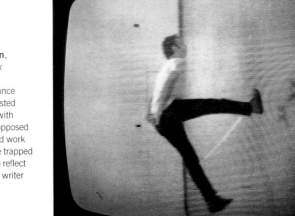

41. (right) **Bruce Nauman**, still from *Slow Angle Walk (Beckett Walk)*, 1968. In his video and performance work Nauman was interested in presenting the viewer with an unfolding process as opposed to a completed, objectified work of art. Clowns and people trapped in extreme situations also reflect his interest in the work of writer Samuel Beckett.

42, 43. (far right) **Bruce Nauman**, two stills from *Clown Torture*, 1987.

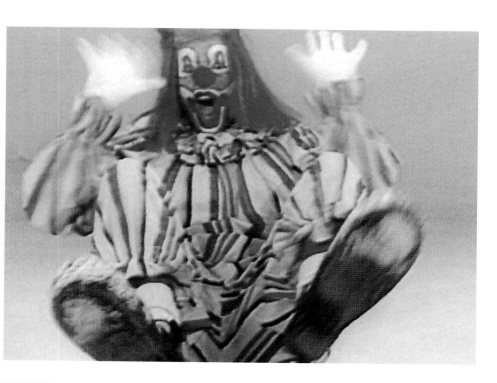

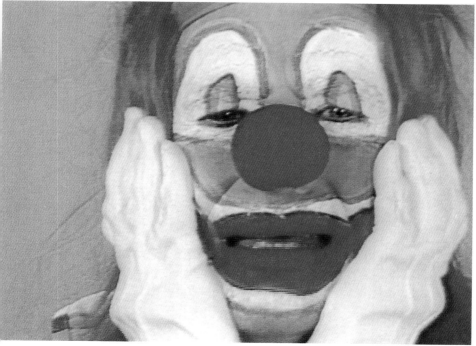

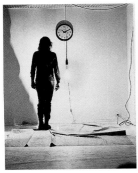

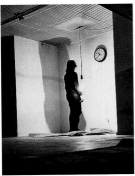

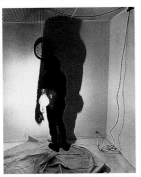

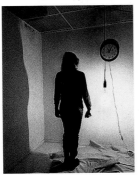

Acconci saw the film or video frame as separating him from the outside world, placing him in an 'isolation chamber,' as he said, where he was intimately connected to his primary material, his body. He made his first video, *Corrections*, in 1970 at the request of American writer and curator Willoughby Sharp, who founded the short-lived *Avalanche*, a magazine devoted to body art, process art, and video. *Corrections* reflected his interest in the immediacy of video. Able to see himself on the monitor as he was recording, Acconci tries to burn off a tuft of hair from the back of his neck using the image on the monitor as a guide. Earlier that same year he made an 8-millimetre film, *Three Adaptation States*, a simple recording of movements in his studio, which he saw as his transition from the page (he had been a poet) to the activity of art. 'I had to leave the page,' he says, 'and I at least got to the floor.' In *Centers* (1971), alone in his studio with a fixed video camera, he points to the lens in a gesture that turns the camera back on the viewer. He stands blindfolded in *Contacts* (1971) with a woman kneeling before him, holding her hand over different parts of his body without actually touching him. Again, a fixed camera records his attempts to name the parts of his own body as she moves her hand around him.

Acconci disliked the term 'performance' for its associations with theater: 'We hated the word "performance." We couldn't, wouldn't call what we did "performance"… because performance had a place, and that place by tradition was a theater, a place you went toward like a museum.' Nevertheless, he did perform in public. In *Pryings* (1971) and *Pull* (1971) Acconci and Kathy Dillon engage in a battle of desire and resistance as Acconci tries to prise open her closed eyelids or each of them tries to mesmerize and control the other with eye games.

Acconci brought his explorations of time and the body into the gallery space in his 1971 collaboration with Dennis Oppenheim and Terry Fox at the Reese Paley Gallery in New York. Facing a large wall clock, his back to the audience, Acconci engaged in private movements as the other artists lay on the floor near a video monitor and sound system. In his 1974 *Command Performance*, Acconci confronts the gallery viewer, by incorporating him into the video environment. In a narrow room, the viewer sits on a stool in front of a monitor, which lies on the floor. The monitor shows a tape of Acconci, also lying on the floor, on his back, straining his head toward the camera, imploring the viewer to seduce him in a rambling monologue that repeats phrases like 'Come on, baby, win me over.' On another monitor behind the stool appears an image of the viewer who is being taped from a camera fixed to the wall above the stool. Everyone becomes a voyeur in this dance of multiple seduction.

Also working in media and performance at this time was Nam June Paik. During his Fluxus period in the early 1960s, in numerous collaborations with musician Charlotte Moorman, Paik created music and video performances that challenged the way music was traditionally played and heard. In *TV Bra* (1968) Moorman is taped, topless, playing the violin, and wearing two circular mirrors on her breasts which reflect cameras focused on her face. He and Moorman were arrested in 1967 for having Moorman perform topless in *Sextronique*, during which Paik's shirtless back became the 'bass' for Moorman's bow string. 'I wanted to stir up the dull waters of sexless men and women in black suits playing music,' he once said. Paik and Moorman collaborated on several such projects, including *Concerto for TV, Cello and Video Tape* (1971) in which she ran her bow across stacks of television sets containing prerecorded and simultaneous images of her running her bow across the televisions. His particular interest was in visualizing time. 'It must be stressed,' he wrote in 1962 prior to his show at Galerie Parnass, Wuppertal, 'that my work is not painting, not sculpture, but rather a Time art: I love no particular genre.'

While Paik abandoned live performance in the 1980s, turning to massive, multi-monitor video constructions, his connection to performance remains evident. It is as if he has made the monitor a

49

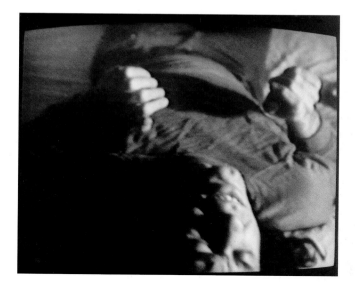

44–47. (left) **Vito Acconci**, *Second Hand*, performance at the Reese Paley Gallery, 1971.

48. (right) **Vito Acconci**, *Command Performance*, 1974. Acconci's first artistic practice was poetry which he thought of as 'movement over the page.' Performance became for him a way to move from the page to an 'outside physical space.'

performer in its own right. He injects such frenzied life into his installations, with images racing across screens, that the video sculptures can appear more like mechanized organisms than inert monitors. He has, in fact, made several 'video robots' since 1964, including *Family of Robot, Aunt* (1986) and *Family of Robot, Uncle* (1986) in which the main visual impression is created by the television sets rather than the images contained in them. He now creates what might be called performative installations.

### Japanese Gutai and Viennese Actionism

Prominent in Japan from 1954 to 1958, though it existed until 1972, was the Gutai Group of painters and performers. In response to the devastation of the Second World War, Gutai artists expressed a violent engagement with their material. Films such as *Gutai on Stage* (1957) and *Gutai Painting* (1960) show artists 'shooting' at canvases with arrows tipped with paint; or pounding canvases with paint-filled boxing gloves; or crashing through paintings with their own bodies. Though eager to have their anti-art actions seen and recorded, the Gutai Group remained involved in painting rather than exploring new media. It was only later that groups in Japan such as Dumb Type fully engaged the media the Japanese, especially the Sony Corporation, had pioneered.

The most radical, postwar expression of media performance was that of the *Wiener Aktionisten*, the Viennese Actionists, principally, Hermann Nitsch (b. 1938), Otto Muehl (b. 1925), Kurt Kren (b.1929 ), and Valie Export (b. 1940), many of whom had begun as painters. Repelled by war, Nazism and its legacy, while rejecting museum-embraced modernism, these artists sought to make an art that was programmatically sensational. They sought inspiration both from Freud's understanding of the unconscious and

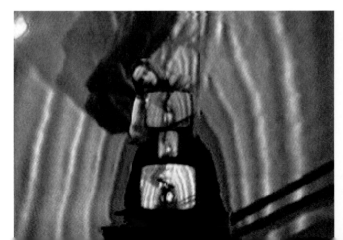

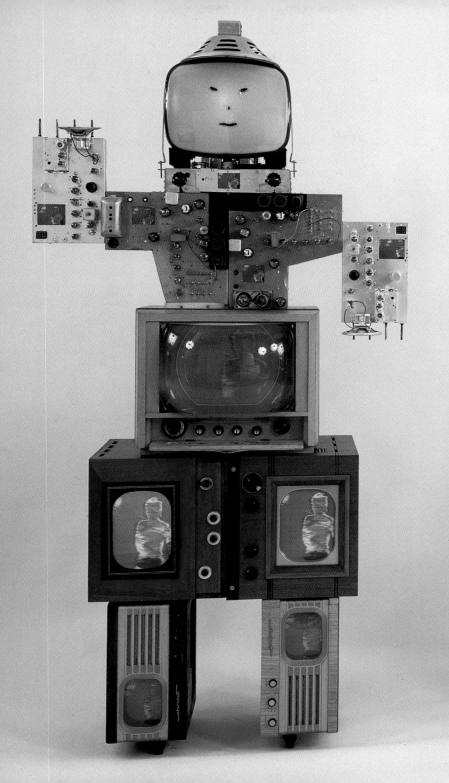

also from the liberated art practices espoused by Fluxus. With the exception of Valie Export, whose artistic reach was perhaps broadest of all of them, extending to sculpture, video, film, photography, installation, as well as performance, the Actionists exalted 'destruction' as a primary pathway to artistic and social freedom. 'I can imagine nothing significant where nothing is sacrificed, destroyed, dismembered, burnt, pierced, tormented, harassed, tortured, massacred... stabbed, destroyed, or annihilated,' Muehl wrote in 1963. The actions which arose from this way of thinking often involved bodily mutilation, sado-masochistic sex, animal dismemberment and misogynist practices all performed for the camera, sometimes with onlookers (audiences), often without. In *Funèbre* (1966), an early filmed action by Muehl, a naked body lies on a bed and is sprayed with pigment and manipulated by other naked figures. Muehl made Yves Klein's early 1960s performances with naked models and paint seem like innocent parlor games. Most extreme was *Scheiss-Kerl* (Shit-Guy, 1969), a 16-millimetre film which graphically depicts acts of coprophilia. Such extreme behavior on film would resurface in the 1980s in the work of Americans Paul McCarthy and Ron Athey.

For Muehl, acts normally seen as perverse or degrading were actually means of escaping the confines of social mores. By 1971 he abandoned art and actions to form a commune, which exists to this day, in which free sexual expression and uninhibited interactions are prescribed. When some of these practices were discovered to involve children, Muehl was imprisoned for seven years, from 1991 to 1998. His alleged utopian practices and transgressions were, not surprisingly, intolerable to the society he saw himself as trying to liberate.

Kurt Kren, who collaborated as a filmmaker with several Actionist artists, was particularly interested in the technical capabilities of editing and image manipulation. He had been making experimental films since the 1950s that were structurally influenced by serial music practices of the same period. Fast editing and single-frame techniques highlighted the material qualities of film, while at the same time providing a new vocabulary for 'time,' as experienced by the viewer. Kren was attracted to the visual complexity of the actions of Gunther Brus (b. 1938) and Muehl, and saw in them the potential for creating his own type of collage on film. As art historian Huber Klocker describes it: 'Kren's films are collage-like pictorial storage media organized in a new form of space and time which compress the pictorial mass like a machine and convert it into pure energy.'

The three-minute color film *Leda and the Swan* (1964), one of Muehl's graphic actions, becomes, in Kren's hands, a syncopated aria of chaos and abstraction.

Valie Export, who participated in the tail end of Actionism, has created performances, videos, films, and media events since the mid-1960s which are bold and often graphic examinations of woman's role in society. She was a founder of Austrian Filmmakers Co-operative and her early experiments in performance and film (*Menstruationsfilm*, 1966, *Orgasmus*, 1966) placed her in the forefront of feminist performance, strongly countering the abuse of women found among other Actionists like Muehl. Her feminist performances and films, as well as her early experiments in still photography, are also marked by technologically sophisticated inquiries into perception, the photographic and filmed image, and the language of the body. By the early 1970s she was using video in performances such as *Bewegungsimaginationen* (Movement Imagination, 1974) which features recorded images and live video. By the mid-1980s she was combining media (still photography, video and 16-millimetre film) in works such as *Syntagma* (1983). Export's long-term aim is to reclaim the female figure in art. 'In film,' she says, 'the woman's body becomes the woman's image to the extent that the history of film and the history of the female body are virtually one.'

As the Viennese Actionists were supposedly exercizing their liberation from National Socialism, artists from the Eastern bloc were consigned to secret activities which, if discovered, were punishable by imprisonment. Cameras and videos were surveillance tools used to spy on citizens and were not to be in the hands of individuals, much less artists, who might use them in subversive ways. Among the most isolated artistic groups in Eastern Europe were the Romanians for whom any type of unauthorized public gathering was prohibited. Thus performances, such as they were, were mostly private actions. Ion Grigorescu created several short films and photographic essays that explored his sense of a self fractured by the lies and secret codes required for survival in a totalitarian state. In Super-8 films like *Boxing* (1977), *Man as Center of the Universe* (1978), and *Dialogue with Nicolae Ceausescu* (1978) he records himself in the seclusion of his own room or in a remote field reflecting the utter confinement of his situation. He often used multiple images of himself within the frame to suggest the fragmented self and the elimination of personal identity imposed by the government.

51

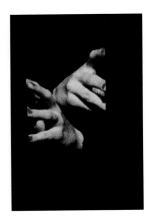

51. **Valie Export**,
*Syntagma*, 1983.
This film opens with a shot of two female hands forcing open a space between two strips of celluloid. The well manicured hands then begin to 'speak' in sign language, spelling out the name of the film.

Still little known outside of his native Hungary was Tibor Hajas (1946–80), whose photo-performances in the 1970s were as dangerous as they were subversive. In *Dark Flash* (1976), he was hung from the ceiling of a darkened room by a rope which was tied around his hands. Holding a camera in one of his bound hands he attempted to photograph light flashes that occasionally pierced the darkness. At the end of the performance there was an enormous flash of magnesium as Hajas, now unconscious, was released from the rope.

Relatively subdued in contrast was the media and performance tableau created by noted postwar German artist Gerhard Richter and his associate Konrad Fischer with the assistance of painter Sigmar Polke. Together they organized *A Demonstration for Capitalist Realism* (1963), during which they occupied a fully decorated corner of a furniture store, and reprogrammed a television set with politically charged images. Certain visual links can be made here with Vostell's *TV De-coll/age*, and Richard Hamilton's collage, *Just what is it that makes today's homes so different, so appealing?* (1956), challenging the seeming tranquillity of domestic life with implications of political and social upheaval.

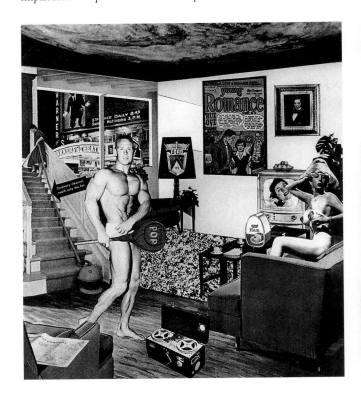

52. **Richard Hamilton**, *Just what is it that makes today's homes so different, so appealing?*, 1956.

58

### Gender and Media Performance

Art historian Moira Roth makes the connection between feminist performance art and so-called 'street theater' engaged in by feminist activists, such as the disruption of the 1968 Miss America beauty pageant. Feminist outrage at constricted gender roles was part of a cultural pattern of liberation movements around the world that included students, people of color, and gays. With Jonas and Schneemann as models, feminist artists embraced media as part of their performance actions.

In her *Video Live Performances* from the 1970s, German artist Ulrike Rosenbach (b. 1944) set up graphic tableaux which were performed for the camera only. Her public multimedia performances, which became in essence feminist actions, included *To Have No Power Is To Have Power* (1978). Here the artist is suspended, trapped in a net, as images from art history and popular culture flash on screens behind her.

Since 1974, French multimedia performance artist Orlan has literally re-sculpted her body using video digitalization and recordings of surgical operations in which she alters the shape of her body and face. She created psychological self-portraits in

54

53. **Gerhard Richter** and **Konrad Fischer**, *A Demonstration for Capitalist Realism*, 1963. Gerhard Richter and Konrad Fischer form a tableau vivant in a furniture store as politically charged images flash on a television screen.

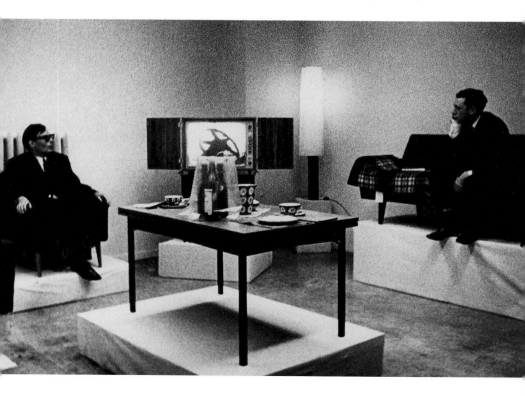

works such as *The Re-Incarnation of St Orlan* and *Image(s)/New Image(s)*, 1991, during which she was videotaped performing, while under local anaesthesia, as her chin was surgically remodelled into the chin of Botticelli's Venus (from *The Birth of Venus*) or her nose into the nose of Psyche, as in Gérard's *Le Premier Baiser*

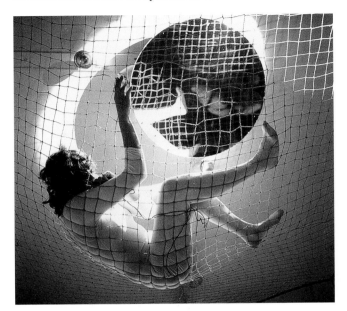

54. (right) **Ulrike Rosenbach**, *To Have No Power Is To Have Power*, 1978.

55. (below) **Orlan**, *Le Visage du 21 siècle*, 1990. French artist Orlan has undergone a series of cosmetic surgical operations to transform herself into the female form most idealized by male artists throughout history.

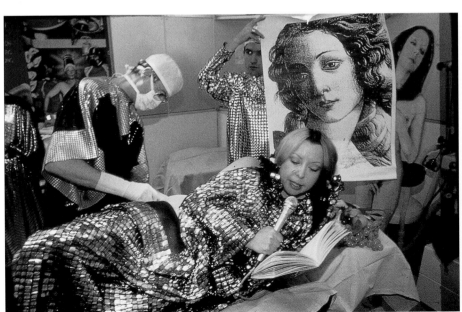

*de l'Amour à Psyche*. She remained conscious in order to 'direct' the surgical performance for the camera. No less committed to a feminist vision is Friederike Pezold, who since the early 1970s has created video performances like *The New Living Body Language of Signs According to the Laws of Anatomy, Geometry, and Kinetics* (1973–76) in which she attempts to shift the focus of architecture, which she sees as traditionally phallocentric, to the female body.

*Minimalist and Conceptual Trends*

A Minimalist aesthetic in media and performance is most evident in the work of Robert Wilson (b. 1941), best known for his monumental stagings of original works such as *A Letter for Queen Victoria* (1974) and *Einstein on the Beach* (1976). Wilson, who trained in interior design, architecture, and painting, actually began his own art work with *Slant*, a ten-minute abstract color film he made in 1963. One of his earliest performances (probably late 1964) was presented in a movie house near the Pratt School of Art and Design in New York, where he was studying, and consisted of choreographed movement accompanied by film. His *Theatre Activity (1)*, 1968, presented at the Bleecker Street Cinema in New York, featured a photograph of a cat superimposed over a film loop of grass. Several other early works, especially *Deafman Glance* (1971), included film. While Wilson continued to make videos and films (his forty-seven minute video *La Mort de Molière*, 1995, was presented at the 1997 Whitney Biennial Exhibition), filmed media were not present in most of his large stage works until 1998 when he and Philip Glass, his collaborator on *Einstein on the Beach*, presented *Monsters of Grace*, based on a text by a thirteenth-century Persian mystic, Jelaluddin Rumi. Combining live stage action and a 3D computer-animated film (made by Jeffrey Kleiser and Diana Walczak), the piece weaves back and forth between illusion and reality, all under the control of a computerized masterboard.

56

58

American composer Robert Ashley (b. 1930) has created experimental operas since the 1970s that combine music driven by the sound of a spoken text and projected video images incorporating abstract images, appropriated images (sometimes from television shows) and words. *Music with Roots in the Aether* (1976) was a fourteen-hour work based on the music and writings of contemporary composers, including Philip Glass, Alvin Lucier, and Steve Reich. Ashley's *Dust* (1999), a fragmented meditation on loneliness in contemporary America, incorporated five electroluminescent screens as well as a large horizontal screen above the performance area, on which were projected a dizzying array of images designed by Japanese artist Yukihiro Yoshihara. For Wilson and Ashley, as for many other artists who incorporate media into their work, video and film provide additional architectural elements to the stage environment and allow for greater manipulations of time.

Eiko and Koma, Japanese-born dance artists associated with Minimalism and Japanese avant-garde theater, used both film and video in their 1998 project for the Whitney Museum, *Breath*, in which they appeared live in the midst of an environment of film and video projections. Fluid landscapes of shapes from nature and changing forms from their moving bodies suggested relationships between the live body and the 'live' film image.

The malleable nature of viewers' perceptions of reality is paramount in the work of Douglas Davis (b. 1933). In 1977, as part of *documenta vi*, Davis devised an international satellite telecast to over twenty-five countries. Davis, who was in Caracas, Venezuela, performed *The Last Nine Minutes*, in which he addressed the audience about the time/space distance between them. Included in the transmission were performances by Nam June Paik and Charlotte Moorman (*TV Bra*, *TV Cello*, and *TV Bed*) and a performance/lecture by Joseph Beuys on one of his utopian theories of art. Davis extended this same practice in 1981 with *Double Entendre*, another live satellite performance, linking the Whitney Museum in New

56. **Robert Wilson**, *Deafman Glance*, 1971.

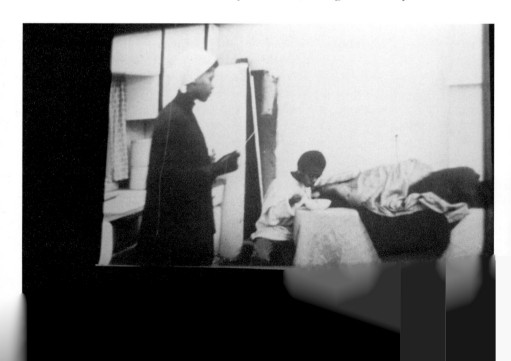

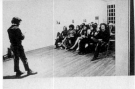

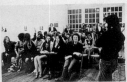

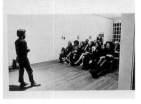

57. (above) **Dan Graham**, *Performance/Audience/Mirror*, December, 1975.

58. (below) **Robert Wilson and Philip Glass**, *Monsters of Grace*, 1998. For Wilson, design elements do not merely support the work, they are the work, the very content of his theater. 'Listen to the pictures,' he says.

York with the Centre Georges Pompidou in Paris, in which Davis explores a transatlantic love affair. Along the way he challenges notions of electronic linkage, cultural and sexual boundaries, as well as language theories; all of which was based on French theorist Roland Barthes' text, *A Lover's Discourse* (first published in France in 1977, English translation, 1978).

Intellectual involvement with architecture, theories of public and private space and issues of perception led Dan Graham (b. 1942) to performance and installation works that engaged viewers by directly focusing on their own position as viewers in a given space at a particular time. He often uses mirrors, closed circuit video systems, and complex viewing environments to engulf the viewer in his ideas about spectatorship and physical space. In *Performance/Audience/Mirror* (1975), Graham positioned himself in a performance space, his back to a mirror, facing an audience. He discussed his audience's movements and what they might signify and then proceeded to face the mirror and discuss his and his audience's movements as 'filtered' through the mirror. Issues of subjectivity/objectivity, the observer and the observed, audience and performer were engaged as varying and very subjective relationships. As he became more sophisticated in his use of video technology, Graham began incorporating video into his mirrored environments. His 1983 *Performance and Stage Set Utilizing Two Way Mirror and Video Time Delay*, created for his retrospective at

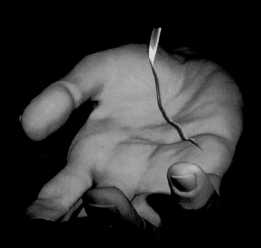

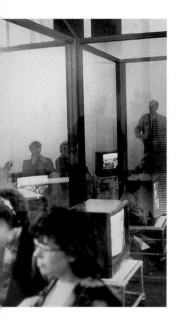

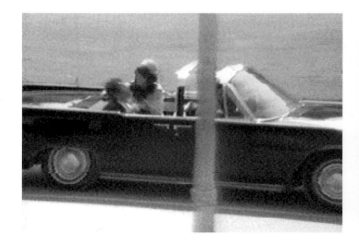

59. **Dan Graham**, *Three Linked Cubes/Interior Design for a Space Showing Videos*, 1986.

the Kunsthalle in Berne, consisted of musicians and audience sitting facing each other through a large two-way mirror. A live feed video with a six-second delay was projected on the mirror, creating a virtual kaleidoscope of perception-bending images during which the audience watched the performers only through the filter of the mirror and video as they were also watching themselves and the performers on a time delay. This sense of disorientation challenged their position as observers. Graham continues to create viewing environments, such as *Three Linked Cubes/Interior Design for a Space Showing Videos* (1986), a space with transparent and mirrored glass, featured in the Guggenheim Museum's 1997 exhibition, *Rooms with a View: Environments for Video*; and an updated version of this, *New Space Showing Videos* (1995). In both cases the environments allow for viewing and being viewed; the viewer becoming at once the performer and the audience.

*Politics, Postmodernism, and the New Spectacle*
Graham's interactive practices reflect the theories of the Situationist International, a loose collective of European artists and intellectuals, whose chief spokesman, Guy Debord (1931–94), had a profound influence on artists in Western Europe and America. Central to Situationist thought (a combination of Marxism, psychoanalysis, and existentialism) was that theory can and should be the locus for 'aesthetic actions' by artists and other concerned individuals. Guided by Debord, especially in his 1967 essay 'The Society of the Spectacle', Situationists, largely through writings, agitated for popular control of urban spaces. One of their publications, *On the Poverty of Student Life* (1966–67), foreshadowed the

60. **T. R. Uthco** and **Ant Farm** (Doug Hall, Chip Lord, Doug Michels, Judy Procter), *The Eternal Frame*, 1975. Abraham Zapruder's amateur 8-millimetre film of President Kennedy's assassination has received more frame-by-frame scrutiny than any other film in history.

worldwide student uprisings of 1968. Artists like Graham and Doug Hall reflected variations on the Situationist manifestos in their own work. Hall became directly associated with political theater as one of the founders of the San Francisco-based, multimedia performance collective T. R. Uthco. Begun in 1970, the group became known for its 1975 collaboration with another media watchdog group, Ant Farm, on *The Eternal Frame*, a filmed re-enactment of Kennedy's 1963 assassination. Combining live performance spectacle, archive footage of the actual assassination, and spectators' filmed reactions to the 're-staging' of the event, this project became a biting record of American fascination with myth, heroes, and the televised image.

Hall also parodied American politics in his video performance *The Speech* (1982), during which he delivered an empty, cliché-ridden stump speech while standing on a platform surrounded by 'media' and 'supporters.' In *Amarillo News Tapes* (1980) and *This Is the Truth* (1982), Hall contested the very notion of 'truth' in the context of media, while engaging his ongoing inquiry into the power of language in the context of 'the public spectacle.' Making no apologies for a lack of intellectual content, Mike Smith (b. 1942), in his performances, videos, and installations since the late 1970s, has skewered the banality of US commercial television in the person of his fictive character 'Mike.' Mike, with no ideas of his own, is a welcome, empty receptacle for all television has to offer. Smith created numerous performance comedies, showcasing his deadpan, conceptual humor in works such as *Down in the Rec Room* (1979), *Secret Horror* (1980), and *Mike Builds a Shelter* (1985). 61-65

Such 'conceptual humor' was evident from the late 1960s and reached an apotheosis in 1980s postmodernism. While scholars still argue over definitions of postmodernism, certain trends in the practice of artists help us to define it. In multimedia theater, the hyperkinetic works of New York's Wooster Group are representative of postmodern performance. The group offers media-mingled interpretations of classic plays such as Eugene O'Neill's *Emperor Jones*, first performed by the group in 1994, *Hairy Ape*, 1995, or *House/Lights*, 1997, based on Gertrude Stein's *Dr. Faustus* 66 *Lights the Lights.* The plays' original texts, though intact, are almost unrecognizable in the midst of high decibel sound scores, amplified voices, and live performers competing for viewers' attention with videotaped versions of themselves on multiple monitors that litter the stage. In capitalizing on the uniqueness of O'Neill or Stein, they offer graphic representation of what social theorist and critic Fredric Jameson cites as the postmodern artist

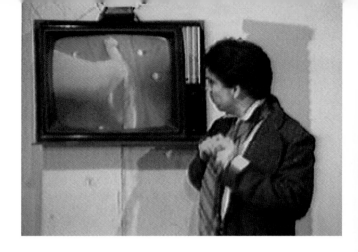

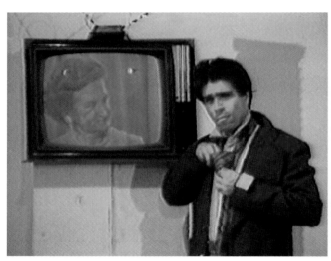

61, 62. (above right, right)
**Mike Smith**, *Down in the Rec Room*, 1979, re-edited 1981.

63. (below) **Mike Smith**,
*Mike Builds a Shelter*, 1985.
Mike Smith's alter-ego 'Mike'
is a living sponge for all that
mass media have to offer.
He easily succumbs to the
lure of advertising but has
nightmares over all that
he's trying to consume.

64, 65. (far right) **Mike Smith**,
*Secret Horror*, 1980.

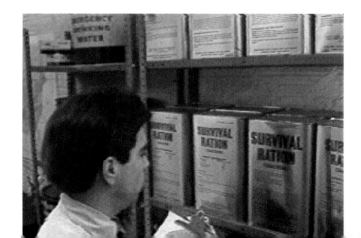

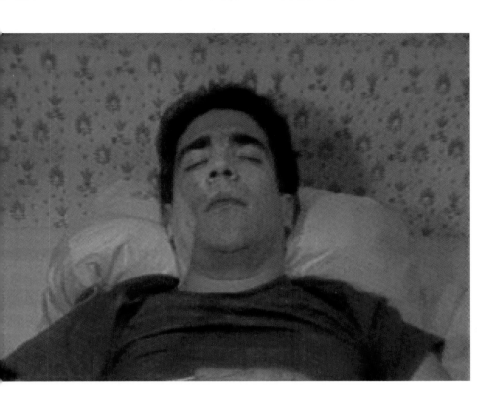

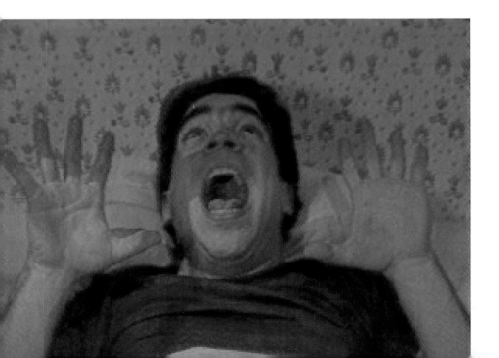

66. **Wooster Group,**
*House/Lights*. Performance at the
Performing Garage, New York,
October 1998.

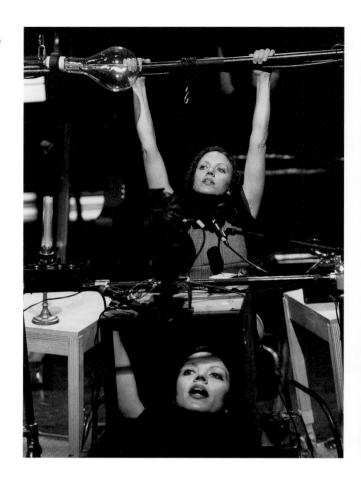

67. **Wooster Group,**
*Brace Up!*, 1991.
Actors including
Willem Dafoe, Kate Valk.
Photograph: Paula Court.
The Wooster Group turns classic
plays into media frenzies with
multiple video monitors and
fractured texts.

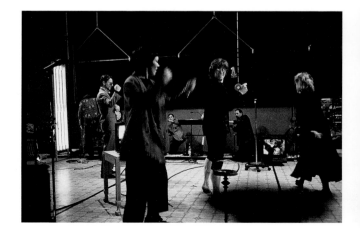

'seizing on their idiosyncrasies and eccentricities to produce an imitation which mocks the original.' But, rather than participate in the banality of media culture, these artists (led by Liz LeCompte who directs most of their productions) actually elevate media culture through their sophisticated use of technology to an artistic level of its own that eschews low-tech associations with the commonplace satirized by Mike Smith. If anything, the Wooster Group creates high-brow art as evidenced by their attraction to writers such as O'Neill or Stein. Among their collaborators is one of the principal architects of postmodern theater, Richard Foreman, founder of the Ontologic Hysteric Theatre, who wrote *Miss Universal Happiness* and *Symphony of Rats* for the Group.

John Jesurun's media theater illustrates another tenet of postmodern genres, namely what French theorist Jean Beaudrillard called 'the death of the subject.' Spewing forth comments on everything from old films, to rock music, to pop psychology, Jesurun's theatrical pieces, which often incorporate multiple video images of the actors, feature characters lost in a universe of words and emotional deprivation. Jesurun's 'subjects', or characters, are in a sense dead, drowned in a sea of free associations and psychobabble that suggest a disembodied mouth in a Beckett play that rambles on eternally. Unlike Beckett, however, whose poetic tracts are more akin to romanticism than postmodernism, Jesurun creates settings which evoke paranoia and hopelessness, like *Deep Sleep* (1985) in which live actors gradually become 'consumed' by filmed images of themselves, or *Slight Return* (1994) in which the audience only sees the projected video image of a performer trapped in a room with a surveillance camera.

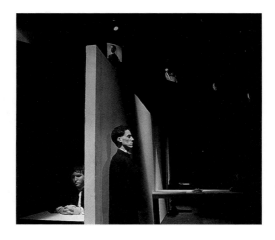

58. **John Jesurun**, *Everything That Rises Must Converge*, 1990. Photograph: Paula Court.

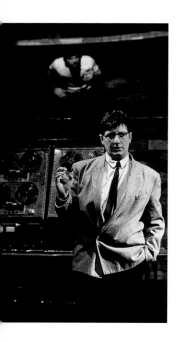

The Wooster Group and Jesurun have influenced many younger artists in the United States and abroad, especially another collective called the Builders Association, whose self-description is a virtual definition of a postmodern media theater: 'We reanimate classic theatrical texts by infusing them with new media, and then re-working them within the chaotic context of contemporary global culture.' Their 1997 *Jump Cut (Faust)*, with texts by Jesurun, and staging clearly influenced by the Wooster Group, involved highly sophisticated interactive video scenes in which characters from Goethe's *Faust* played off scenes from a silent era film of *Faust* (1926) by F. W. Murnau, and reacted to live video feed from a camera placed on stage.

Like Robert Wilson, French-Canadian director Robert Lepage works in large, multimedia formats. With his company Ex Machina, he has created several media-based theater works, including *Polygraph* (1990), *Needles and Opium* (1992), and *The Seven Streams of the River Ota* (1996), a seven-hour work that combined film, video, music, and Japanese Butoh and Kabuki-inspired dance. This elegy for the twentieth century was inspired by his visit to

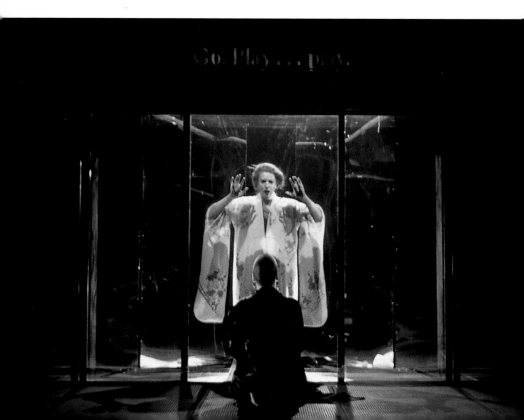

Hiroshima; it is a complex work which collapses time by weaving together lives of people who experienced the Holocaust, the bombing of Hiroshima, and the AIDS epidemic. 'The theater is implicitly linked to technology,' Lepage has said. 'There is a poetry in technology, but we try to use it in a way that does not eclipse the action on stage.' La Fura dels Baus, the international performance group founded in Barcelona in 1979, confronted media head on in their phantasmagoric *F@usto: Version 3.0* (1998). Bloodied bodies and hellfire projected onto huge screens and actors swinging from the ceiling or floating through the air in water-filled, mechanized 'wombs' made boldly graphic representations to illustrate Goethe's tale of the pact between a man and the devil.

Lepage states that he was influenced by the improvisatory working methods of British theater director Peter Brook (b. 1925), whose Paris-based international company has created works often based on literary and classic sources ( e.g. *The Mahabarata*, a nine-hour epic developed over several years in the 1980s). Although Brook was also a film director early in his career, he is not associated with media. Nonetheless, he made significant use of large format, live video in his

69. (left) **Robert Lepage**, *Polygraph*, 1990.

70. (below left) **Robert Lepage**, *The Seven Streams of the River Ota*, 1996. For theater and opera director Robert Lepage, video and film become living characters alongside actors in his technology-based stage works.

71. (below) **La Fura dels Baus**, *F@usto: Version 3.0*, 1998.

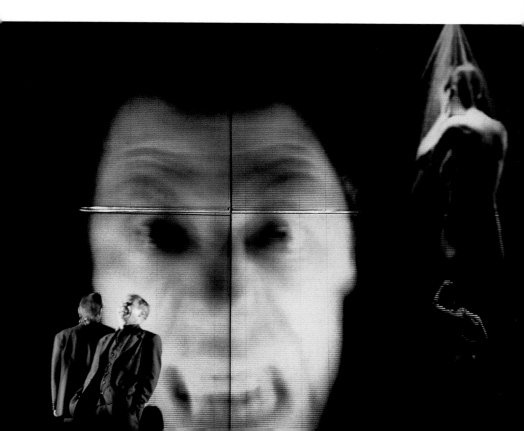

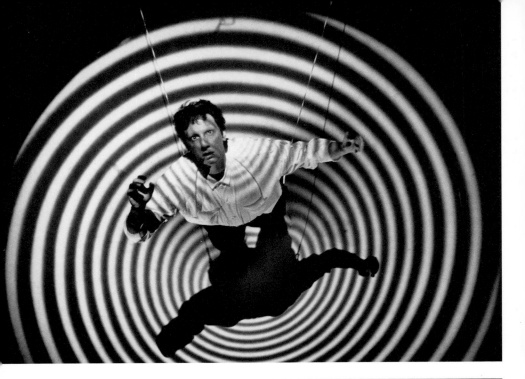

72. (above) **Robert Lepage**,
*Needles and Opium*, 8–12
December, 1992.

73. (right) **Peter Brook**,
*The Man Who*, 1992.
In Brook's adaptation of Oliver
Sacks's *The Man Who Mistook
His Wife for a Hat*, video images
function as mirroring devices for
the central character who forgets
moments as soon as they pass.

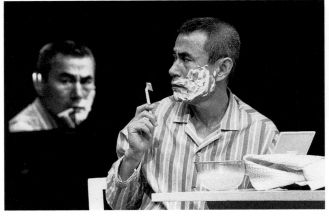

1992 production, *The Man Who*, based on Oliver Sacks's book *The
Man Who Mistook His Wife for a Hat* about a man with brain damage.

Several other experimental theater companies that often use
media in their work include groups like Squat Theater (founded
in Czechoslovakia), Japan's Dumb Type, Impossible Theater
(a 1980s American collective whose use of sophisticated media
methods in productions like *Social Amnesia*, 1986, was intended
as a critique of technology) and companies associated with

74. (right)
Ping Chong, *Deshima*, 1993.

75. (below)
**Kristin Lucas**, *Host*, 1997.
The video camera functions as an extension of her own body for Kristin Lucas, who often straps small cameras and projectors on her head during live performances.

alternative performance spaces, like LaMaMa ETC in New York, for which artists like Ping Chong, trained in film and dance, and the author of this book, who trained in theater and photography, use media as poetic elements in abstract works that combine music, dance and texts, in imagistic visual environments.

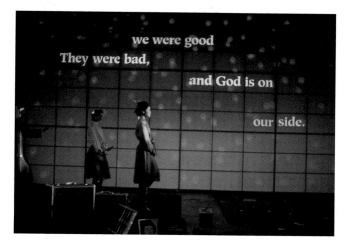

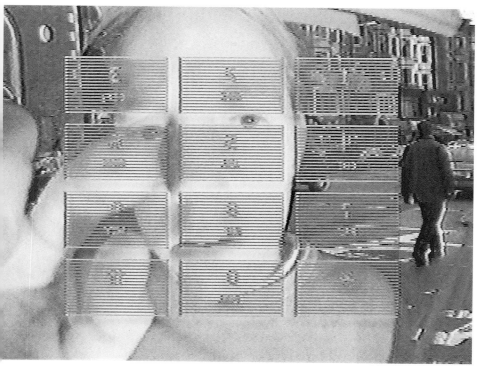

Though sophisticated use of media entered experimental theater productions in the 1980s, plenty of low-tech performance is practised by younger artists whose pared-down presentations are more akin to Fluxus events than theater. In the United States Kristin Lucas (b. 1969) is representative of an energetic young breed for whom the hi-8 video camera functions like a found object, allowing the creation of media collages (or 'video improvs,' as she likes to call them) that are elegant in their simplicity. Strapping a camera or a small projector to a helmet, Lucas, often dressed in a pair of orange workers' overalls, as in *Host* (1997), makes real-time performances, projecting recently recorded images of encounters with policemen or other

76. Broadway staging of the musical *Tommy*, 1995.
Video technology has become a trademark of rock music shows and many large-scale commercial theater productions such as The Who's *Tommy*.

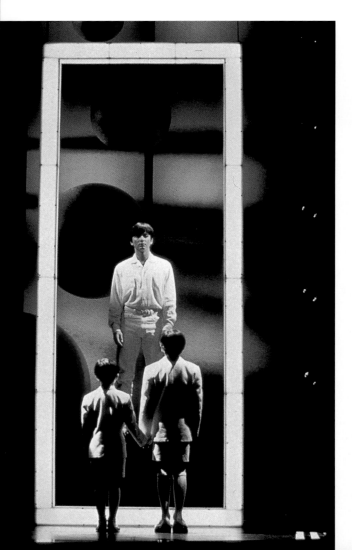
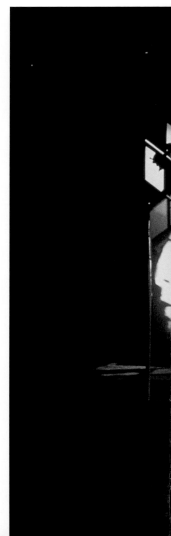

people she meets onto the walls of makeshift gallery or performance spaces.

By the late 1990s, multimedia techniques, begun so spontaneously by experimental dance and theatre groups in the late 1960s, had infiltrated mainstream theater and stadium spectacles, especially rock music shows. The Broadway musical *Tommy*, written as a rock opera by The Who in the 1970s and presented on Broadway in 1995, featured multiple video projections around the theater's proscenium. Nearly every rock show now offers live feed video projection of the performers, which serves to expand the viewing field for large crowds and also adds to the feeling of a hyperkinetic, 'significant' event occurring on stage.

77. (below) Samuel Beckett's *Foirades/Fizzles*, adapted and directed by **Michael Rush**, 1994. Moving and still camera images add layers of time and memory to the voices of Beckett's characters.

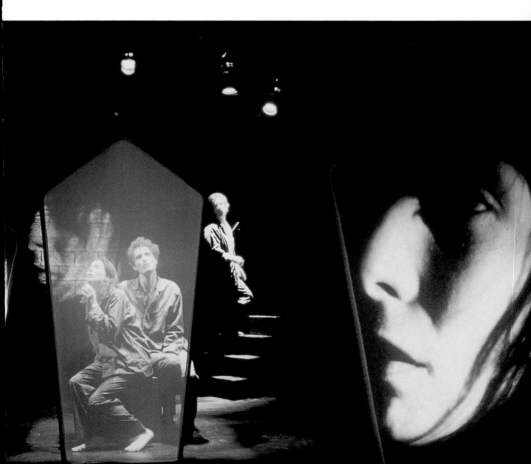

Located behind the scenes of most contemporary, large-scale media-infused performances are digital control boards that, with a touch of a button, control lights, sound, videos, films and much else. The British-based performance company Complicite, founded in 1983 by Simon McBurney (b. 1957) and a few collaborators, demonstrated the highest level of media sophistication in their 2003 production *The Elephant Vanishes*. Based on the short stories of Japanese writer Haruki Murakami, McBurney and company explored the emotional turmoil of contemporary city life through surreal events occurring to three characters whose routine, everyday lives appear anything but. Objects, projection screens, videos, and all manner of technology conspire to visualize the dreamy scenarios of Murakami's narratives.

Reflecting on the complexity of this project, McBurney writes: 'His [Murakami's] stories are extraordinary, springing out of ordinary, mundane urban life. People iron their clothes, make dinner, go to work, watch TV, listen to Haydn and Mozart, get into bed and start again the next day. Yet extraordinary things happen to his characters. They cease to sleep, monsters crawl out of the ground or the television and change their lives. The effect of these intersecting events is to slice through to the heart of what it means to live in this ultra-consumer, disconnected world of ours.'

78. **Complicite**, *The Elephant Vanishes*. Performance at the Lincoln Center Festival, New York, 2004.

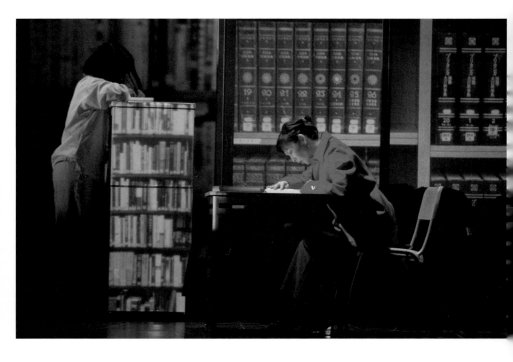

McBurney describes Complicite's work as a series of 'intricate collisions' with stories, memories, movement, technologies, and everyday objects.

The American artists Paul Kaiser (b. 1956) and Shelley Eshkar (b. 1970) have been pushing the boundaries of dance into the realm of new media since the late 1990s with works such as *Biped* (1999) and *Motion-e* (2002–5). In *Biped*, an otherworldly dance project choreographed by Merce Cunningham, Kaiser and Eskar projected digitally animated figures that interacted with live dancers on stage. In a similar vein, *Motion-e* is a series of virtual dances Kaiser describes as 'realtime, interactive, motion-capture-based performances,' made in collaboration with US choreographers Bill T. Jones (b. 1952), Bebe Miller (b. 1950), and Trisha Brown. Brown, who has been at the forefront of experimental dance for more than forty years, created one of the first media dance performances in 1966. In *Homemade*, a collaboration with artist and filmmaker Robert Whitman, she attached a projector to her back which thrust prefilmed images of the same dance she was perfoming live onto a screen at the rear of the stage. This self-reflexive act operated on many levels. It was both spectacle and challenge. How could the live performer compete for viewers' attention with both the mystery and beauty of the filmed image? Which performance was more 'real,' the filmed or the live? The filmed dancer was, in a sense, both a ghost and a companion, a reflection and a mirage.

In contemporary dance, the artist most identified with media and choreography is Cathy Weis who has been staging dances with interactive video projections for several years (e.g. *Face to Face*, 1996; *A Bad Spot Hurts Like Mad*, 2001).

Not all artists work at such a level of technological wizardry. Some are decidedly and determinedly low-tech. The German-born but US-based Oliver Herring (b. 1964), an artistic descendant of John Cage, who built an artform around highly aesthetic and conceptual chance encounters, believes in the potential artfulness of everyday gestures and mundane objects. *Spit Reverse* (2003) is a multi-screen, videotaped performance that explores his interests in the ever-new 'vocabularies' that emerge when a group of strangers (previously unknown to the artist as well) come together for a self-generated, unscripted performance. Here participants are filmed playing a water-spitting game and the action is projected in reverse.

Herring's video projects link his performances to the sculpture and painting he has practiced in other contexts. For Herring artistic media, whether paper, Mylar, videotape, or the body, serve his need to explore ideas, emotions, and new modes of communication. A painterly sensibility permeates his videos. From his earliest *Videosketch #1* (1998), through *The Sum and Its Parts* (2000), *Little Dances of Misfortune* (2001), and *Sleepless Nights* (2001), among several others, performers appear with bodies painted in Mondrianesque patterns or shielded with fluorescent paint. Herring films the performers often through grueling hours of minute gestures and physical interactions. Eschewing digital after effects, he creates his complex-appearing choreography through stop-motion filming, much like early cinematic innovators Buster Keaton and Charlie Chaplin.

The South African-born artist Robin Rhode (b. 1976), who now works in Berlin, also uses the stop-action technique in his videos, which are taped street performances that incorporate drawing and movement. In *White Walls* (2002), for example, the artist is taped drawing a car (in the manner of early Jean-Michel Basquiat or Keith Haring) on a large street wall. In the animated video, Rhode jacks up the car to fix a tire. For viewers, this is as close to a live performance as a tape can get. The same can be said of the Indian artist Sonia Khurana's (b. 1968) video *Bird* (1999), in which, nude and unselfconsciously porcine, she engages in a wild dance that is her attempt to fly.

The pervasive presence of Performance in contemporary media art is undeniable. The link between video and the body from the early 1970s to the present day has been central to the work of numerous artists, including, to name a few, Vito Acconci, Bruce Nauman, Joan Jonas, Robert Rauschenberg, Carolee Schneemann, Nam June Paik, Valie Export, Marina Abromovic and Ulay, Robert Wilson, Martha Rosler, Jurgen Klauke, Steve McQueen, Lucy Gunning, Tony Oursler, Paul McCarthy, Gary Hill, Klaus Rinke, Nayland Blake and Pipilotti Rist.

It has been the availability of affordable technology that has always paralleled developments in art and media. At the same time that artists were taping performances in their studios or incorporating film and video into Performance art and theater, artists were making single-channel videos that were often personal responses to a medium that rarely professed to be art: television.

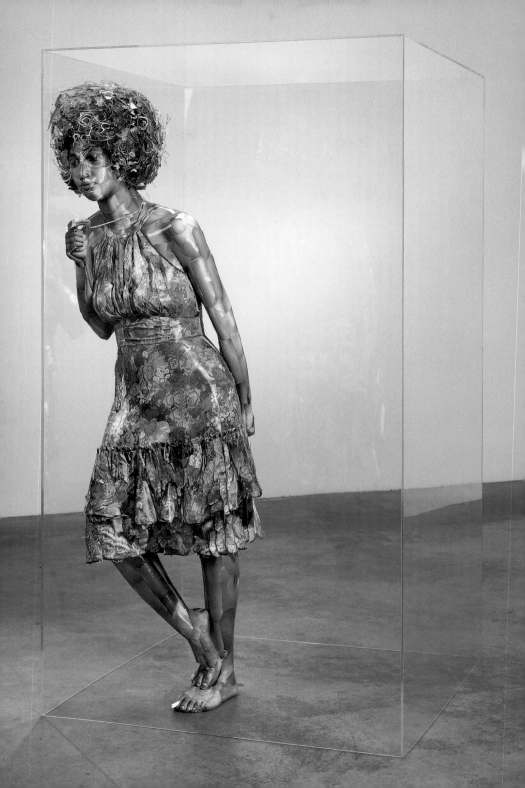

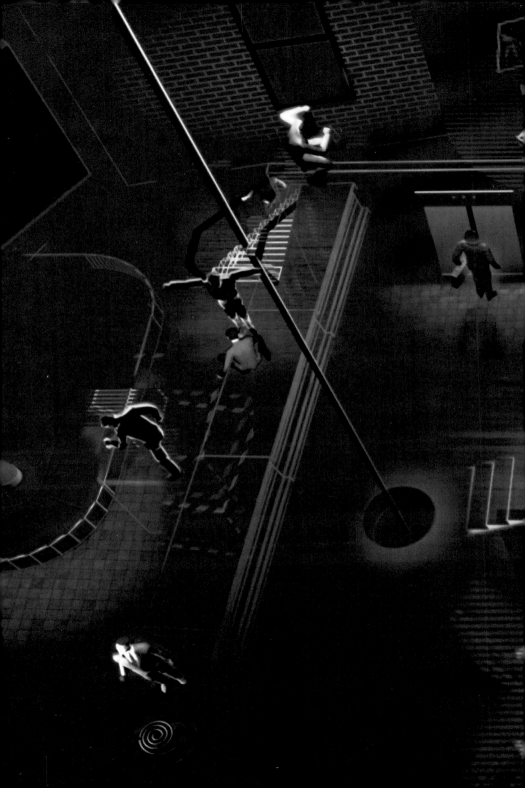

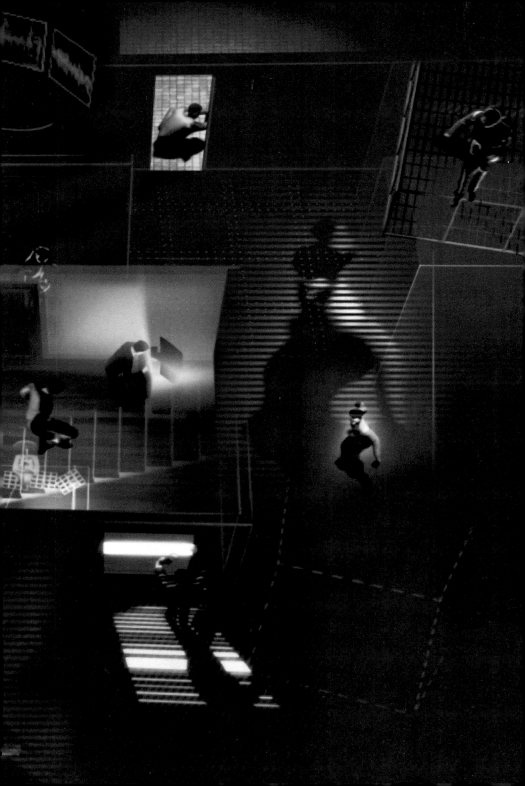

# Chapter 2:    Video Art

*A New Medium*

Critics may still have been (indeed still are) arguing over the aesthetic viability of Marcel Duchamp's *Fountain* (the upturned urinal submitted to an art exhibition in 1917) in the mid-1960s, but by this time the boundaries of art had been stretched so far that there were no more 'boundaries.' Readymades like *Fountain* turn out to have been just the beginning. In New York the Happenings of Allan Kaprow, Claes Oldenberg, and Jim Dine, the mixed-media canvases (with beds, stuffed chickens and wires) of Robert Rauschenberg, the body installations of Carolee Schneemann, and the neon panels of Dan Flavin are but a few examples of the multiplicity of art works on display at that time. Critic Clement Greenberg's dictum that the meaning of art (by which he meant a painting or a sculpture) was to be found within the object itself, was being challenged now by the notion that central to the practice of art was concept and context.

Minimalism and its offspring, Conceptualism, were the dominant forms of the period. 'Unfettered by object status,' art critic Lucy Lippard wrote, 'artists were free to let their imaginations run rampant.' In the visual arts, illusionism was rejected in favor of a pared down simplicity that was closer to industrial design than to pictorialism. This attitude reflected the ever increasing tendency in art toward eliminating the boundaries between art and everyday life, or, as history has come to treat it, between 'high' and 'low' art. And beyond the confines of the art world, the medium that predominated in mass culture at that time was television.

Art histories of the period often begin by considering Jasper Johns's *Flag* (1954–55), Frank Stella's *Stripe Painting* (1959), or Andy Warhol's *Brillo Boxes* (1964); not with any discussion of video art. It is partly because video art, which emerged in the mid-1960s, must be considered from the perspective of a world increasingly dominated by the media, especially television; and this, to many critics, is too far afield from the concerns of art. However, as San Francisco Museum of Modern Art curator Christine Hill notes, 'a fundamental idea held by the first generation of video artists was that in order to have a critical relationship with a televisual society, you must primarily participate televisually.'

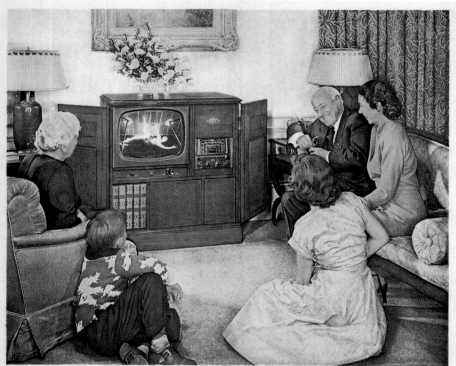

Paul Hesse photo

Here's Mr. Showmanship himself—Cecil B. DeMille—enjoying
Magnavox Big-Picture TV at home with his family in Hollywood.

# *Magnavox* graces America's finest homes

ONE of the things which makes many American homes so envied is television, and magnificent Magnavox Big-Picture TV ranks highest where gracious living is a daily habit. For Magnavox instruments are showpieces inside and out, combining advanced engineering with stunning cabinetry of heirloom quality. Each superb furniture piece is the ideal sounding chamber for glorious Magnavox tone. Sharp, clear Magnavox pictures are specially filtered for pleasing contrast. No matter how proud your home, or how modest your budget, you'll find a Magnavox meant just for you. See this great value at one of the fine stores listed under Magnavox in your classified telephone directory. The Magnavox Company, Fort Wayne 4, Indiana.

**THE MAGNAVOX EMBASSY** (also shown above) AM-FM radio-phonograph in rich mahogany finish. Add 20-inch TV now or later.

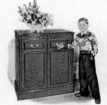

**Better sight...better sound...better buy**

*the magnificent*
# Magnavox
*television* J *radio-phonograph*

**Ultra High Frequency Units Readily Attachable**

81. 1960s advertisement
for Magnavox Televisions.
By 1960, ninety per cent
of American households had
television sets.

Images from around the world, which had only been available in the newsreels in movie houses, were now filtering into the average home, not only in black and white but now also in color. The moving image had entered the common household with a vengeance: by 1953, two thirds of American households had televisions; and by 1960, it was up to ninety per cent, a fact which was to have a profound effect on the film industry. Nonetheless, despite some notable exceptions on television in the US like the serious dramas on *Playhouse 90,* 'art' was to remain the domain of cinema. This century has established a kind of media technology pecking order, with cinema still on top, followed by television, then video, and now computer-transmitted images; all of which, arguably, derived from theater, which has suffered the most from loss of audiences and loss of artists to the other media.

By the 1960s the total commercialization of corporate television had been accomplished, and, to media watchdogs and many artists, television was becoming the enemy. Americans were watching up to seven hours of it daily and a new consumer society was forming, generated by an advertising oligarchy, which is what keeps television going. In addition worldwide political upheavals and dissident awareness, the student revolts in Paris, New York and many other parts of the world, and a sexual revolution all contributed to the cultural contexts in which video art emerged.

No one conceptualized the broad effects of the media explosion better than Canadian author Marshall McLuhan (1911–80). In his many writings, especially *The Medium Is the Message: An Inventory of Effects* (1967), he helped a generation to understand the tremendous impact of the media on daily living. 'Any one of our new media,' he wrote in 1960, 'is in a sense a new language, a new codification of experience collectively achieved by new work habits and inclusive collective awareness.' 'The new media,' he went on to say in 1969, 'are not ways of relating us to the old "real" world; they are the real world and they reshape what remains of the old world at will.' His critiques of advertising and commercial television became rallying points for 1960s artist/activists.

Though there has been argument over the exact origins of video art (especially targeted critiques from feminist critics in the US like Martha Gever and Martha Rosler), in the very beginning there were two types of video practices: activist-driven documentaries linked with alternative news reports and more properly so-called art videos.

Among the former camp are the political activities of so-called guerilla videographers like the Canadian-born Les Levine (b. 1935) and US artist Frank Gillette (b. 1941), who forced their way into political conventions and other newsworthy events without the proper credentials customary to news media. Levine was one of the first artists to use half-inch video equipment when it became available in 1965. *Bum* explored the street life of the down-and-out occupants of New York's so-called Skid Row on the Lower East Side. In 1968, Gillette also took to the streets, taping a five-hour documentary on hippies who congregated around St Mark's Place, the main thoroughfare on the Lower East Side in New York. Both Levine and Gillette utilized a gritty, you-are-there improvisational style of filming, which did not place any preconceived artistic or directorial overlay on the material. The subjects were starkly presented and were in no way 'artistic.'

In the US video collectives also sprang up quickly, spearheaded by groups such as Videofreex, Raindance Corporation, Paper Tiger Television (in New York) and Ant Farm in San Francisco. Strongly influenced by French and American *cinéma vérité* filmmakers who preceded them by ten years, these early video users were adapting a style that was soon to be very appealing to mainstream television stations in their 'on the spot' news coverage.

A case in point, Top Value Television (or TVTV) produced alternative coverage of the 1972 Democratic and Republican conventions in the United States. Using a half-inch, open reel, black and white Portapak, several TVTV 'correspondents' infiltrated the main convention floors, interviewing everyone from politicians to commercial television reporters in what amounted to an entertaining, provocative look at the foibles of American political and news gathering processes. The link between early alternative television (which actually received government funding) and mainstream television has its own, vital history. Suffice it to say, by the end of the 1970s, as US video historian Deirdre Boyle points out, network television, realizing their entertainment value, had absorbed many of the guerilla television camera and interviewing techniques. It even won over several of its members, including one activist/producer, Jon Alpert, who became a producer for NBC Television News.

The more purely 'art'-oriented video histories will usually point to the day in 1965 when Korean-born Fluxus artist and musician Nam June Paik bought one of the first Sony Portapak video sets in New York, and turned his camera on the Papal entourage that day making its way down Fifth Avenue. That, in this view, was the day video art was born. Paik apparently took the footage of the Pope, shot from a cab, and that night showed the results at an artists' hangout, the Cafe à Go Go.

84

82. (above right) **Andy Warhol**,
*Factory Diaries: Paul
Johnson*, 1965.

83. (right) **Andy Warhol**,
*Factory Diaries: Chinese Dinner
on Couch*, 1965.
Warhol's Factory was the defining
locus for multiple art practices.
In the mid-1960s Warhol was in
possession of his first hand-held
video camera with which he taped
all manner of activities in the loft,
including quotidian ones like
people eating or sleeping or
simply talking to the camera.

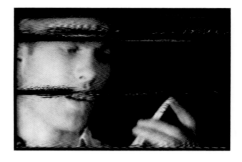

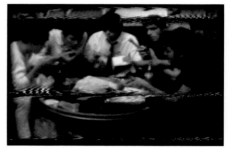

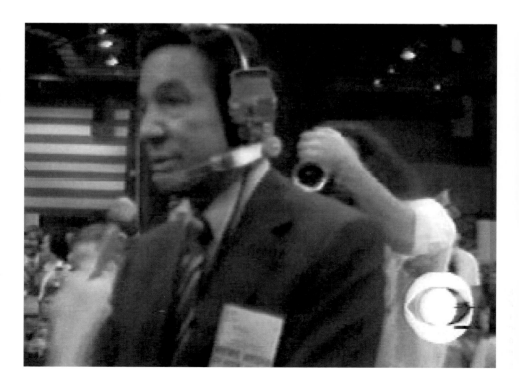

As video art history keeps getting re-written, we now know that Andy Warhol was most likely the first artist in the US to show what has become 'video art.' Warhol was among the first to use portable video cameras. In 1965, he was asked by *Tape Recording* magazine to experiment with the portable Norelco slant-track video recorder, a remote-control television camera with a zoom lens, and a Concord MTC 11 hand-held video camera with a Canon zoom lens. He made two thirty-minute tapes of a member of his cohort, Edie Sedgwick, and incorporated the tapes into his first double-projection film, *Outer and Inner Space* (1965). However, on September 29, 1965, just weeks before Paik's presentation at the Café à Go Go, Warhol presented videos at a party in a large, underground railroad space (it was important that the party be 'underground' for the presentation of 'underground' tapes) below the Waldorf-Astoria hotel in New York.

What makes Paik's filming of the Pope or Warhol's taping of one of his 'superstars' video art? At the most basic level, they are considered so because recognized artists (Warhol and Paik), already associated with visual art, music, or performance made the tapes as an extension of their artistic practice. As opposed to a newsperson on the beat with the Pope, Paik created a rough, non-commercial product that was a personal expression. Paik was not 'covering' the news of the Papal visit; Warhol was taping the way he might have been silk-screening or photographing. For Paik, this was the beginning of a career-long use of video as a preferred medium. He became the first 'spokesman' for video art. 'As collage technique replaced oil paint,' he is quoted as saying, 'so the cathode-ray tube will replace the canvas.'

At issue here is the intentionality of the artist, as opposed to that of the television executive or even commercial filmmaker or video maker: the work is not a product for sale or mass consumption. The aesthetics of video art, as intentionally loose as they may be, demand an artistic starting point from video artists that is akin to the aesthetic enterprise in general. Video, as an art, should be distinguished from the uses of video, however artfully executed, in documentaries, news reporting, and other purposeful, that is, applied, arenas. 'Art' and 'artful' are separate, though linked, terms that exist to help us differentiate between what can and cannot be considered to be art. Artful techniques may enliven commercial television, advertising, etc., but these techniques are not in themselves what we would normally call art. Art lies in the intentionality of the artist: to make or conceive of something without the constraint of some other purpose. The

84. (left) **TVTV**,
*Four More Years*, 1972.
The look of low-tech, portable camera interviews were soon admired by mainstream television news because of the authentic immediacy they suggested.

87

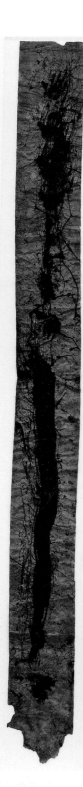

intention of the activist videographers, no matter how artful in execution, was not to create a moment of personal expression regardless of a practical application (here an alternative to traditional news reporting).

This is certainly not to suggest that the only legitimate historical analysis of video art must begin with those artists who came from more traditional media, like painting or music, and incorporated video into an essentially painterly art culture. But we must recognize, as John Hanhardt, curator at New York's Guggenheim Museum points out, that it is a curatorial museum culture that has become the ultimate validating source for all works of art. The artists whom that system recognized often came from the established media of painting and sculpture.

Paik, who studied aesthetics and music in Japan in the 1950s, is clearly representative of the video *artist*, as opposed to activist or reporter. A native of Korea, he moved to New York in 1964 from Germany where he had been a student, specifically, as he says, because of John Cage, whose experimental work in music and performance had a tremendous impact on many young artists at that

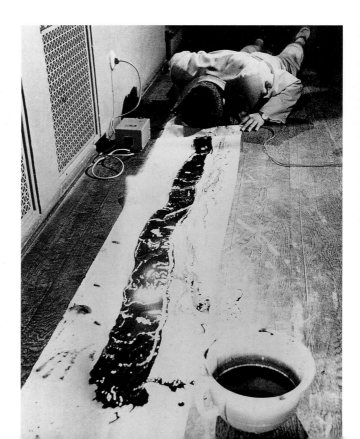

time. While in West Germany he met Cage and other Fluxus artists, and participated in what is considered the first Fluxus festival, the *Fluxus International Festival of Very New Music*, held in the auditorium of the Städtisches Museum in Wiesbaden. At the festival, Paik 'enacted' a 'score' by composer LaMonte Young that consisted entirely of the direction 'Draw a straight line and follow it.' Paik dipped his head, hands, and necktie into a bowl of ink and tomato juice and dragged them across a long horizontal piece of paper. Paik later returned to this single straight line in his 1968 *Video Buddha*, which features a Buddha sitting in front of a television screen showing only a black horizontal line.

For Paik and other early practitioners of video art, including Dan Graham, Bruce Nauman, Joan Jonas, and John Baldessari, it was video's capacity for instantaneous transmission of image that was most appealing, in addition to its relative affordability. For these artists, all of whom were preoccupied with themes concerning time (and often memory as well) the spontaneity and instantaneity of video were crucial. Video recorded and revealed instant time, whereas film had to be treated and processed. According to

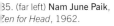

35. (far left) **Nam June Paik**, *Zen for Head*, 1962.

36. (left) **Nam June Paik** performing La Monte Young's *Composition 1960 #10* to Bob Morris as his *Zen for Head* at Fluxus Internationale Festspiele Neuester Musik, Wiesbaden, Germany, 1962.

37. (right) **Nam June Paik**, TV installation at Galerie Parnass, Wuppertal, 1963. The single line on Paik's television screens actually reflected the very first image to appear on the first television set in the late 1930s.

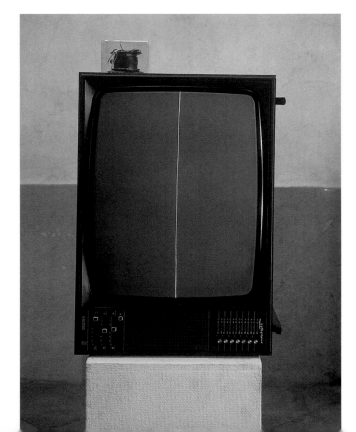

Graham, 'Video feeds back indigenous data in the immediate, present-time environment. Film is contemplative and "distanced;" it detaches the viewer from present reality and makes him a spectator.' Furthermore, as multiple projection devices were formulated, especially by Paik, it was possible to represent the often chaotic and random feel of multiple images competing constantly for our attention.

Video also afforded a sense of intimacy usually not realizable in film. In the hands of artists like Vito Acconci and Bruce Nauman, who literally turned the camera on themselves in fabricated situations (Acconci) or in their studio (Nauman, Howard Fried), video became an extension of the artistic gesture so long associated with painting, and especially with the Abstract Expressionists who had emphasized the physical act of painting itself. With video, the artist's gesture could be recorded and his or her body could be observed in the act of creation.

By the time he bought his Portapak, Paik had already been involved with using television in his art. In 1963, at the Galerie Parnass in Wuppertal, Germany, Paik filled a gallery space with televisions, some on the floor, some placed on their sides, all in an

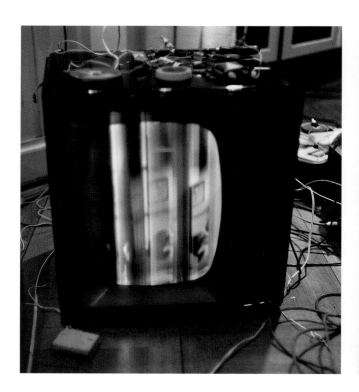

88. **Nam June Paik**,
*Zen for TV*, 1963–75.

effort to disrupt the normal relationship of the viewer to the television set. Though the distorted images in this early media sculpture were not Paik's own, this reconfiguring and displacing of the television set from its normal setting in the living room of a home has remained a central preoccupation of the artist.

Also in 1963, German artist Wolf Vostell (b. 1932) placed television monitors amidst what he called his 'De-coll/ages' magazine covers and announced that the television set had now been appropriated by an artist. Earlier in his first *TV De-coll/age* (1958) Vostell placed six television monitors in a wooden box behind a white canvas. 'The TV set is declared to be the sculpture of the twentieth century,' he said at the time of the exhibition, sounding as confident as Paik had about the death of the canvas. Their early enthusiasm provided a rallying point for the new electronic art. Vostell and Paik recontextualized the monitor, thus inaugurating a new way of viewing the small screen divorced from the familiar, commercial locus of the home. Now that the television medium had been liberated, so to speak, from the control of the commercial producers, artists could explore what to put on it in place of mostly commercial-driven content.

89. **Wolf Vostell**,
*TV De-coll/age No. 1*, 1958.

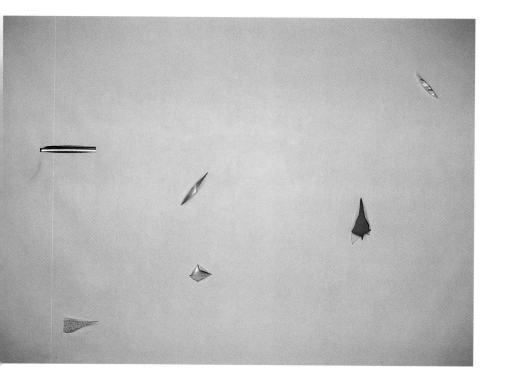

A critical attitude toward television was dominant in video art from its inception and into the mid-1980s. Like the Fluxus film artists before them, video artists took it upon themselves to comment, often in the ironic tones of postmodernism, on the cultural wars surrounding television and its prevalence in the twentieth-century household. Richard Serra's (b. 1939) *Television Delivers People* (1973) features a scrolling text criticizing television as corporate entertainment. To highlight his cultural critique Serra uses a soundtrack of musak, a bland hybrid music played in elevators and malls throughout the world. In a series of tapes from the early 1970s, including *Studies in Black and White Videotape 1* (1971), *Talk-Out* (1972), and *Street Sentences* (1972) US artist and critic Douglas Davis tackled received assumptions of television's use of time and space by breaking the 'fourth wall' and addressing the viewer directly. Like Acconci, he debunks the presumed intimacy of the medium and reveals it for the distancing device it really is. Taka Iimura (b. 1937) grappled with the illusory nature of language and recorded image in his perception-bending videos from the early 1970s. In *Double Portrait* (1973), utilizing delayed audio playback

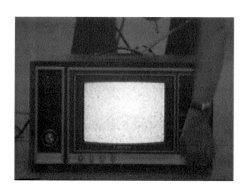

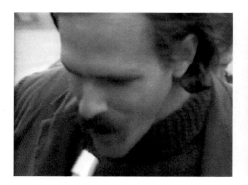

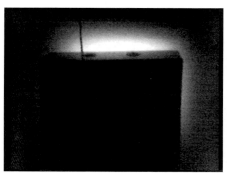

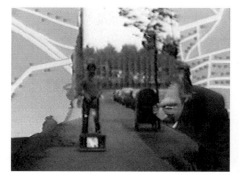

94. Mako Idemitsu, *HIDEO,
t's Me, Mama*, 1983.
More than fifteen years ahead
of the popular film *Truman*,
in which the life of the main
character is unwittingly taped
and projected onto television
sets worldwide, Mako Idemitsu
created a character called
Hideo who is constantly watched
and judged by his mother,
who appears on video screens
wherever he goes.

and reverse image playback, Iimura exposes the questionable reality' of electronic images.

The numbing effects of television commercials are interspersed with disturbing war footage in German artist Klaus vom Bruch's (b. 1952) *Das Softiband* (The Softi Tape, 1980). Seemingly endless repetitions of an ad for facial tissues highlights the power of television to trivialize even the most poignant events as archive war footage competes with the commercial for the viewer's attention.

Cultural and media critiques reach a Kafka-esque synthesis in Japanese artist Mako Idemitsu's (b. 1940) videos of tortured family members, who can never escape the watchful eye of the mother because she is always watching them from a television monitor wherever they go. Idemitsu reflects the corseted nature of Japanese life through the melodramas of television soap-operas which play continuously in the background of her psychological narratives such as *HIDEO, It's Me, Mama* (1983) and in the trilogy, *Great Mother* (1983–84).

In addition to criticizing the television medium, several early video artists engaged the technology of the camera and created innovative means of expression that were both used by other

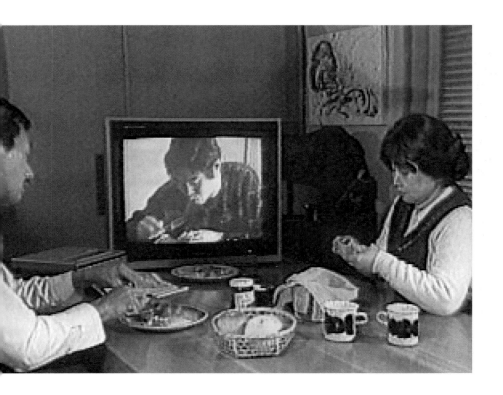

95. **Ed Emshwiller,**
*Thermogenesis*, 1972.

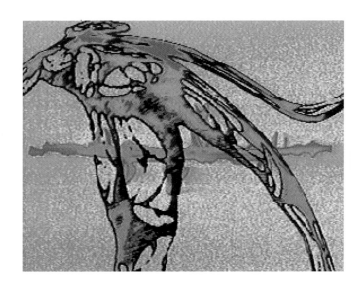

96. **Keith Sonnier,**
*Animation II*, 1974.

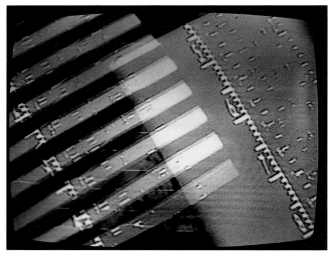

artists, and commonly usurped by mainstream media and advertising. American Ed Emshwiller (1925–90), who was an Abstract Expressionist painter as well as filmmaker and teacher, exploited the capabilities of video synthesizers and computer systems with his own original artistic and electronic strategies. In *Scape-mates* (1972) Emshwiller utilized a form of computer animation which resulted in an almost psychedelic dance of figurative and abstract elements. Earlier that same year he took his own black and white drawings and, with the assistance of engineers at Dolphin, one of the first corporations involved in computer imaging in the US, created *Thermogenesis*, a videowork that dances with imagery in a sound environment made with a Moog Audio Synthesizer in collaboration with Robert Moog himself.

Dan Sandin, whose interests in video grew out of his involvement with student protests in the late 1960s, developed the Image Processor in 1973. The IP, as it is called, is an analogue computer for the manipulation of video images. In his *Spiral PTL*, Sandin uses the IP to move a linear spiral made of dots in a musical rhythm with an accompanying soundtrack of electronic buzzes and running water. In a decidedly abstract vein, US artist Keith Sonnier (b. 1941) used an early version of a computer scanner, the Scanimate, to create sensuous multiple image collages. *Painted Foot: Black Light* (1970), and *Color Wipe* (1973) both show extensive formal experimentation with light and color. His *Animation II* (1974) is a record of abstract shapes and colors which serve as metaphors for the properties of paint and paintings.

Also prominent among early technological innovators of video art was the husband and wife team of Steina and Woody Vasulka, who emigrated to the United States in 1965 (she was born in Iceland in 1940, he in Czechoslovakia in 1937). Seizing the reins from commercial television, they set out to advance the technology of video by creating devices for artists, especially in the fields of digital processing and electronic image processing. In keeping with the age-old practice of artists' constantly exploring the tools of their medium, the Vasulkas possessed a passion for understanding the inner workings of video: electrical energy organized as voltages and frequencies in a temporal event.

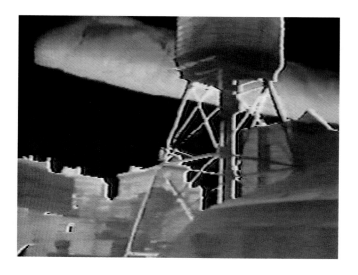

7. Steina and Woody Vasulka, *Golden Voyage*, 1973.

Like painters involved with the contents of their palette, these innovators probed the video medium in much the same way that abstract artists or colorists did. Distinguishing themselves from the electrical engineers of commercial television, they were interested in the mechanisms of video as they function artistically, not how they can enhance the transmission of images of a commercial product. In a sense the Vasulkas embody the notion that video art was to television what studio painting was to early forms of drawn or painted advertising. In works such as *Home* (1973) in which the Vasulkas artfully incorporate colorizing and electronic imaging techniques to glamorize everyday objects, and *Golden Voyage* (1973), a multilayered homage to Magritte, the Vasulkas invented new means of electronic manipulation that altered viewers' perceptions, as Pointillism and Impressionism had done in painting a century before. *Vocabulary* (1973–74) resulted from their experimenting with digital manipulation of images that closely resemble today's floating, computer-based images seen everywhere on computer monitors and on television. Using the image of a hand filmed in close-up as a metaphor for artistic creation, the artists fashion an electronic sculpture from which light emerges and through which other objects are shaped and imbued with a life of their own.

Nam June Paik, who has been influential in virtually every area of video art, contributed one of the first new technologies with his Paik/Abe Synthesizer, a device for image manipulation and colorization, developed with electronics engineer Shuya Abe. His *Suite 212* (1975, re-edited 1977) is Paik's personal New York notebook. Essentially a monumental electronic collage of altered images accented in dizzying colors, this piece set the stage for Paik's later investigations of imagery and culture, a classic example of which is *Butterfly* (1986), a vibrant amalgam of collaged images and music.

Several artists, taking their cue from Paik and the Vasulkas, incorporated sophisticated technology in their critiques of technology. Max Almy (b.1948), a Los Angeles artist, uses computer animation and digital effects in her postmodern renditions of a world dehumanized by technology. In *Leaving the 20th Century* 1c (1982) Almy creates a futuristic landscape in which human relations and attempts at communication completely fail. Time travel is imaginatively accomplished through the computer chip in this early experiment in computerized video art.

Television also benefitted artists. Public television stations in the United States and Europe fostered experimentation by

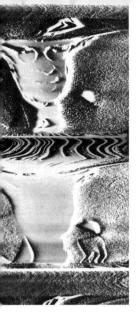

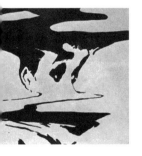

allowing access to fully equipped studios. Starting in the late 1960s, Boston's public television station, WGBH, with funding from the Rockefeller Foundation, produced the New Television Workshop under the leadership of Fred Barzyk. In 1969 six artists (Nam June Paik, Allan Kaprow, Otto Piene, James Seawright, Thomas Tadlock, and Aldo Tambellini) made videotapes using WGBH equipment for a program called 'The Medium is the Medium' which aired nationally. This was the widest exposure the new practice of video art had yet received.

Robert Zagone, working at public television station KQED in San Francisco, created eerie disintegration of abstract forms through multiple camera feedback techniques in *Videospace* (1968). He also replicated a dream state in his multilayered tape of a dancer, *Untitled* (1968), which resembles an updated and animated version of a Muybridge chronograph. Swedish artists Ture Sjölander, Lars Weck, and Bengt Modin produced *Monument* (1967), a program for experimental television which combined pre-recorded film, slides, and videotapes in a process that distorted images during the transmission of the image from the tape to the television. After seeing these for the first time, historian Gene Youngblood said, 'We see the Beatles, Charlie Chaplin, Picasso, the Mona Lisa, the King of Sweden, and other famous figures distorted with a kind of insane electronic disease.'

Peter d'Agostino's (b. 1945) *TeleTapes* (1981), produced by the influential Television Laboratory at New York's Public Television Station, WNET, incorporates card games, tricks, and a broad assortment of television effects, to confront the viewer with 'experiential reality' and 'television reality.'

8, 99. **Ture Sjölander,**
**ars Weck** and **Bengt Modin,**
*ing of Sweden* (top) and
*harlie Chaplin* (above).
.vo distorted TV film clips from
ιe film *Monument*, 1967.
Ίany innovations in what later
ιecame computer animation were
ιaugurated by video artists who
arly on developed electronic
ιnaging techniques.

00. **John Baldessari,**
*Am Making Art*, 1971.
.onceptual artists like John
ιaldessari made several
ιomespun videos whose
ιtentional lack of polish took
ιm at the pretenses of high art.

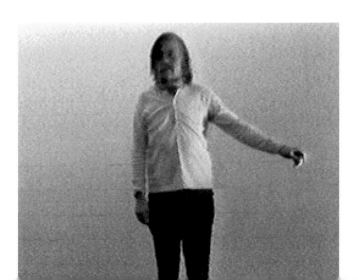

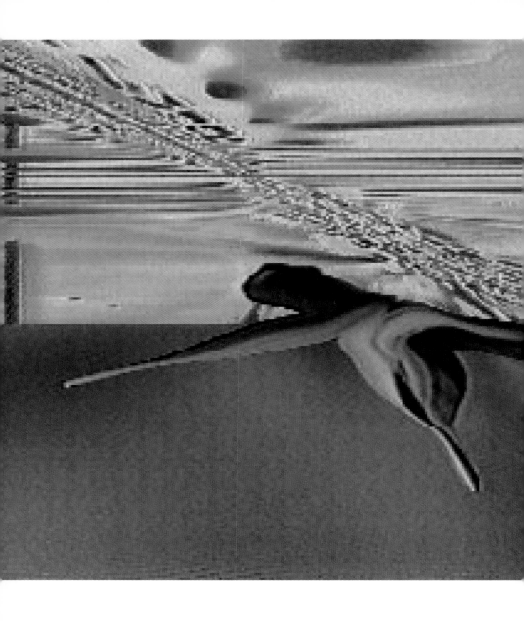

101. **Nam June Paik**, *Butterfly*, 1986.

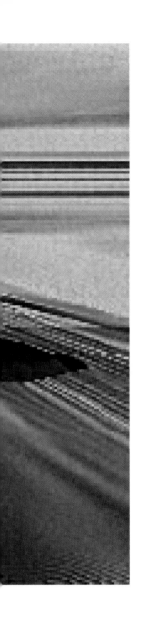

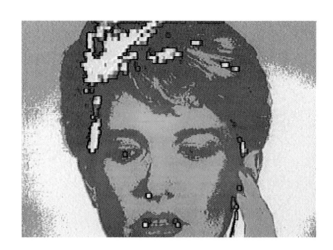

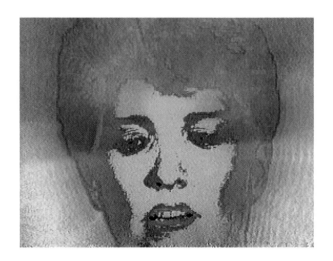

02–104. **Max Almy**, *Leaving the 0th Century*, 1982.

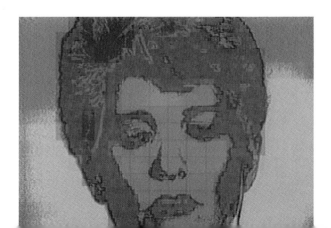

### Conceptual Video

Some other early explorations in video art came from artists who were already practising their own forms of Conceptual and Minimal art, mingled with the strong influence of Performance art. Much of early video art can in fact be seen, on one level, as the recording of a performance, or what came to be dubbed 'performative' actions. John Baldessari (b. 1931), a California Conceptual artist who used photography and language in his work of the early 1960s, made a series of roughly shot, but conceptually rigorous black and white videos, many of them in 1971. In *I Am Making Art*, Baldessari films himself in his familiar dishevelled state, dressed in white, standing in front of a white brick wall. As he makes small, discreet movements (decidedly unchoreographed) he repeats over and over the words of the title. For almost twenty minutes he allows one gesture to lead to another as he systematically debunks all the pretenses of 'high' art (such as Abstract Expressionism) and even some of the 'low' art of 1960s performance.

Another California artist associated with Conceptualism is Howard Fried (b. 1946) whose *Inside the Harlequin* series (1971) anticipated the work of Matthew Barney twenty years later. In this series, presented in multi-screen projections, Fried scales the walls of his studio with the help of suspension wires and harnesses. He presents the studio as a place to be entered fully and conquered.

Vito Acconci, in addition to the performative works discussed in the previous chapter, explored the place of the body in art and life in several black and white single-channel video works in 1971. Isolated inside a box, or in the corner of a room, Acconci focused the camera on himself and, in direct address, engaged the viewer in

105. **Vito Acconci**,
*Theme Song*, 1973.
The notions of viewer and voyeur are interconnected in Acconci's ironic videotaped monologues in which he crudely tempts the viewer to join him inside the camera.

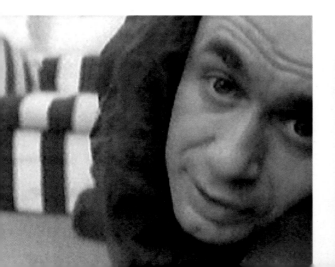
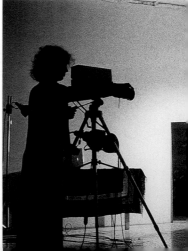

psychological word games that probe the relationship of the viewer (or the voyeur) to the subject being watched. He thus manufactures (and reflects) the medium's false sense of intimacy. In *Theme Song* (1973) Acconci lies on the floor, just inches from the camera, in front of a black and white striped couch, and attempts to seduce the viewer to join him. 'I want you inside me,' he pleads repeatedly as he smokes an endless cigarette and shifts position on the floor. In *Filler* (1971), on the floor inside a cardboard box and facing the camera, Acconci coughs at odd intervals suggesting a pathetic come-on. Intentionally or not, Acconci's narcissistic video performances are a perfect foil for those obsessed with celebrity, whose habits are fed by tabloid television.

If Acconci revealed the false intimacy of the televised image from a male perspective, in the 1970s several female artists drew attention to the representation of women common in television, films, and pornography. A commonly heard battlecry, 'the personal is

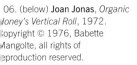

06. (below) **Joan Jonas**, *Organic Honey's Vertical Roll*, 1972. Copyright © 1976, Babette Mangolte, all rights of reproduction reserved.

07. (right) **Joan Jonas**, *Organic Honey's Vertical Roll*, 1973. Jonas, like Acconci, upsets the relationship between viewer and televised image by confounding any sense of perspective through the use of multiple mirrors.

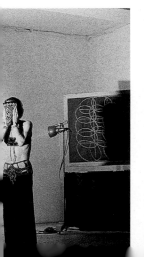

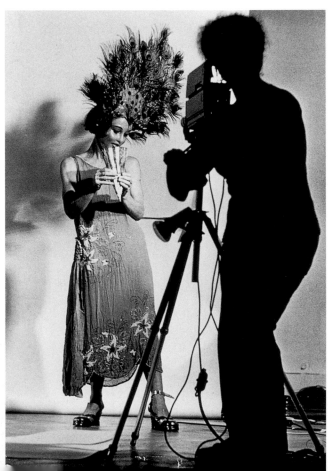

108. (below) **Joan Jonas**, *Left Side, Right Side*, 1972. Jonas, like Acconci, upsets the relationship between viewer and televised image by confounding any sense of perspective through the use of multiple mirrors. 'From the beginning,' she says, 'the mirror provided me with a metaphor for my investigations as well as a device to alter space…and to reflect the audience, bringing them into the space.'

109. (opposite) **Hannah Wilke**, *Gestures*, 1973. What at first looks like a commercial for a skin cream becomes a grotesque send-up of the idealized female image.

political,' resulted in opening artistic discourse more broadly to include female perspectives. Issues of gender, sexuality (homosexual and heterosexual) and the role of women in art and society became ubiquitous in art.

Known for her performance work, Joan Jonas's (b. 1936) large body of video work has come to define the medium in its complexity. *Vertical Roll* (1972), which refers to an interrupted electronic signal that causes a televised image to keep rolling incessantly on the screen, utilizes the power of repetition, so often seen in choreography and in minimal sculpture, to fragment and disorient perceptions of the female body. As Jonas is filmed, now as a belly dancer, now as a 1930s movie star, her image is ripped from view by the unrelenting electronic roll. Throughout she bangs a spoon, a simple metaphor for domestic life, against what seems like the front of the camera, to further disorient the viewer and convey the rage she feels.

In a more whimsical mode, in *Left Side, Right Side* (1972) Jonas performs tricks with the camera and a mirror, further to confuse the perception of left and right when looking at a reverse image. Jonas exaggerates this dilemma, repeating all the while, 'This is my left side, this is my right side,' until the viewer can no longer

106

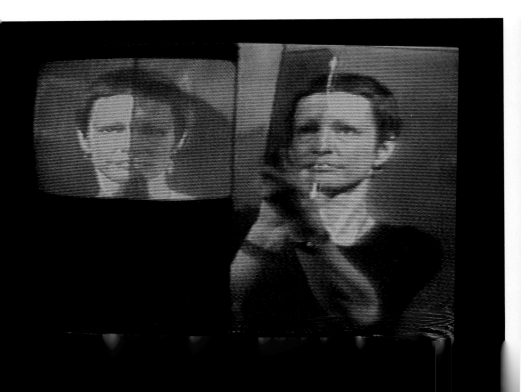

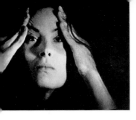

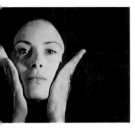

tell which is actually her left or her right side. Like Acconci she turns the medium on itself, by confusing conventional perspective, at the same time creating a striking personal, feminist landscape by using her own body in ways the female body was rarely seen in conventional media. 'Working with video,' she says, 'enabled me to develop my own language, a poetic language. Video was something for me to climb into and explore as a spatial element and with myself inside of it.'

German-born artist Hannah Wilke (1940–1993) also explored the dynamics of the artist and her body in relation to conventional portrayals of women, as in *Gestures* (1973). In this work she focuses the camera close-up on her face and engages in sexually suggestive gestures involving her fingers and her tongue. Gradually these gestures become grotesque as she distorts her face, thus demystifying the female body as portrayed on screen. In a similar vein, the American artist Lynda Benglis (b. 1941) in *Now* (1973) projected pre-recorded images of herself, in facial close-up, and performed in real time for the camera, interacting with her own image, exploring the possibilities of this new medium even as she engaged in a criticism of the use of the medium to degrade the female body.

10. (below) **Dara Birnbaum**, *Technology Transformation: Wonderwoman* (1978–79). Birnbaum takes a popular TV character and debunks the 'Wonderwoman' myth.

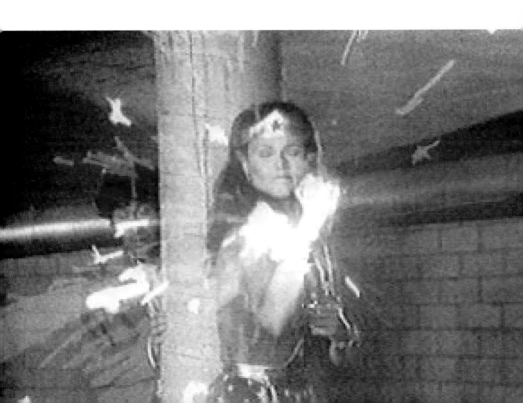

Dara Birnbaum (b. 1946) in her *Technology Transformation: Wonderwoman* (1978–79) manipulated images from a popular 1970s US television show, *Wonderwoman*, and countered the myth of woman as beautifully chiseled miracle worker and lover. Through careful editing of single images, Birnbaum has Wonderwoman spinning and whirling in an orgy of repeated and fragmented images that literally deconstruct the conventional televised myth.

Often overlooked in historical surveys of feminist media art is Cuban-born Ana Mendieta (1948–86). During her graduate training in the Intermedia Department at the University of Iowa, Mendieta created performances, videos, and films that expressed the visceral connections she felt between her own body and the earth. She would perform for the camera distorting her body pressed onto large pieces of glass or pouring large amounts of animal blood on herself and imprinting part of her body on paper or other surfaces. In her 1974 film *Burial Pyramid*, shot on desolate terrain in El Yaagul, Mexico, a pile of rocks starts to move as if being shaken by an earthquake. As the rocks become displaced, Mendieta appears, lying naked on her back underneath them, shifting them with the movements of her body. These performative videotapes, begun in 1972, are collected in the series *Body Tracks* (1974).

111. **Ana Mendieta**, *Body Tracks (Blood Sign #2)*, 1972–74. In many of her performances Mendieta used her bloodied body as a spiritual metaphor for sacrifice.

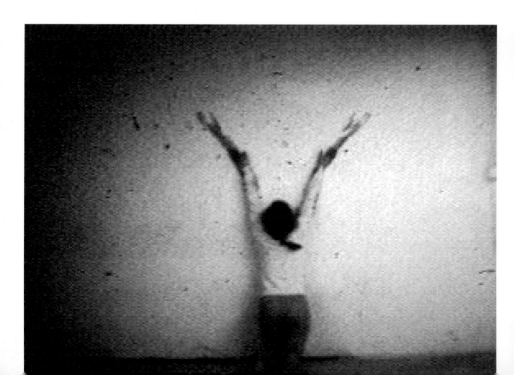

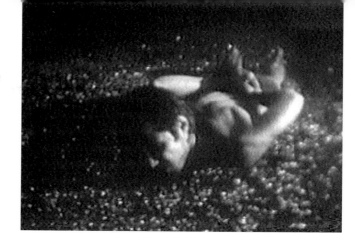

**112. Chris Burden,**
*Through the Night Softly*, 1973.
Burden often challenged the art-making process by using his body as art in extreme situations such as crawling on glass or having himself shot in the arm.

**113. Peter Campus,**
*Dynamic Field Series*, 1971.

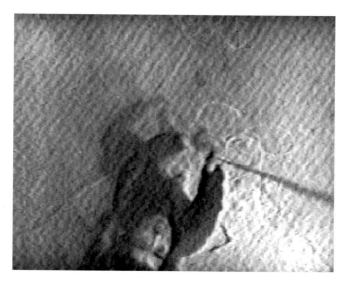

Explorations of the body were not limited to women artists, however. The American Chris Burden's (b. 1950) radical explorations of the body-at-risk subverted any 'high-art' notions of the artistic work process. His performance-based work aimed to shock viewers into a new relationship between the performer and the audience, in which the viewer becomes implicated in the performer's extreme actions. Burden's early videos and films were documentations of his often shocking performance actions, including *Shoot* (1971) in which a bullet was shot into his arm, and *Through the Night Softly* (1973) in which, lying on his stomach, hands tied behind his back and dressed only in a pair of shorts, he pulls himself along a street full of broken glass. In *Icarus* (1973)

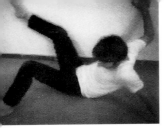

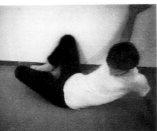

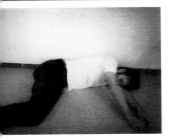

he is taped lying naked on the floor of his studio in front of a few invited friends who serve as audience/witness while he narrowly escapes being set on fire as the curtains that hang above and around him are ignited. As is always the case with such video art work, Burden narrated these tapes himself, coming across as a youthful daredevil Conceptualist. His voice suggests no irony. He clearly believed that his risky actions revealed psychological insights into his own body's relationship to the world and to art.

Other early practitioners of video art who explored personal and spatial identity through video performance include Peter Campus (b. 1937) whose *Dynamic Field Series* (1971) features the artist in his studio engaging in a set of self-imposed feats of endurance, like climbing a rope, while the camera engages him from so many different angles that the viewer is never sure what is real or imaginary. His *Three Transitions* (1973) is considered a classic tape. Using the video medium as a metaphor for the internal and external selves, Campus creates illusions of transformation in which he appears to be stabbing himself in the back, erasing the surface of his face, or climbing through his own ruptured back.

Bruce Nauman (b. 1941) also made videos using his own body: in *Wall/Floor Positions* (1968) he assumes sculptural poses on the wall and floor of his studio. The viewer is invited into a voyeuristic encounter with the artist in his workspace as he defines the physical space of his studio with his body. Several of his tapes, which are literal enactments of their titles (*Bouncing in the Corner no. 1, Revolving Upside Down, Stamping in the Studio*, all 1968) reveal the body as

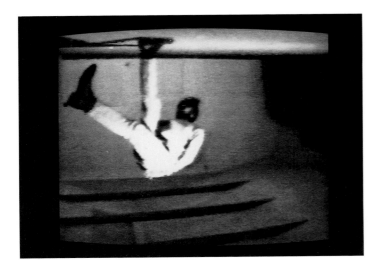

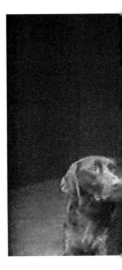

114–16. (left) **Bruce Nauman**, *Wall/Floor Positions*, 1968.

117. (below left) **Bruce Nauman**, *Revolving Upside Down*, 1968. Nauman saw a relationship between the activities, however mundane, he performed in his study and his sculpture. Performance and sculpture were linked in his work. 'I think of it as going into the studio,' he says, 'and being involved in some activity. Sometimes it works out that the activity involves making something, and sometimes that the activity is the piece.'

118. (below) **William Wegman**, *Selected Works: Reel 6*, 1975.

119. (below right) **Juan Downey**, *Moving*, 1974. Artists like Juan Downey have used video as a form of diary or visual recording of personal thoughts and impressions.

sculptural material as he moves about his studio in different configurations. These tapes also reflect the common practice among early video artists to simply let the tape run on to the end, thus deliberately rejecting conventional editing. It was not until 1975 that more affordable editing equipment became commercially available.

Nauman is a good example of an artist who turned to video as only one other medium of his artistic practice. For Nauman and for others of his generation, new modes of expression were constantly and ruthlessly pursued in order 'to figure out how to proceed,' as he says. Uninterested in simply re-hashing traditional problems with painting (he admired the way De Kooning explored in paintings his own reactions to Picasso), Nauman was 'interested in what art can be, not just what painting can be.' The materials, therefore, were at once unimportant and all important in that there were no limitations on what could be used to make art.

Yielding to the more humorous side of self-exploration in the studio, while capturing the exuberance of a newly developing medium, was the American William Wegman (b. 1943), who has become known for his funny and touching photographs of his pet dogs. Wegman began videotaping his dog, Man Ray, in the late 1960s, producing an early body of work, ironic in its juxtapositions of the dog's movements with Wegman's textual overlays on life and art. In *Selected Works: Reel 6* (1975), Man Ray and another dog become fixated on an off-camera object that makes the two seated dogs move their heads from side to side in a synchronized rhythm that mimics the crowd at a tennis match. Wegman often invokes the

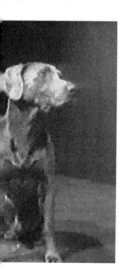
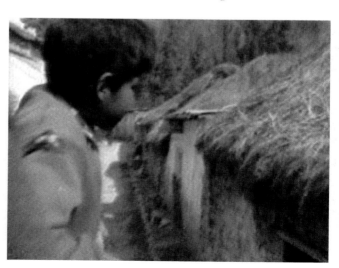

history of modern art in his work. In *Split Sandwich* (1970) he appears in drag in one sequence like Duchamp as his invented character Rrose Selavy, and his *Man Ray Man Ray* (1978) is a 'biography' of the artist Man Ray as played by Wegman's pet dog of the same name.

Other significant early video artists used the medium as a form of diary. Andy Warhol, who bought a Sony Portapak in 1970, began shooting his *Factory diaries*, which recorded hundreds of hours of activity in his studio through 1976. Juan Downey (b. 1940), a Chilean artist who has lived in New York for many years, uses video in his self-exploration as an artist who chose cultural discontinuity as a way of life. In *Moving* (1974) Downey, accompanied by his Portapak camera, travelled across the United States and through into South America (Peru, Bolivia), down to the southern tip of his native Chile, all the while creating a video diary of his attempt to recover his lost self.

Several other artists in the 1970s reflected Conceptualism's use of language in their videotapes. Gary Hill (b. 1951), who began working in video in 1973, uses language and texts in as integral a fashion as others use music in video art. In *Electronic Linguistics* (1977) he attempts to interpret the shape of an electronic sound visually by picturing in fast succession moving electronically generated shapes (lines, curves) on the screen. Hill sees the image as a language that he is continuously re-inventing through the medium of video art.

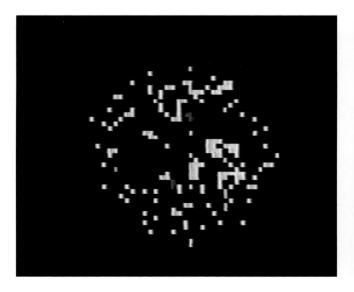

120. **Gary Hill**, *Electronic Linguistics*, 1977. Words, sounds, images, movements are all languages for Hill. Much of his work tries to visualize human attempts to attain consciousness through varieties of language.

121, 122. **Ken Feingold,**
two stills from *Purely Human
Sleep*, 1980.
Feingold unearths unconscious
fears that creep into our lives
from news reports, advertising,
and television.

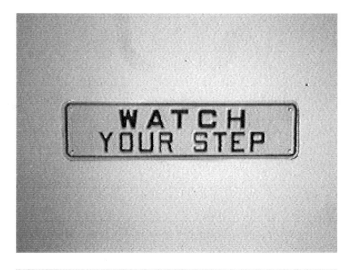

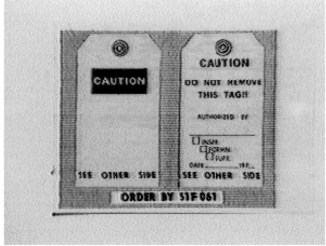

Hill also provides a useful link to the second generation of video artists who have come of age since the mid-1980s. As artists rapidly accustomed themselves to the availability of ever more affordable cameras, especially color cameras, and processing techniques, the art of video progressed from what had been an art that reacted to television, or that merely translated trends in visual art to the video medium (Conceptualism, body art, Process art), and began taking on its own identity. Artists emerged who were or became primarily video artists, not sculptors, photographers, or painters who dabbled in video (the way, say, Serra or Baldessari had). Although Hill had been a sculptor, his conversion to video was a complete move. His sculptural influences remain evident in his video installations, but his primary explorations have remained in the realm of electronic art.

Ken Feingold's (b. 1952) career in electronic art began in video and continues in sophisticated computer-based work. While Hill's imagery often derives from the philosophical writings of Ludwig Wittgenstein, Feingold's videos from the early 1980s (*Water Falling From One World to Another*, 1980, *Purely Human Sleep*, 1980, 121-2 and *Allegory of Oblivion*, 1981) reflected his interests in Lacanian psychoanalysis and semiotics, emphasizing a certain intimacy between language and image, the self and the other, whether real or imagined. Feingold used language symbols to portray postmodern existence as a world 'fractured by philosophy, the news, and art.'

Intellectual explorations of language, sound, and image, so favored by filmmaker Jean-Luc Godard beginning in the 1960s, are also reflected in the work of Robert Cahen (b. 1945), one of France's most influential video artists. His affinity with Godard is evident in tapes like *Juste le Temps* (1983) and *Boulez-Repons*

123. **Robert Cahen**, *Juste le Temps*, 1983. Cahen's images often feel like they belong in films instead of videos, but he manages to combine the feeling of the textural depth of film with the real-time immediacy of video.

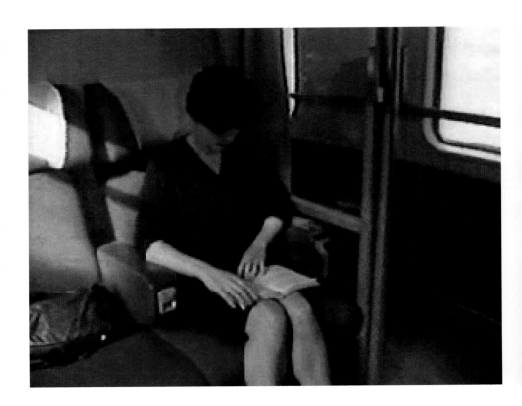

(1985). In the former, Cahen creates an abstract landscape of multiple images that appear and disappear through the window of the train in which his female protagonist is sitting. In *Boulez-Repons*, Cahen applies electronic processing techniques to engulf a musical composition by Pierre Boulez in images of water, sky, and trees.

Video artists of the 1980s and 1990s have largely, though not exclusively, turned their attention to personal narratives that reflect a quest for identity (particularly cultural or sexual) and political freedom. These developments are often expressive of economic realities. Western European, North American, and some Japanese artists, living in a time of relative peace and economic prosperity, from which some artists feel excluded, have turned to video to communicate their intense desire to achieve personal social equality (in the case of women and sexual and racial minorities); whereas in the East (including Eastern Europe and the Middle and Far East), political struggle remains at the forefront of artistic and economic preoccupation. Partly for economic reasons, but largely due to artistic differences, video art did

24. **V. Bukatin, B. Galeyev** nd **R. Sayfullin**, *lectronic Painter*, 1975–80. he Soviet art and technology roup SKB Promotei managed ɔ create visually compelling xperiments in video during a me when artistic exploration ⱱas officially frowned upon in heir country.

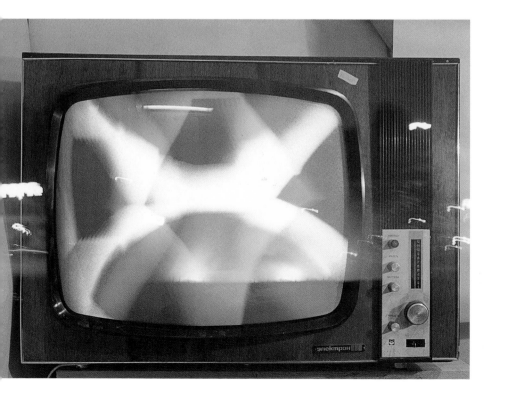

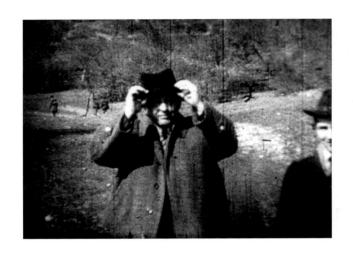

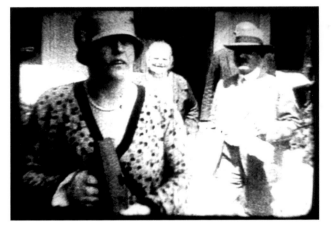

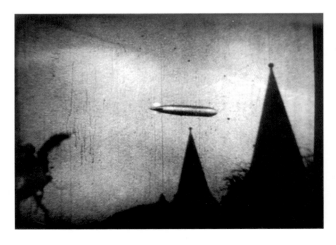

125–27. **Péter Forgács,**
*Private Hungary:*
*The Bartos Family*, 1988.
Rare footage of life under Stalin
was assembled by Hungarian
video artist Forgács from family
films shot by Zoltan Bartos.

not catch on in the former Soviet Union until the 1990s, after the fall of Communism. Bulat Galeyev, a founder of the art and technology group SKB Promotei, has said that video was not considered 'art' in the Soviet Union. It is also likely that potential surveillance uses of video kept the form dormant in Russia during the Soviet era. Galeyev's group did, however, experiment with the use of the television monitor in a series of works called *Electronic Painter* (1975–80); these involved programming images of color through electronic generators placed inside the monitor. Their *Space Sonata* (1981) is an abstract exploration of the body in an outerspace context. In Hungary, beginning in 1988, Péter Forgács created a record of life under Stalin in *Private Hungary: The Bartos Family*, using footage shot by Zoltan Bartos, the eldest son.

124

In the slowly emerging video art of Communist China, which largely takes the form of documentary, artists like Ma Liuming, Li Yongbin, and Wang Jinsong explore the 'individual' in a country where anonymity has been rewarded over declarations of the self. Shi Jian and Chen Jue's *Tiananmen Square* (1991), a series of tapes filmed in the neighborhoods around the square in Beijing where historic student uprisings occurred in 1989, were banned by the Chinese government from domestic and international distribution until 1997 when they were shown at New York's Museum of Modern Art.

*Personal Narratives*
Bill Viola (b. 1951), whose video art will be discussed in greater detail in the next chapter, began his long exploration of the physical and spiritual self in his single-channel videos of the 1970s and 1980s. For Viola, perhaps more than any other video artist, video is an intensely personal medium that contains within its power a full range of expressive possibilities. Like a young painter experimenting with the feel of different paints on a canvas, Viola toyed with the electronics of a videotape recorder in his 1973 video, *Information*. He used a technical mistake (a self-interrupting signal) to create a sequence of images he could control from the outside. Trained in music and acoustics, Viola places sound and the interplay of light and dark at the center of his art. He performed for the camera with a loudspeaker superimposed on his back (*Playing Soul Music to My Freckles*, 1975) and with his own image, reflected in a coffee cup, gradually disappearing as he drank from the cup (*A Non-Dairy Creamer*, 1975). The self and non-self, fundamental concepts of Eastern

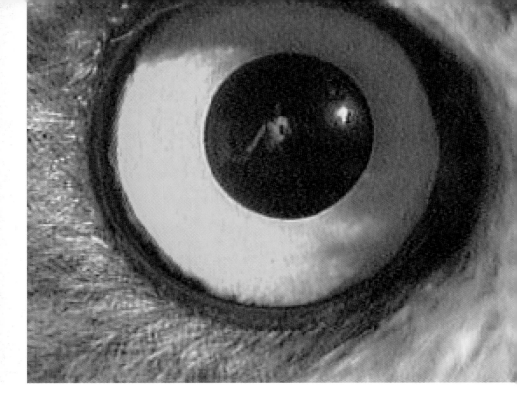

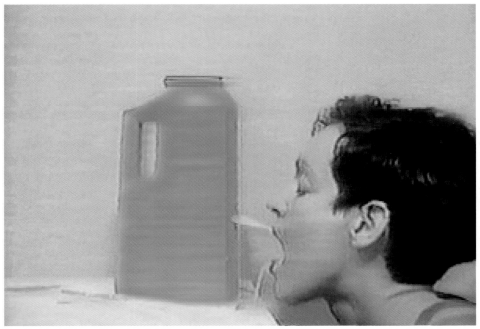

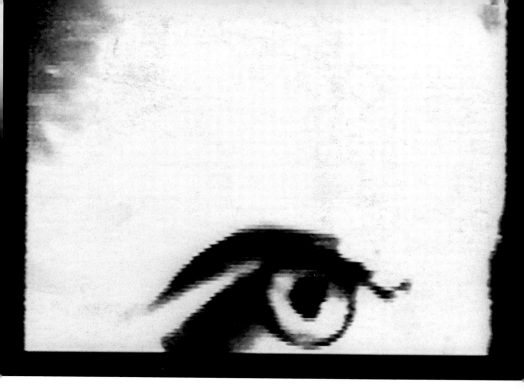

28. (above left) **Bill Viola**, *Do Not Know What It Is Am Like*, 1986. Viola has engaged in rigorous self-examination through video since 1975. Here the artist films his own image in the eye of an owl.

29. (left) **Cheryl Donegan**, *Head*, 1993.

30. (above) **Sadie Benning**, *Every Girl Had a Diary*, 1990. Sadie Benning, as a sixteen-year-old, used a toy pixel camera to make a 'diary' of her sexual awakening.

mysticism, have long interested Viola and play a central role in all of his work to the present day. The artist's reflection, captured in the eye of an owl, became a signature mark of the artist with his heralded 1986 video, *I Do Not Know What It Is I Am Like*. Based on a Sanskrit text that investigates the connectedness of all living beings, Viola's search for self-knowledge is visualized in this five-part metaphysical journey.

The low-tech performative style of 1970s artists such as Acconci and Jonas reverberates especially in the work of several female artists. Placing the body squarely in the personal/political realm are artists like Swiss-born Pipilotti Rist (b. 1962) and the Americans Cheryl Donegan, Sadie Benning (b. 1973), and Phyllis Baldino (b. 1956). In her 1986 video, *I'm Not the Girl Who Misses Much*, Rist, echoing the early work of Marina Abramovic, dances frenetically in front of the camera while repeating the words of the title (also a pop tune). As her gyrations become more grotesque, this critique of MTV becomes a biting comment on the degrading of the female body in popular culture. In a slower-paced, more ironic vein, Cheryl Donegan's 1993 work, *Head*, the artist, while drinking white liquid from a plastic detergent bottle,

1–3

makes exaggerated sounds of pleasure in this send-up of the pornography industry. Her *Line* (1996) follows the plot of Godard's film *Contempt* (in which a woman played by Brigitte Bardot becomes embroiled with egomaniacal film directors) in a tightly composed send-up of male posturing in art.

The diaristic work of American artist Sadie Benning, a self-described lesbian videomaker, keeps the improvisational spirit of early video alive in her very personal narratives, begun in the late 1980s. Using a toy camera manufactured by Fisher-Price, Benning records the feelings of a young woman emerging into sexual maturity in tapes such as *A New Year* (1989), *If Every Girl Had a Diary* (1990), and *Flat Is Beautiful* (1998). *Living Inside* (1989) records Benning's three-week period when she took off from high school as a sixteen-year-old and taped herself in her room by herself. Innocence and pathos unite in this tale of the teenager as outsider. The incongruities of more 'grown-up' life are

131. **Seoung Cho**, *robinson or me (From the Far East)*, 1996.

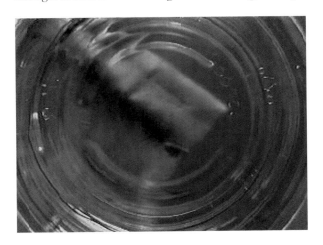

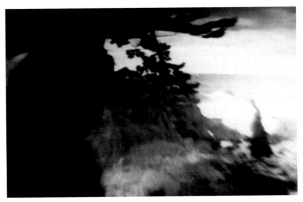

132. **Alexandr Sokurov**, *Oriental Elegy*, 1996.

explored by Phyllis Baldino's performative tapes in which she constructs and deconstructs everyday objects in front of a continuously recording camera. Her questioning of the stereo-typical female preoccupation with make-up is featured in *Cosmetic/Not Cosmetic* (1993–94) in which she destroys a vanity case with a power drill even as she is all 'made up' and dressed in a satin slip.

Several male video artists appear to have taken a more lyrical track in work that tackles questions of identity. Their work is less angry, often expressing longing. Korean-born Seoung Cho explores domestic activities, but in a reflective and imagistic manner. In his 1996 tape, *robinson or me*, ritualized activities like drinking tea or showering become metaphors for the solitary life. A sense of searching for an identity in a world in which the artist feels displaced links the work of British artist George Barber (*Withdrawal*, 1996) and Canadian Nelson Hendricks (*Window*, 1997). A profound search for the self dominates the videos of Russian filmmaker Alexandr Sokurov (b. 1951), especially *Oriental Elegy* (1996), a dreamscape filmed on a misty, remote Japanese island in which the characters appear suspended somewhere between life and death.

Sokurov and Viola represent what might be called the 'high end' of video production, employing sophisticated, film-like technology (occasionally mixing film with video) and resulting in a highly polished end product. What is so vibrant about video art is the fact that it embraces both high and low end budgets in equal measure, at least in terms of what is shown in festivals, museums, and galleries. There is strong curatorial interest in conceptual, often performative, technologically primitive work, evident, for example, in the Museum of Modern Art's exhibition, *Young and Restless* (1997), which featured several low-budget videos by young female artists (among them Cheryl Donegan, Kristin Lucas, Alix Pearlstein) who engage the camera in direct, personal ways. Several British artists, especially Sam Taylor-Wood (b. 1967) and Gillian Wearing (b. 1963), also maximize the single-channel video format in their provocative, often humorous, tapes. Sam Taylor-Wood's *Brontosaurus* (1995) features a nude man dancing alone to frantic music. Wearing, in a type of alternative television commercial, films women of different ages and ethnic origins making music by blowing into Coca-Cola bottles in *I'd Like to Teach the World to Sing* (1996).

Single channel video, at least as viewed on a small monitor, has less and less appeal among artists today, most of whom favor wall projections of works that have most likely been shot with a digital camera and certainly edited with digital equipment.

133

ollowing pages:
33. **Gillian Wearing**, *I'd Like to each the World to Sing*, 1996. Wearing uses non-actors in her e-configured commercials as in nis personal interpretation of a oca-Cola ad.

*117*

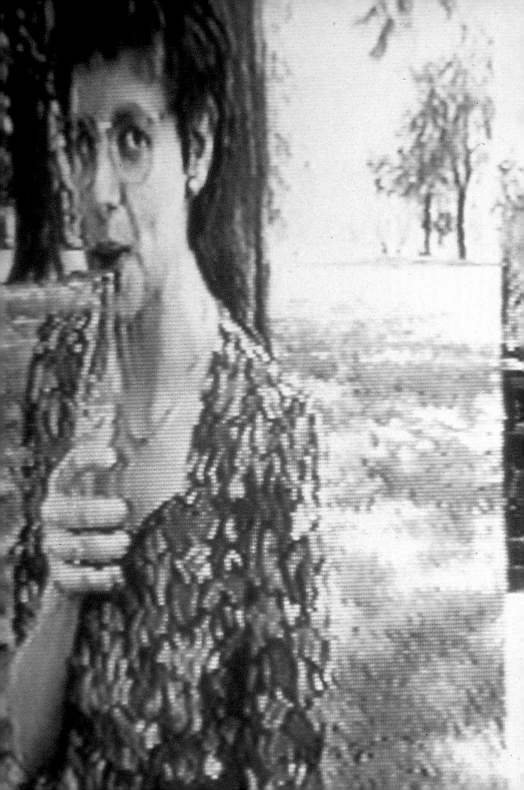

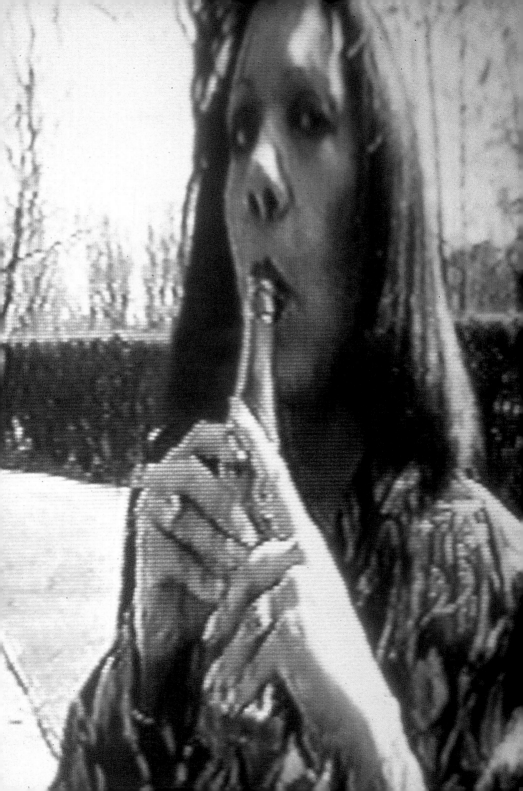

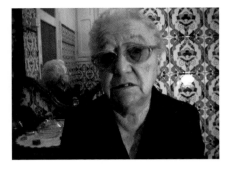 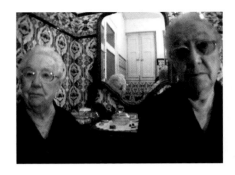

134–36. (above) **Pedro Ortuño,**
*Reina 135,* 2001.
Despite the increasing prevalence of large-scale projections, many artists, for both artistic and economic reasons, still favor the single-channel format that can be screened on a television set. These images are from a video shown in the exhibition 'Monocanal' ('Single-Channel') at the Museo Nacional Centro de Arte Reina Sofía in Madrid in 2003.

137. (far right) **Douglas Gordon,**
*Fog,* 2002.

Anna Gaskell's (b. 1969) *Floater* (1997), a single-channel video projected onto the floor, shows the body of a young girl (looking at first like a life-size doll) suspended, lifeless in water. As the camera lingers on her, her body floats onto its back and her head arches toward the camera, which in turn zooms into her open mouth. Even though we know the girl is dead, Gaskell creates an eerie expectation that perhaps she isn't. This undelineated boundary between the known and the unknown is characteristic of Gaskell's work with girls and young women. That the video is projected on the floor heightens the voyeuristic participation of the viewer.

The world of the Japanese artist Mariko Mori (b. 1967) is futuristic and in it the girls get to dress up in the most outrageous costumes, a combination of rock-star Grace Jones and the dolls named Diva Starz. In *Miko no Inori* (1996), the artist, fully decked out in a silver wig and a shiny white space outfit, rolls a glass ball around in her cupped hands . Throughout the new-age electronic soundtrack (not unlike one of Pipilotti Rist's) the one discernible phrase to Western ears is 'wait and see'. Mori, in her installations, photos and videos seems to be the supreme escape artist: creating clothes and contraptions designed for time travel to far-off lands. Actually, she is the most earthbound of artists, designing fantasies for people all too grounded in the everyday. She offers a way to feel singular in a homogenized world, much like her glam-rock predecessor David Bowie, a.k.a. Ziggy Stardust.

Scottish-born artist Douglas Gordon's (b. 1966) installation *Fog* (2002), can almost be seen as an elegy for single-channel video. In it, images of a young man, shrouded in mist, are seen on both sides of a large projection screen. The videos are actually the same, but they play out of sync, in a roundelay of digital prowess, resulting in a mysterious study of individual identity, a recurring theme in Gordon's work.

Following pages:
138. **Mariko Mori,**
*Miko no Inori,* 1996.

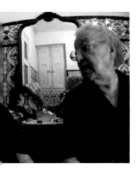

Whether it be through narratives, formal experimentations, short humorous tapes, or large-scale meditations, video art has assumed a position of legitimacy, even prominence, in the art world that few would have predicted even in the 1980s. Its seeming endless possibilities and relative affordability make it increasingly attractive to young artists who have been raised in an era of media saturation. Video is a way of participating in and reacting to media overkill; it is also a manageable means to communicate personal messages.

The physical size and scope of artists' projects have grown ever larger, while themes have become increasingly personal or individualistic. Several of the artists mentioned here have gone on to create complicated media installations in which they can control not only the image but also the context of viewing the image in complete environments of their own devising.

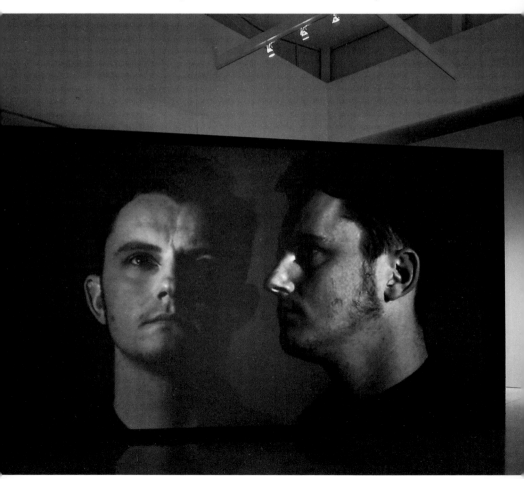

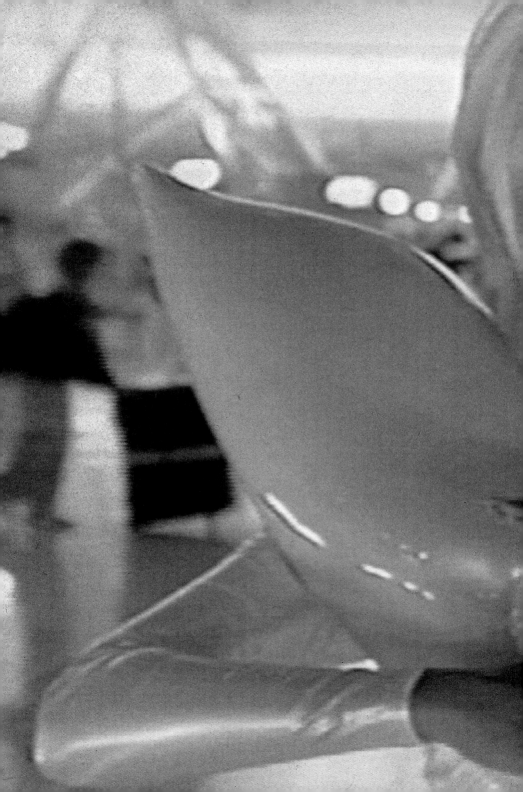

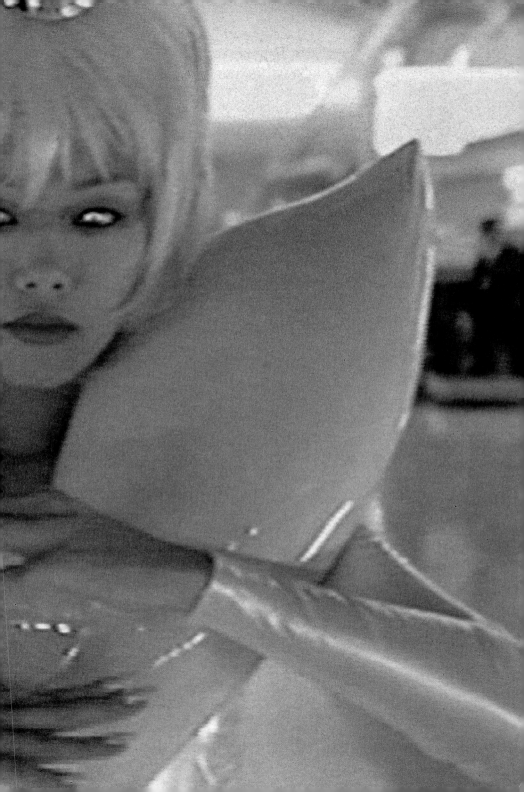

# Chapter 3:    Video Installation Art

Historical precedents for Installation art can be traced at least as far back as painted triptychs in Renaissance churches and the establishment of 'museums' in the West in the eighteenth century. As art emerged as something to be viewed by an audience beyond the confines of the home of wealthy patrons, spaces for the showing of art developed. While one may not want to call the Eisenheim Altarpiece an installation, its multiple parts placed in a public place of worship are recalled in terms of presentation in the diptychs and triptychs that are found on the walls of video projections. To present day Installation artists, who are intensely conscious of their work as extensions of the self, the physical presentation and surroundings of their art have become part of the art itself. Context, for these artists, is paramount; and they wish to exercize control over the context by explicitly creating an environment which, in its totality, constitutes the art. As critic Brian O'Doherty wrote in *Inside the White Cube: The Ideology of the Gallery Space* (1970): 'As modernism gets older, context becomes content. In a peculiar reversal, the object introduced into the gallery "frames" the gallery and its laws.' Ironically, while much of Installation art, following the lead of Belgian artist Marcel Broodthaers (1924–76), possessed an anti-museum attitude characteristic of the 1960s and early 1970s, it is museums and galleries that support such art. 'Context art,' as we might call it, itself needs an institutional context to be seen. Rooted in expanded notions of 'sculptural space' in Perfor-mance art and the trend toward greater viewer participation in art, Installation is another step toward the acceptance of any aspect or material of everyday life in the making of a work of art.

Installation art's association with sculpture has also eased its acceptance in museums and among critics. 'Perhaps,' US critic Cynthia Chris suggests, 'video installations have been gracefully annexed into the lexicon of visual art criticism because of certain of their ties to sculpture and other familiar practices.'

In common with other types of Installation art which extend the creative process beyond the studio into social space, the media installation, to use Gary Hill's sense of it, is a recognition of the space outside the monitor. Of equal importance is the extent to which Installation enhances the exploration of 'time,' a concept central to video artists. If time can be manipulated in multiple ways within the single-channel video, the possibilities are expanded dramatically in video installations which utilize several monitors or projection surfaces, and often several tapes, vastly increasing the amount of imagery.

*Sculptural Space and Surveillance*
Multimedia video installations appeared virtually at the same time as single-channel video art, even a little earlier. German artist Wolf Vostell's *TV De-coll/ages* (begun in 1958) would be considered an installation today, consisting, as one did, of a group of television sets showing distorted images and arranged on furniture and desks in the window of a Parisian department store. In common with other Fluxus practices of the period, Vostell was calling into question both the materials of art and the practices of culture, in this case the ubiquitous intrusion of television into everyday life. In reflecting on his work, Vostell noted,

*Marcel Duchamp has declared readymade objects as art, and the Futurists declared noises as art – it is an important characteristic of my efforts and those of my colleagues to declare as art the total event, comprising noise/object/movement/color/& psychology – a merging of elements, so that life (man) can be art.*

Vostell declared thus the essential underpinning of what the US critic Lucy Lippard later called the 'dematerialization of the object of art:' work in which the material form is secondary to the notions or ideas behind the art. Rooted in this conceptual approach, and incorporating the practices of performance, body art, and sound art, as well as other aspects of Fluxus, multimedia installation developed, both as a response to the inclusiveness of multiple objects and ideas into the realm of art, and a challenge to the prevailing media institutions, principally television and its bedmate, advertising. This 'total event' that Vostell spoke of, reflecting the performance influence in video art, recognized that art takes place in a context. Context quickly enough became content as sculptural effects were incorporated into the video presentation.

Sculptural approaches were and continue to be utilized to dramatic effect by Nam June Paik. Paik's 1963 Wuppertal exhibition at Galerie Parnass contained television sets on the floor of the gallery on which he projected distorted images in an attempt to disrupt the viewers' complacency in front of the television set. 'TV has attacked us all of our life,' Paik is quoted as saying, 'now we're hitting back!' Paik's preoccupation with television images is visible in many of his video sculptures from *Video Jungle* (1977) in which multiple television sets were arranged among jungle flora, to *Electronic Superhighway: Bill Clinton Stole My Idea*, Paik's massive entry in the 1993 Venice Biennale. Dozens of monitors packed the German pavilion from floor to ceiling, projecting a barrage of images from what looked like a universal data bank: mundane to political, nature shots to nuclear explosions.

Shigeko Kubota (b. 1937), who participated in Fluxus with John Cage, Paik, and others, has created a large body of work

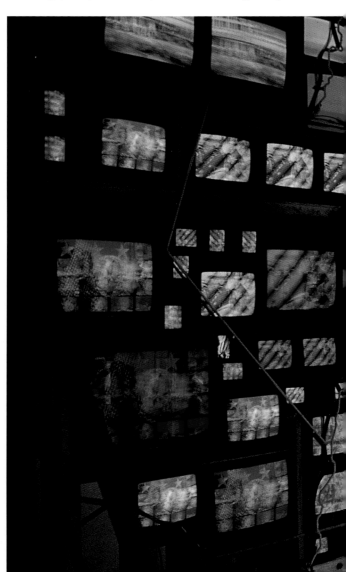

139. **Nam June Paik**,
*Electronic Superhighway*, 1995.
Continental USA is made up
of 313 TVs; Alaska – 24 TVs;
Hawaii – 1 TV per island.
50 laserdisc players, 50 laser
discs, approximately 60 video
distribution amps, approximately
20 fans, 1 video camera,
scaffolding, 'state borders'
fabricated in steel, neon,
200 watt audio system.
Paik's superhighway is strewn
with the detritus of media culture,
but his images still flash warnings
of wars and cultural upheavals.

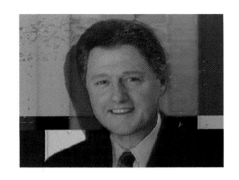

40. **Nam June Paik**,
*Electronic Superhighway*, 1993.
Part of Paik's 'video catalogue'
produced for the national
touring exhibition *The Electronic
Superhighway*, which premiered
at the Museum of Art in Fort
Lauderdale, Florida.

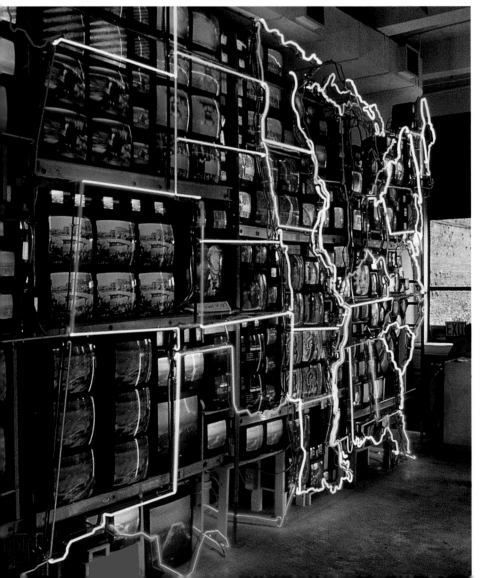

ranging from the sculptural to the diaristic (including video notes from a trip across Europe in the early 1970s (*Europe on ¹/₂ Inch a Day*, 1972). She often incorporates art-historical references, as in her homage to Marcel Duchamp, *Duchampiana: Nude Descending a Staircase* (1976), in which the image of a nude woman moves from screen to screen in a series of monitors configured like a staircase. Paik's influence is also evident in the work of New York artist Ray Rapp (b. 1948), whose whimsical video sculptures, which often incorporate several television sets, refer to Marcel Duchamp, Richard Artschwager, Joseph Beuys, Meret Oppenheim and others. In *Fur Wrap* (1997) a video of an artist sweating is seen within a disassembled television set wrapped in fur, a take on Oppenheim's furry *Object* (1936).

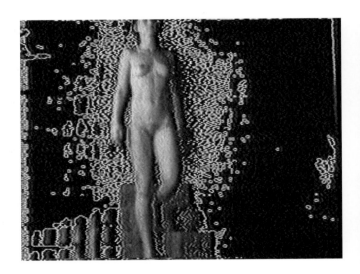

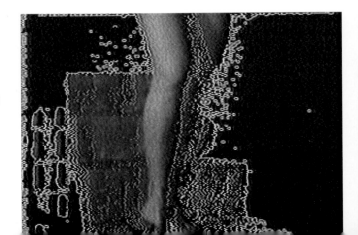

141. **Shigeko Kubota**,
*Duchampiana: Nude Descending a Staircase*, 1976.
An active member of the Fluxus international art movement, Kubota pays homage to Marcel Duchamp and John Cage, both of whom strongly influenced Fluxus artists.

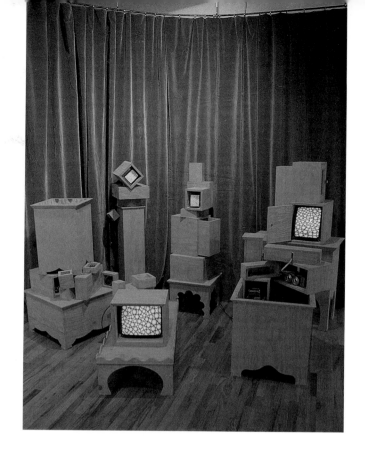

Other early practices of video installation involved viewer participation, however unwittingly, in the form of surveillance cameras. Les Levine's first installation, *Slipcover* (1966) at the Art Gallery of Toronto, showed viewers recorded images of themselves on a series of monitors. Never done before, this experience was at once eerie and exhilarating. Bruce Nauman, who, as we have seen is another early single-channel video artist, exhibited *Video Corridor* in 1968. This claustrophobic enclosure consisted of two floor-to-ceiling parallel walls forming a tunnel, with two monitors on top of one another at one end. The viewer walks into the corridor to see the videos which turn out to be simultaneous surveillance shots of the viewer. The impact of the video is dependent on the context of displacement, even fear, created by the wall constructions.

Critic Margaret Morse, upon encountering *Video Corridor*, the first video installation she had seen, wrote: 'To me it was as if my body had come unglued from my own image, as if the ground of my

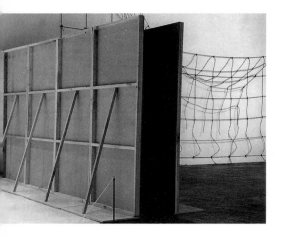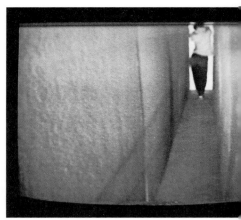

143. (above) **Bruce Nauman**, *Performance Corridor*, 1968–70.

144. (above right) **Bruce Nauman**, still from *Walk with Contrapposto*, 1968.

orientation in space were pulled out from under me.' Nauman explored video surveillance in other works during the early 1970s. In *Corridor Installation* (1970) a series of walls divided the Nicholas Wilder Galleries in Los Angeles into six passages, only three of which were passable. Visitors attempting to work the maze were taped, always from the back, by cameras mounted on top of the walls and their images were projected on monitors throughout the passages.

Peter Campus, who along with Nauman and Acconci was an influential first-generation video artist, explored psychological aspects of perception in interactive installations such as *Negative Crossing* (1974) in which visitors were knowingly videotaped performing actions in front of a mirror that were then projected onto large screens.

The surveillance technique was utilized by German-born Dieter Froese (b. 1937) in his *Not a Model for Big Brother's Spy Cycle* (1987) in which the artist combined closed-circuit television with a two-channel pre-taped video. Viewers were taped as they entered the installation room, their bodies projected on monitors as they watched others being interviewed about their political activities. need another word here

Interest in surveillance arose not only from public revelations in the news media about actual policing practices, but also from the nature of television itself which appears to be constantly watching the viewer even as the viewer is watching it. 'Surveillance art' installations directly confronted this reflexive quality of the television and flipped responsibility for viewing back to the viewer lolled into a passive relationship with the television screen. Video

145. (right) **Dieter Froese**, *Not a Model for Big Brother's Spy Cycle (Unpraezise Angaben)*, 1987.

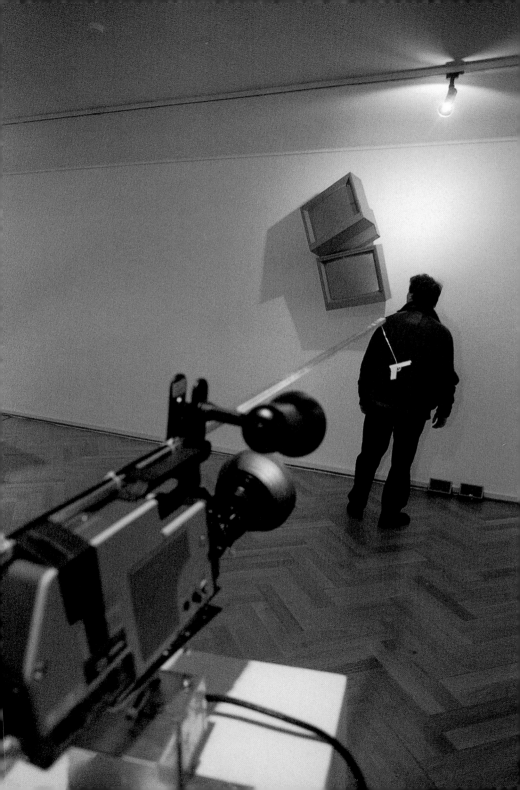

installations took an active role in energizing the viewer to respond to the object viewed. By showing viewers themselves, the artists engaged them intentionally in a very direct way, sometimes to the point of anger or shock. Even more importantly, the viewer became a performer, a totally new viewing experience. Unlike performative strategies in Happenings, where viewers went to the event expecting or hoping to become a part of it, the viewer of a work installed in the museum has no such expectation. The privacy of the viewing experience is invaded and, willingly or not, the viewer becomes the viewed not only by herself but also by others.

As a time-based medium (the recording in real time), video art allows for multiple manipulations of the experience of time. Present tense is no more readily felt than in seeing oneself all of a sudden on a monitor in the middle of an exhibition. Time lapse can also provide immediate experience of time just passed as when a viewer's previously recorded image plays on one monitor as their present image is shown on another. In a 1992 exhibition at the London Museum of Installation, David Goldenberg had his video

146. **David Goldenberg**, *Microwave and Freezerstills*, 1992. Surveillance cameras which are ubiquitous in contemporary culture (in stores, banks, parks, etc.) appeared in art galleries in the 1970s in anticipation of what was to come.

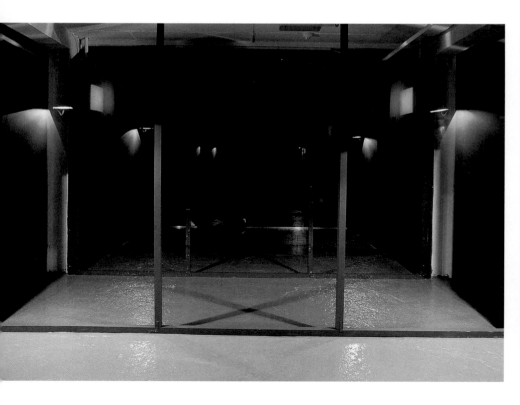

cameras monitor audiences who could see their images in mirrored chambers they were unable to enter. Past, present, and future were collapsed in a maelstrom of self-projections.

It is a short leap from looking (fixing one's gaze upon another) to voyeurism (taking delight in extended gazing) to spying (surreptitiously studying the actions of another). Surveillance, a type of spying, has interested artists and fascists alike since the birth of video technology. Clearly derived from the uses of video in military technology, surveillance highlights the sinister flip-side of the photographic gaze: intruding upon the unwitting subject with a camera. It is a strange alliance between the techniques of law enforcement control systems and art.

Present-day, so-called 'Reality TV' shows, with names like *Survivor* and *Big Brother*, feature participants willingly displaying their every move for the camera in hopes of claiming the jackpot at show's end. Surveillance, it seems, has actually ceased being sinister. It is now a means to a million-dollar grab bag, at least for some. For all of us, however, in the words of media theorist Thomas Levin, 'Now more than ever we are under surveillance. When we use a credit card or an ATM, when we call on our cell phones or use EZ Pass, when we surf the web or simply walk down the street, we leave traces.' It is here, in the traces, that art surfaces.

Nauman and Acconci initially turned the video camera on themselves in what might be described as self-imposed surveillance performances that were both solitary and reflective of their interest in sculpture, poetry and performance. Acconci's *Following Piece* (1969), is an example of spying both on the other and on the self. In it, the artist follows a man as he goes about his daily activities. In common with Dan Graham, Nauman and Peter Campus, Acconci was interested in collapsing boundaries between public and private space.

The French artist Sophie Calle's (b. 1953) *The Shadow (Detective)* (1985), represents a perfect melding of Nauman's perception-altering devices and Acconci's auto-performances. The artist asked her mother to hire a detective agency to follow her, report on her activities and, in the artist's words, 'to provide photographic evidence of my existence.' It's a set-up, for sure, but one that guarantees multiple layers of interpretation: the artist as subject; the voyeur as artist; the viewer as witness to the unreliability of images. The British artist Jamie Wagg (b. 1958) created haunting and disturbing surveillance photographs from video footage that he manipulated into rather beautiful large-format prints. In them two boys, silhouetted in black in a luminous orange background, are seen walking with a toddler in a crowd of people shortly before brutally killing him.

Jordan Crandall (b. 1960) has utilized military target-finding technology, tracking systems, border surveillance and his own cameras to make multi-screen installations (*Drive*, 1998–2000, *Heatseeking*, 1999–2000) that address the inclusion of hi-tech spying techniques in the lives of ordinary people and military personnel alike. In his fictional film *Trigger* (2002), the artist used an eye-tracked synchronization system which automatically aligns weapon and human gaze. 'In this case,' Crandall says, 'seeing literally does become firing. With such increasingly automated tracking systems, the status of the 'seer' is an open question. Is the camera-weapon manned or unmanned, and where is the body that connects to its viewfinder? As humans become ever more closely integrated with machines, the boundaries are not so easy to draw.'

Julia Scher (b. 1954) has been unmasking the power games inherent in surveillance video for several years in museum and gallery installations involving elaborately staged security systems (complete with pink security costumes). Visitors are invited to make printed copies of their own image as it is then appearing on surveillance monitors or to make prints of anyone else's image from half a dozen other monitors placed throughout the space. The visitors can look at themselves, spy on others, and become paranoid about who else might be watching them from some unseen venue in the gallery, all at the same time. In a 2002 interview with novelist Lynn Tillman, Scher said, 'My interest has always been with the necessity of watchfulness,' which suggests some positive filters through which this artist explores surveillance.

147–49. Jordan Crandall, *Trigger*, 2002.

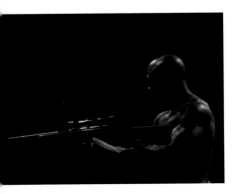
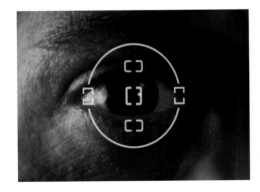

**50.** Julia Scher, *Security by Julia II*, 1989.

**51.** Julia Scher, *Security by Julia IX*, 1990.

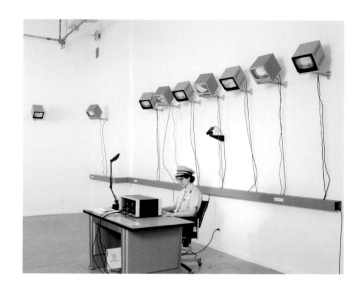

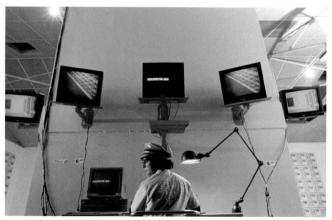

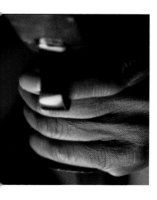

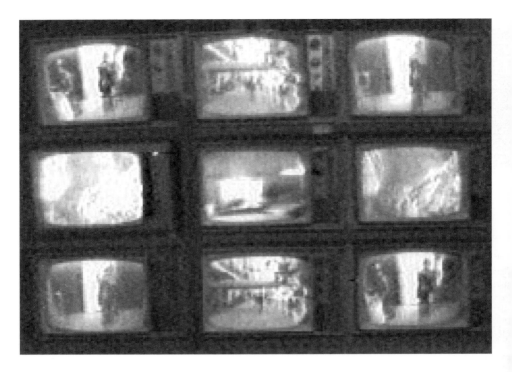

152. **Frank Gillette** in collaboration with **Ira Schneider**, *Wipe Cycle*, 1969.
*Wipe Cycle* utilized a closed-circuit television system that taped gallery visitors, thus integrating them into the information being seen on the monitors.

*Exploring the Political*

While Doug Hall and Sally Jo Fifer, in their book *Illuminating Video* (1990), warn that video art defies categorization in familiar art-historical terms, there are recognizable trends in video installation. Closely linked to the early sculptural installations of Vostell and Paik are the politically charged multi-channel installations of US artists Les Levine, Frank Gillette, and documentary filmmakers John Reilly, Arthur Ginsberg, and Skip Sweeney.

As if responding to the late eighteenth-century French critic Saint-Simon, who urged artists to become the advance guard of political sensitivity, artists of the 1960s and 1970s responded to political unrest in a multitude of ways that included performances, events and installations, fostering interactivity in making and viewing art.

Frank Gillette's installation, *Wipe Cycle* (1969), produced in collaboration with Ira Schneider and presented in the influential exhibition, *TV as a Creative Medium*, at the Howard Wise Gallery in New York, resulted from Gillette's experiments with image feed-back and time-delay. Integrating pre-recorded information with a live feed of the viewer's image, Gillette challenged the traditional passive viewing experience. 'The most important function of *Wipe Cycle*,' Schneider told critic Gene Youngblood, 'was to integrate the audience into the information. It was a live feedback system which enabled the viewer standing within its environment to see himself not only now in time and space, but also eight seconds ago and sixteen seconds ago.' Gillette added, 'It was an attempt to demonstrate that you're as much a piece of information as tomorrow morning's headlines.'

Members of US underground video groups such as TVTV and Global Village occasionally made installations as part of their video work. John Reilly, co-founder of Global Village, created a multi-channel installation of his controversial *Irish Tapes* in 1974. Bombarding the viewer with images of conflict in Northern Ireland on multiple screens, Reilly created an energetic installation which furthered his purpose of presenting as many images as possible of his hundreds of hours of unedited tape.

As the use of video in installation grew, the distinctions between artists and activist dissipated, and many artists engaged in media and society critiques within the framework of their art. Dara Birnbaum (b. 1946), whose aforementioned single-channel video *Technology Transformation: Wonderwoman*

53. **John Reilly** and **Stefan Moore**, still from *The Irish Tapes*, 1974.

54. **Dara Birnbaum**, *PM Magazine*, 1982.

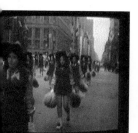

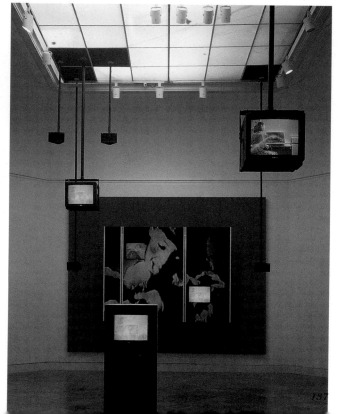

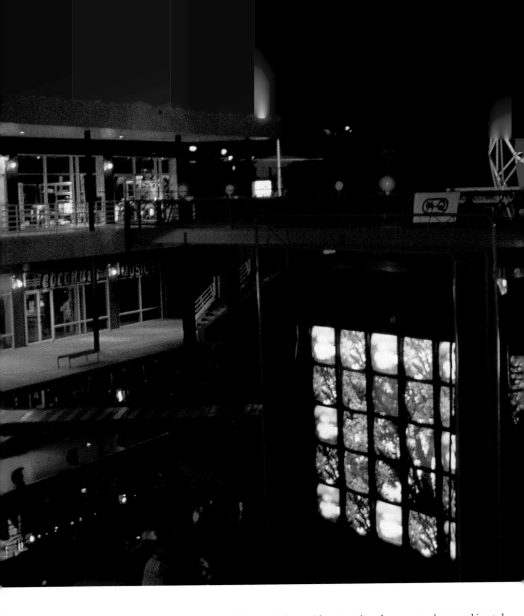

(1978–79) brought her wide attention, has created several installations that engage the politics of television: *PM Magazine*
(1982–89), a virtual assault of appropriated, banal images from
the mass media; and world politics: *Tiananmen Square: Break-In
Transmission* (1990), a fast-paced examination of the role of
the media in the highly publicized student uprisings in China
in 1989. Birnbaum was one of the first to make video 'walls' that
followed the lead of television merchandisers who pile their

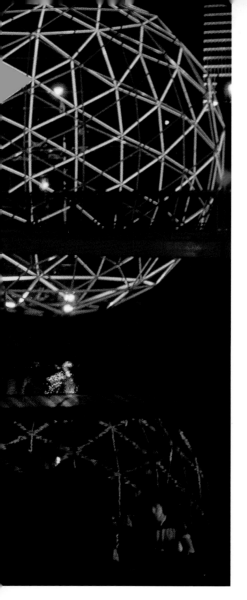

155. **Dara Birnbaum**,
*Rio Videowall*, 1989.
Installation view of videowall
within the context of the public
plaza, Rio Shopping/Entertainment
Complex, Atlanta, Georgia, USA
(permanent outdoor installation).
Video art breaks out of the gallery
and into the public arena in
Birnbaum's multi-monitor work.

television sets one on top of the other in store displays. Her *Rio Videowall* (1989) installed in a shopping mall in Atlanta, Georgia, is a permanent outdoor video installation consisting of twenty-five monitors. The structural enormity of installations such as these gives new weight to the union of sculpture and architecture in the medium of installation. Furthermore, the moving video image expands the notion of the field of sculpture, rendering it more fluid and active.

156. (below) **Fabrizio Plessi**, *Bronx*, 1985. Suggesting that death comes to all things, even machines, Fabrizio Plessi here contemplates the end of technology.

157. (right) **Judith Barry/ Brad Miskell**, *Hard Cell*, 1994. Discarded computer monitors function as projection devices for videotaped conversations among machines and humans.

Following pages:
158. **Judith Barry/Brad Miskell**, *Hard Cell*, 1994 (detail).

The public function of art and media has been subjected to broad scrutiny in the installations of US artist Judith Barry (b. 1954). Emerging from the Feminist movement of the 1970s, Barry explored issues of female identity in early videos like *Kaleidoscope* (1979), in which familiar family characters argue feminist theory. Her repertory of themes has expanded to include large-scale installations that take on the entire spectrum of modern technologies. In *Hard Cell* (1994), video monitors, projectors, discarded computers, a defibrillator, and other detritus from the modern age spill out of a corroding shipping crate. A veritable grave-digger's site for old television sets was fabricated by Italy's Fabrizio Plessi (b. 1940) at the 1986 Venice Biennale in his installation, *Bronx*. He upturned twenty-six televisions in rusted metal containers and plunged shovels into their screens. The shovels were in turn reflected in a projection of blue water on each of the sets. Plessi, for one, sees the portable camera as simply part of his artistic practice, like paint or wood. 'The TV is a material the artist submits to his poetic ideas,' Plessi said in relation to his work, particularly his installation *Matria Prima* (1989). 'A moment of pause, of thought, a silent fossil, in the end technology ceases. Its form is no different from the form in marble.' American artist Peter Fend's (b. 1950) *Development Plan to Build Albania* (1992) features numer-

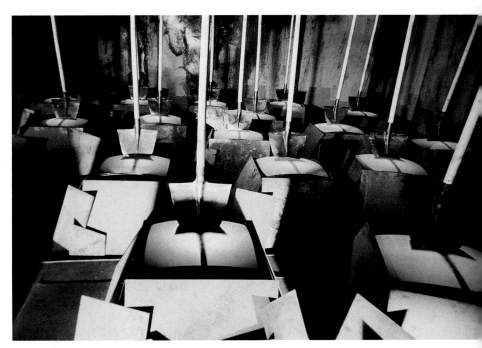

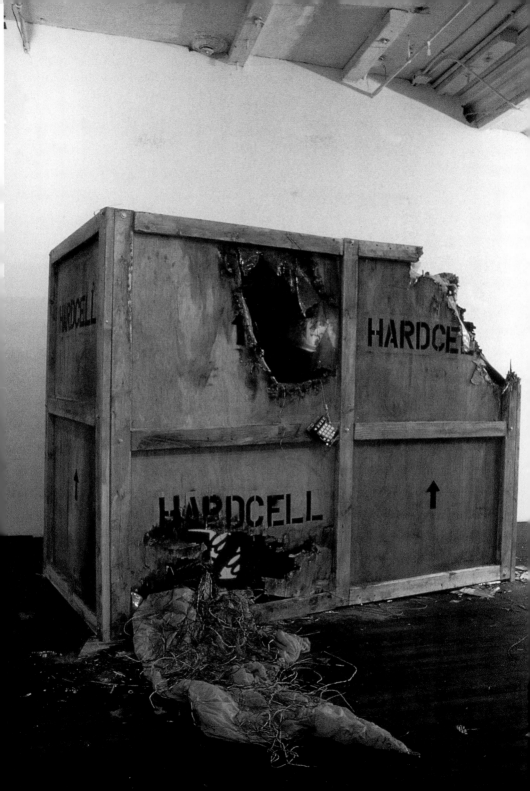

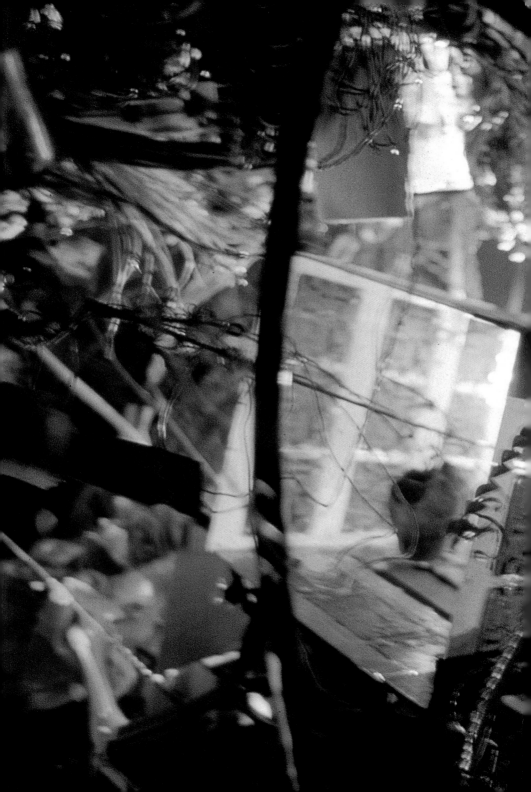

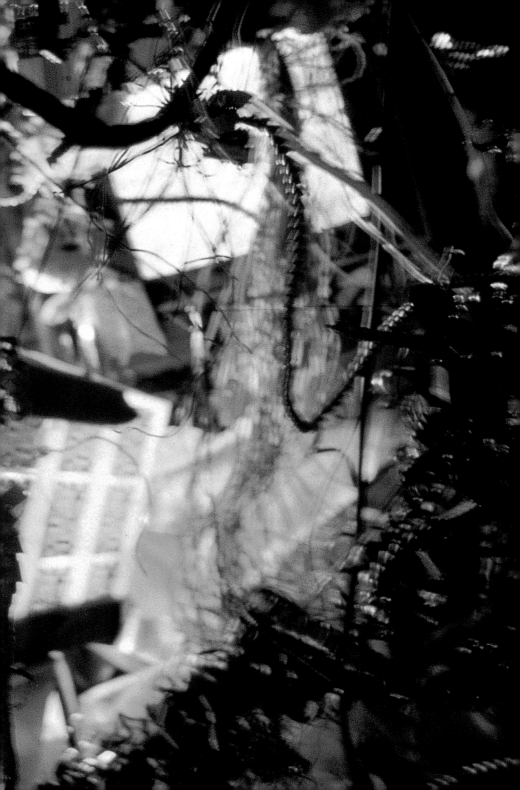

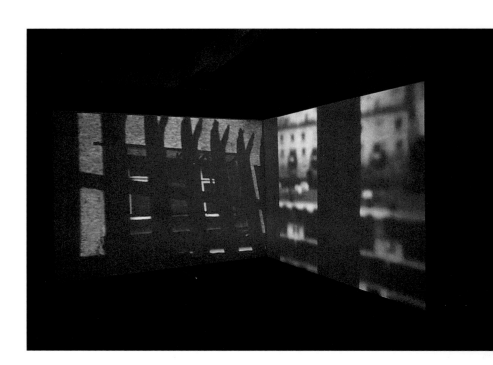

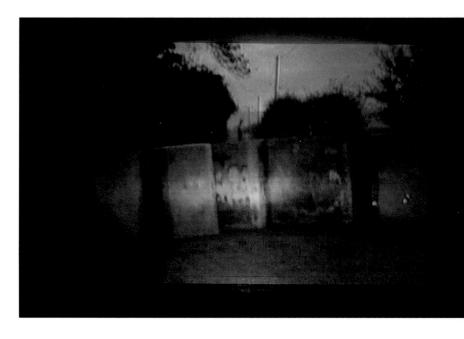

ous video monitors with live satellite broadcasts of the terrain of Albania and parts of Yugoslavia. Fend sees his installations as 'workstations' for a global redistribution of power and resources.

The longstanding political turmoil in Northern Ireland is the subject of Irish artist Willie Doherty's installations *At the End of the Day* (1994), and *Somewhere Else* (1998). Doherty uses full wall projections of burnt-out cars, roads leading to nowhere, pure darkness and looped voice-overs of phrases like 'At the end of the day there's no going back' to illustrate the pathos of war.

Taking direct aim at popular contemporary media is Canadian artist Stan Douglas (b. 1960), whose cool, understated installation *Evening* (1994) re-enacts the ritual of the family watching the evening news in the 1960s and 1970s. Using archival footage from the period as background and actor/newsmen in the foreground, Douglas has his 'anchors' smiling regardless of the horrors (Vietnam War stories, interracial riots) they may be reporting.

The ubiquity of broadcast news, raised to an unprecedented international level by Ted Turner's Cable News Network (CNN), which can be seen in virtually every country on earth, has made the image of a world event (starving children in Somalia; war in Iraq; the death of Diana, Princess of Wales) instantly recognizable the world over. Many international artists reflect this preoccupation with the news image in their own video installations. French

159. (left) **Willie Doherty**, *Somewhere Else*, 1998.

160. (below left) **Willie Doherty**, *At the End of the Day*, 1994. Doherty's videos capture the traces of desolation left by war in his native Ireland.

161. (below) **Fabrice Hybert**, installation in the French Pavilion at 1997 Venice Biennale. Hybert, a former participant in the films of Andy Warhol, reconstitutes a television studio for a performance installation.

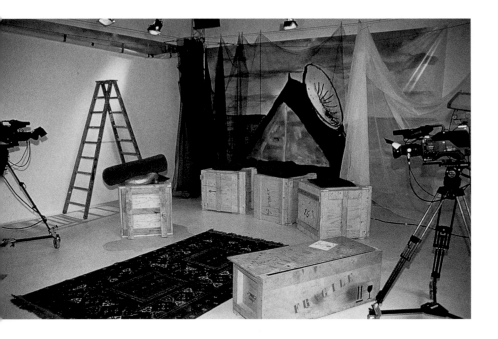

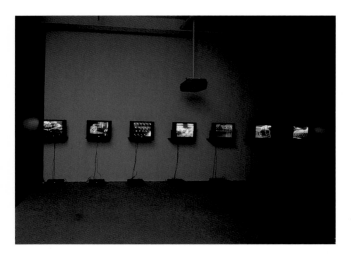

162. **Marcel Odenbach**, *Eine Faust in der Tasche Machen* (Make a Fist in the Pocket), 1994. The use of multiple monitors in an installation suggests a sculptural environment artfully removed from the 'living room' atmosphere associated with the single monitor.

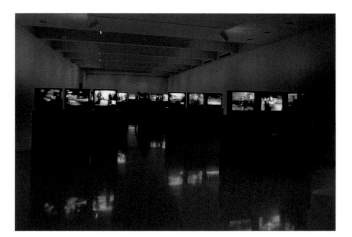

163. **Chantal Ackerman**, *Bordering on Fiction: Chantal Ackerman's 'D'Est'*, 1993/1995. Large-screen projections that meet in corners or intersect on walls became common in video installations of the late 1990s.

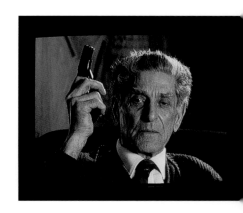

artist Fabrice Hybert created an entire broadcast studio, complete with monitors, furniture, editing and control rooms, at the 1997 Venice Biennale. Performing within his own installation, Hybert conducted interviews, did commercials, and had 'production meetings' in this ersatz broadcast outlet.

*Eine Faust in der Tasche Machen* (Make a Fist in the Pocket), a 1994 installation by German artist Marcel Odenbach (b. 1953), portrays how seven countries (Germany, USA, England, France, Italy, Czechoslovakia, and Mexico) maintained order during the political upheavals of 1968. Seven monitors, lined up next to each other, showed period news clips from each country, intercut with archival footage of the Third Reich's burning of books. This multi-monitor strategy was used by Belgian artist Chantal Ackerman (b. 1950) in a video deconstruction of her 35-millimetre film *D'Est* of 1993. Ackerman arranged twenty-four monitors in eight groupings of three and projected fragments of her film diary of a trip through Eastern Europe, the birthplace of her parents and grandparents. Shooting from the open window of a slow-moving car she records in dreary detail the everyday lives of people walking to work, waiting for buses, or standing in bread lines. In his ongoing video project *Xenology: Immigrant Instruments* (begun in 1992), Polish-born artist Krzysztof Wodiczko (b. 1943) combines interviews with immigrants in different countries with images of the same people riding subways or standing in front of public buildings in their newly adopted countries. Another approach to the immigrant experience is taken by Turkish artist Sukran Aziz in her installation, *Reminiscences* (1998). Projected on walls are video-taped interviews with people in Istanbul, New York, Paris, and other cities, while suspended from the ceiling are hundreds of minuscule speakers, concealed in

64–66. (below, left to right) Marina Abramovic, *Balkan Baroque (Father)*, 1997.

Marina Abramovic, *Balkan Baroque (Marina Abramovic)*, 1997.

Marina Abramovic, *Balkan Baroque (Mother)*, 1997. Abramovic's multi-screen installations are a very personal response to the ethnic battles in her homeland in former Yugoslavia.

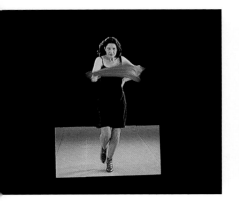 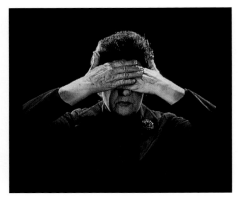

metal containers, that project pre-recorded conversations about memory and displacement.

Douglas Gordon re-examines archival film footage, extracting and dissecting images, often in slow motion, and, in the process, reveals psychological and sociocultural aspects of history. His *Hysterical* (1995) recycled a turn-of-the-century medical film in which a masked woman, apparently suffering from hysteria, was maltreated by doctors supposedly engaged in a cure. In *Through the Looking Glass* (1999) he excerpts a seventy-one second scene from Martin Scorcese's film *Taxi Driver*, in which the lead character talks to himself in the mirror and 'rehearses' a confrontation with some unnamed enemy. In Gordon's installation, projected on opposite walls of a gallery space, the character, Travis Bickle, played by Robert De Niro, repeats 'You talking to me?' as he slips an automatic pistol from under his shirt and points it at the camera. The viewer feels caught in a random act of violence by an armed madman.

167. **Douglas Gordon**, *Hysterical*, 1995.

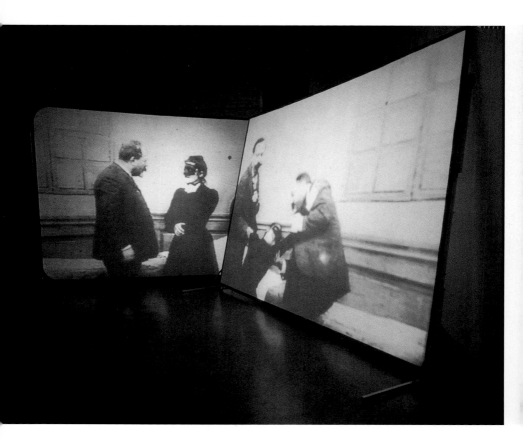

Always one to tackle a multitude of social and critical issues in her multi-disciplinary art, musician/artist Laurie Anderson tackled our relationship with modern technology in her installation *Dancing in the moonlight with her wigwam hair* (1996), a video and sound installation at New York's Guggenheim Museum, which incorporated talking parrots, projected animation, telephones, a moving model airplane, and an illusionistic video of the artist in a circus of images and sounds reflecting the multiple competition for our attention in the modern world. Fluxus and Pop are married here in Anderson's installation, fulfilling American art critic Thomas Hess's notion that such theatrical art requires an audience to complete it.

Belgrade-born artist Marina Abramovic (b. 1946) presented *Balkan Baroque* at the 1997 Venice Biennale. A three-screen instal- 164–66 lation, accompanied by three large, water-filled copper vessels, features Abramovic on one screen delivering a lecture about rats who slaughter their own kind, as images of the artist's parents

68. **Laurie Anderson**, *Your Fortune One $ Animatronic parrot from Dancing in the moonlight with her wigwam hair*, 1996.

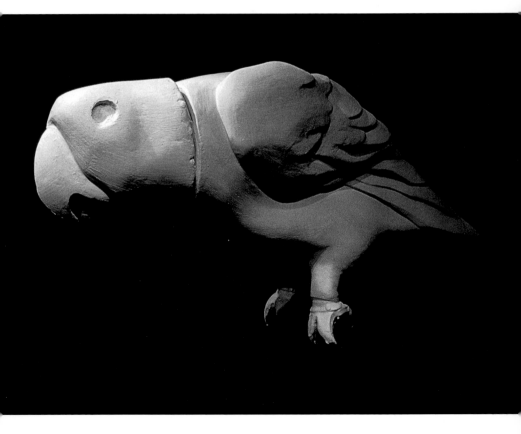

occupy the other screens. As Abramovic changes from lecturer to frantic, dancing seductress, her father, who, like her mother, had been silent and motionless during the lecture, raises a gun to his head and the mother covers her eyes. Iranian Shirin Neshat (b. 1957) examined her country's unbalanced treatment of men and women in *Turbulent* (1998). On opposite walls of a room were projected two videos, one of a man performing songs for an enthusiastic male audience, the other of a woman, dressed in chador, her back to the camera, singing a string of notes to an empty auditorium. The notes turn into wails as her hands flail in the air.

American artist Doug Aitken (b. 1968) filmed the devastation from the eruption of the Soufrières volcano on the Caribbean island of Monserrat. Taking his camera through what looks like a landscape destroyed by a nuclear bomb, and then presenting the footage as a multi-wall installation, he captures the silver-grey emptiness of a lifeless country.

Installation has become a formidable conduit for political meaning because, by virtue of size and visual complexity, it offers a charged environment for viewers to enter.

*Exploring the Lyrical*

'Like Jean Cocteau, I am a poet who also made films,' wrote experimental filmmaker Stan Brakhage in 1967. Citing this remark, US critic David James maintains that avant-garde film from the 1950s and early 1960s was most commonly understood in terms appropriate to poetry. Explorations of mood through color, lingering camera shots, even fragmentation and replication of images, all, he argues, have their root in French symbolist poetry. The same may be said of Bill Viola, Mary Lucier, Steina and Woody Vasulka, among others, whose lyrical video installations reflect the artists' preoccupations with memory, loss, mysticism, and aesthetics.

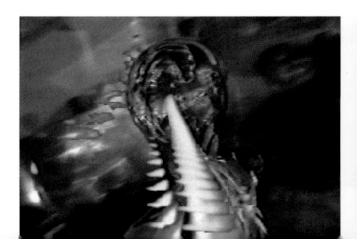

169. **Steina and Woody Vasulka** in collaboration with **Bradford Smith**, *Progeny*, 1981.

The poetic ruminations of Woody and Steina Vasulka extended to installation even before the term was widely used. At the Kitchen Live Audience Test Laboratory, New York (now simply called The Kitchen), which they founded in 1971, the couple created what Steina refers to as 'environments' consisting of multiple monitors and cameras. In *Machine Vision* (1976) two video cameras on a motorized turntable interacted with two mirrors and two monitors, creating a camera view beyond the restrictions of the human eye. Regarding this early work, Steina remarked,

*I was horrified by the idea that if you hold the camera you control the image the viewer sees; so I put the camera on a tripod and left the room. With the turntable, the image would move continuously, without a cameraman. I wanted people to think of 'point of view;' that they are in a space controlled by the machine.*

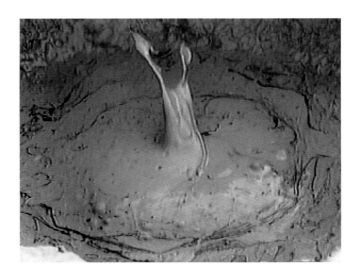

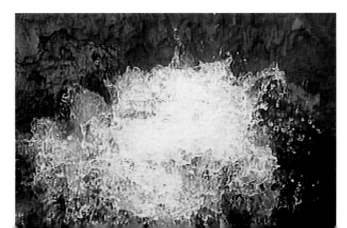

172. **Bill Viola**,
*Stations*, 1994 (detail).
Bodies submerged in water hang
limp, suspended in space in this
five-channel installation. Different
images appear on cloth screens
and on polished granite slabs
beneath each screen.

In time Steina, for many years working apart from Woody, became more lyrical in her expression. In her installation for the 1997 Venice Biennale, *Orka*, the Icelandic word for 'force,' she paid 155–8 homage to her birthplace. On three double-sided screens and carefully placed mirrors, Vasulka projected large images of rolling surf, burning lava, and all manner of birds in flight along with an overpowering soundtrack of noises generated by each of these images. Estonian artist Jaan Toomik evokes his homeland in a similar vein in his installation *The Sun Rises, The Sun Sets* (1997). Bouncing off a mirror in the bottom of a tin pan and onto a wall is the image of the sun rising over the Baltic sea, then setting over the waters of Venice.

Bill Viola's work, perhaps more than any other, represents the tendency toward the lyrical in art. Viola has been creating a wide range of single-channel and installation videos since the early 1970s. He himself describes his videos as visual poems in which he grapples with issues of identity and spiritual significance in the modern world. Installation has become his preferred method of presentation since the mid-1980s. His explorations of light and form, matched by his interests in spiritual source material (the

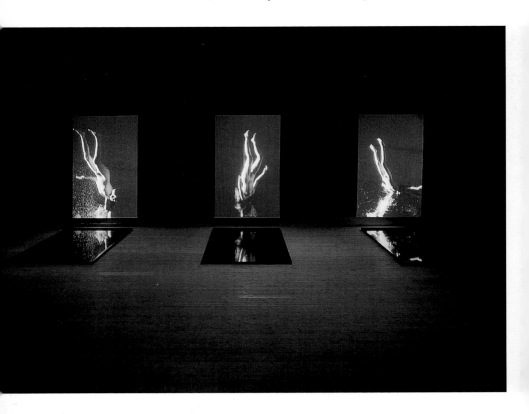

173, 174. **Bill Viola**, *The Messenger*, 1996. A man repeatedly rises from the water, inhales deeply, then sinks back, suggesting the recurring cycle of birth and death.

Koran, Buddhist texts, and Sufi mysticism), find expression in large-format projections which have been exhibited in many parts of the world. With *Slowly Turning Narrative* (1992) Viola utilized a spinning, mirrored projection surface to suggest a constantly turning mind absorbed with itself. The artist intended for 'the room and everyone in it to become a continually shifting projection screen, encompassing images and reflections' as seen through the mind of the man represented on the turning wall. In *Stations* (1994), a computer-controlled, five-channel video/sound installation, images are projected onto vertical slabs of granite and, in turn, reflected on mirrored slabs placed on the floor perpendicular to the granite ones. Bodies appear to fall through air or topple into the water in this rendition of the Stations of the Cross. *Fire, Water, Breath* (1996), a three-part installation, a section of which, titled *The Messenger*, was initially projected onto the ceiling of Durham Cathedral in England, features man in contact and/or conflict with the three basic elements: a naked man is submerged in water, rises to the surface, releases a deep breath and sinks back again. In its original setting in the church dome,

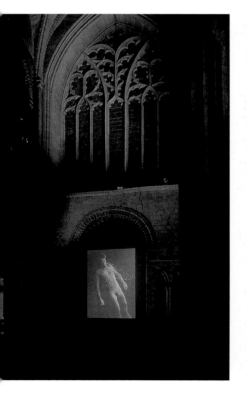

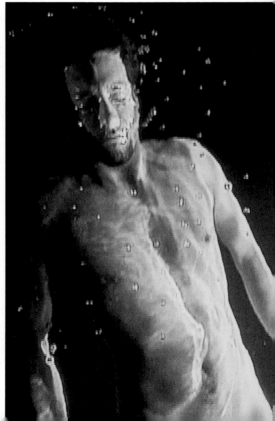

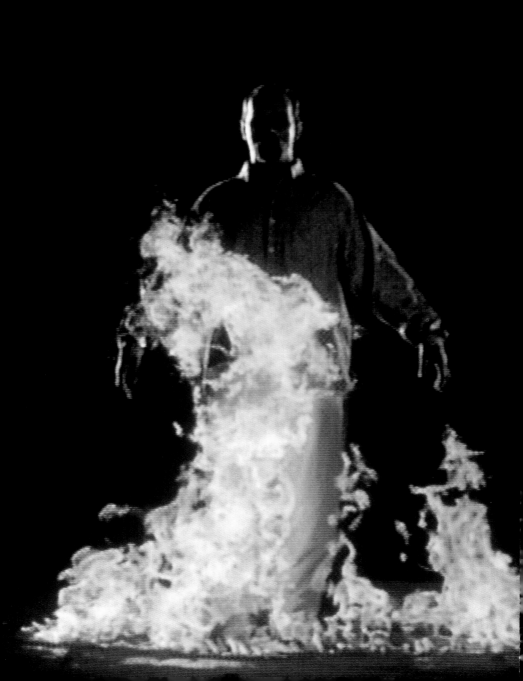

viewers too are engulfed in the projected image and accompany-ing sounds of this ritual. In a museum context, opposite *The Messenger* Viola has arranged *The Crossing*, two floor-to-ceiling projections of a man gradually consumed by flames and the same man drowned by slowly accumulating drops of water. While these images may seem horrific, with Viola there is always the feeling that, somehow, a redemption is also taking place. Slow motion, piercingly loud sounds, rich coloration and grand scale all con-tribute to a cinematic experience of man immersed in nature.

Viola's 1997 retrospective at the Whitney Museum of American Art in New York demonstrated Viola's romantic kinship updated to the era of electronic art. Like pioneering video artist Nam June Paik, Viola studied music and audio design. All of his work places sound and image on equal footing. *The Stopping Mind* (1991), a four-screen installation, and the first one the visitor encountered in the Whitney retrospective, features a barely audible voice mur-muring sentences about the body and loss of sensation as images

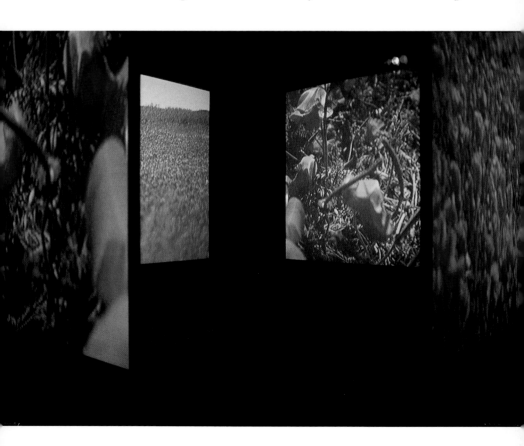

(close-ups of trees, meadows), once frozen, suddenly move, then stop. Loud bursts of noise accompany the movement. This piece serves the viewer as a primer for what is to come: unexpected jolts of imagery and noise that awaken our minds to new ways of perceiving the present moment. Echoes of Jean-Luc Godard and Samuel Beckett are present as Viola engages one of his common themes: a single man dwarfed by the enormity of nature; a nature that can sometimes consume, as it does in *The Crossing*.

For the mystics of old, whom Viola reveres, flames and water are symbols for an all-consuming love that annihilates the old self in a new contemplative union. This is most evident in his *Room for St John of the Cross* (1983), an imagined recreation of the cell in which the sixteenth-century Carmelite mystic was imprisoned by the Inquisition. A voice is heard reciting the Saint's poems in Spanish, some of which speak of ecstatic flights of the soul out of the dark night and over snow-capped mountains. At one point a

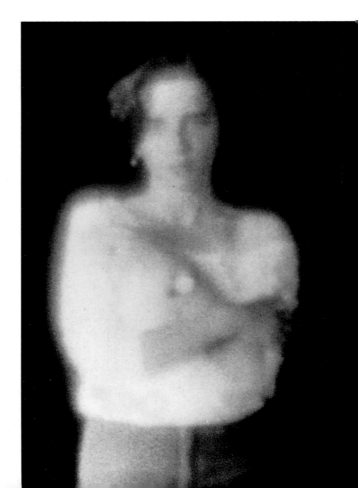

177. **Gary Hill**, *Tall Ships*, 1992. Hill utilizes interactive technology in *Tall Ships*. Visitors to the narrow gallery space trigger the projections of images on screens suspended in the space.

mountain shifts violently accompanied by a roaring sound as in an earthquake. During that same year Viola confined himself to a room in a house where he attempted to stay awake for three days. The taped chronicle of this self-imposed entrapment, *Reasons for Knocking at an Empty House*, illustrates how harsh the passage of time can be. 'My work,' Viola says, 'is centered on a process of personal discovery and realization. Video is a part of my body; it's intuitive and unconscious.'

Gary Hill thought of his first video installation, *Hole in the Wall* (1974), as a transition from sculpture to video. He taped himself knocking out the wall of a gallery and projected the tape on a monitor placed in the wall opening. Where a sculpture might have been, he placed, in his words, 'the video memory of a performance.' From the start Hill has been concerned with the poetics of language and image. His intellectually rigorous multiple-screen projections often make reference to semiotics, the philosophy of

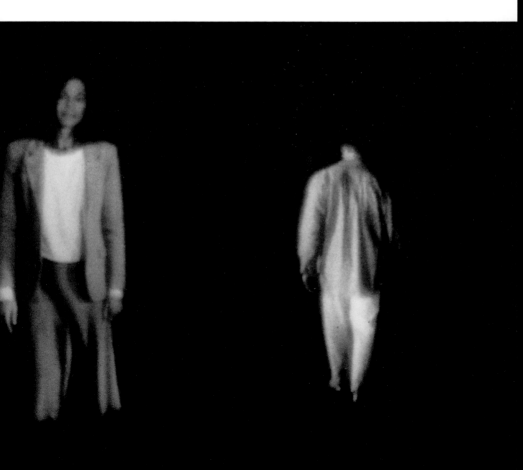

Ludwig Wittgenstein, French postmodern theory, and the history of cinema. *Tall Ships* (1992) is an interactive installation consisting of multiple projection surfaces, whose images of various people are triggered by the entrance of a viewer into the installation room. As the viewer walks in, figures appear as if from 'nowhere,' approaching him and murmuring barely perceptible sentences.

Language, image, and a strong sense of the unknown is characteristic of the video installations of American artist Susan Hiller

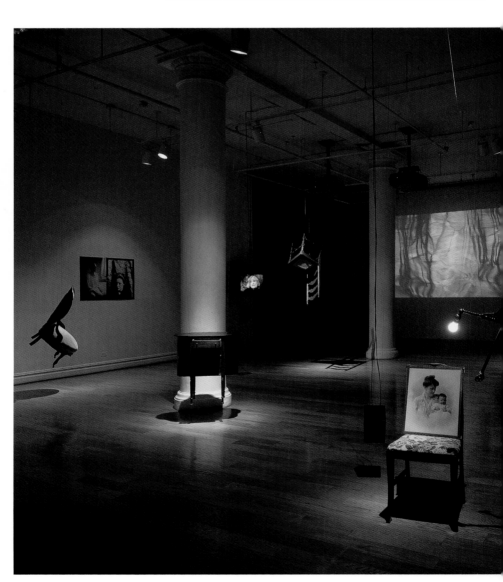

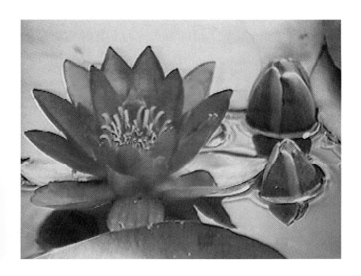

(b. 1940), who has been creating video installations since 1983. Her *Wild Talents* (1997), inspired by the reputed telekinetic and telepathic abilities of Polish psychic Stefan Ossowiecki, incorporated fragments from American and European films from the 1960s to the present, largely from the horror genre, that featured the otherworldly powers of children. Utilizing the Minimalist strategy of repetition, Hiller's installation, which wrapped around two corners of a gallery wall, created a mesmerizing ritual at the intersection of popular religious beliefs and mass media.

Light and landscape (both internal and external) suffuse the video installations of American artist Mary Lucier (b. 1944). In works such as *Ohio at Giverny* (1983) and *Wilderness* (1986) Lucier pays homage to Monet and the nineteenth-century American Luminists. In two earlier works, *Dawn Burn* (1975) and *Bird's Eye* (1978), she pointed a laser directly at the camera's eye, burning the vidicon tube. She then changed the focal length of the lens and moved the laser, all in an attempt to 'record' changes in light, thus associating her technological work with the Impressionists' observations of light. *Oblique House (Valdez)*, 1993, featured the reconfigured empty inside of a former car dealership in Rochester, New York, which Lucier turned into a plasterboard house with no windows, only monitors. For Lucier, this architectural environment was 'about image and sound: outside the house is blind; inside, television monitors provide windows which look not out to landscape, but further inward to the human soul.'

### Exploring Identities

Following the lead of early single-channel video artists (Joan Jonas, Vito Acconci, Hannah Wilke, Dara Birnbaum) video installation artists have used the medium for ever-deepening examinations of the self. The camera has the unique property of being a conduit for real-time images of the self; when placed in a designed environment like an installation it has the power to present an encompassing view of the self. As Tracey Moffatt (b. 1960), an Australian media artist, stated rather boldly: 'I am not concerned with verisimilitude…I am not concerned with capturing reality, I'm concerned with creating it myself.'

The installation environment also allows for greater participation of the viewer in the process of 'completing the art object,' in Duchamp's famous phrase. In many installations, the viewer actually enters the artwork in a literal sense to experience it. For artists occupied with issues of identity, this ultimate merging of viewer and viewed is especially pertinent. The collapse of boundaries also reflects certain artists' influence by the Freudian and Lacanian inspired psychotherapeutic environment so dominant in 1970s art-critical circles. Combined with Conceptualism's principle that artists be responsible for the context of their art, this fed

180. **Adrian Piper**, *What It's Like, What It Is #3*, 1991. Piper engages racial stereotypes in her often confrontational installations. Taped characters speak directly at viewers, challenging their presumptions and prejudices.

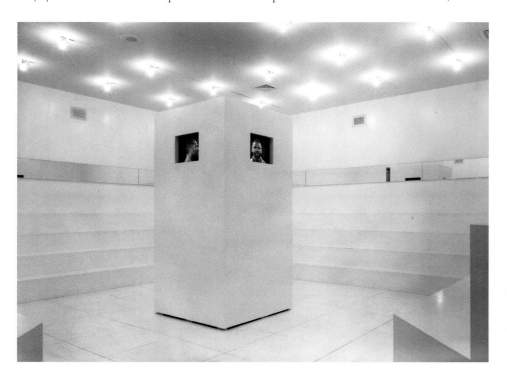

directly into the new realism of Installation in which the mundane and the personal are re-imagined in very direct ways.

As the technical capabilities of media have expanded, the integration of different elements (sound, image, sculptural setting) in the service of the artist's telling his or her own story has become more widely practised. To some critics as well as to some artists this has brought the practice of art close to that of theater. It is not surprising, however, given the influence of Fluxus performance actions and Happenings on the development of late twentieth-century art, that 'the theatrical' would be embraced in multimedia Installation art, particularly in the case of those artists whose work is identifiable as lyrical and poetic, or indeed political.

Trained in art and philosophy, Adrian Piper (b. 1948) works at the intersection of several cogent themes in contemporary art. Gender, race, presence, absence, text, and image all are dealt with in her work which, since the late 1960s, has included performance, sound, drawings, photomontage, and since the 1980s, video installations. A fair-skinned black woman whose original preoccupations were with a purely rationalistic conceptualism, Piper eventually gave up her stern sculptures for confrontative installations which offered direct challenges to viewers' prejudices. In *What It's Like, What It Is #3* (1991) Piper integrated her early work in minimal sculpture with video by constructing a white, vertical box, in which monitors showed a black man's head from different angles. Viewers were seated on white bleachers surrounding the box (like the Romans watching the lions devouring Christians, Piper said; and also like sitting on late 1960s Minimal sculpture). The man spews forth retorts to common racial slurs: 'I'm not lazy,' 'I'm not vulgar,' 'I'm not horny,' and so on. In this almost totemic installation Piper operates on the many levels that inform her own identity: intellectual, artistic, racial, and personal.

In her 1997 installation, *Out of the Corner*, consisting of seventeen monitors, photographs, and overturned chairs, Piper confounded viewers' associations with all manner of racial and ethnic stereotypes by having the talking heads on the monitors address challenging questions directly to the audience.

Turkish artist Kutlug Ataman's (b. 1961) multi-screen installation *Stefan's Room* (2004) was notable almost as much for its sculptural design as it was for the identity issues it dealt with. In it five screens were suspended from the ceiling, some with one edge pointed near the floor, some on a diagonal with the gallery's walls. The artist described these juxtapositions as central to his depiction of his subject, Stefan, a Berlin man obsessed with moths. He has 30,000 of them in a small apartment. The work is a colorful but highly disturbing portrait of an isolated personality living a schizoid life among dead specimens.

Of all the video installation artists who confront identity issues, perhaps Matthew Barney (b. 1967) has gained the most worldwide attention with his surrealistic explorations of male identity beyond conventional boundaries. Barney quickly moved from Nauman and Acconci-inspired videos of himself naked

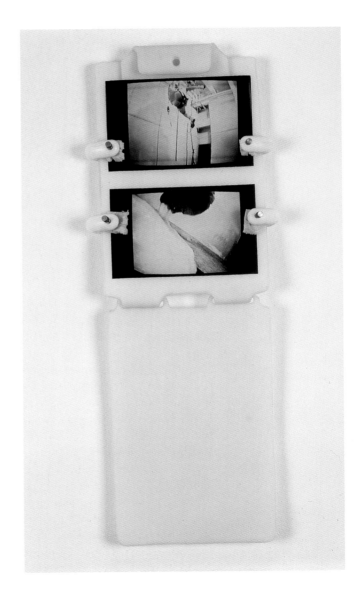

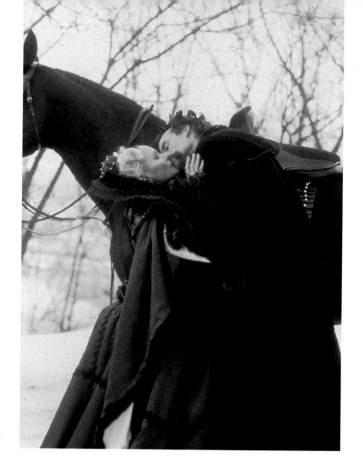

scaling the walls of his studio – *Field Dressing (orifill)* (1989) – to full color and lavish scenarios of his *Cremaster* videos and installations, begun in 1994, in which elaborately costumed fairies, satyrs and other assorted creatures enact private scenarios that spring from Barney's preoccupations with body parts and fluids, hetero- and homosexual relations, athletics, and alchemy. The word 'cremaster' (the thin suspensory muscle of the testicles) invites associations with an enclosed world that is primed for sexual activity, fueled by fantasy and desire. With Barney, explorations of the body in late twentieth-century art reach Baroque proportions in production values of costumes, make up, prosthetic devices, fantastical camera images, and sculptural oddities that suggest a breathless search for identity and pleasure under the constant eye of encroaching death. *Cremaster 5* (1997) especially, with its elaborate black costumes and dark music, has the feel of an extended funeral, despite underwater images of sea nymphs at play.

Combining a strong sense of the theatrical with advanced technologies is characteristic of the Japanese group Dumb Type, formed in 1984 while its members were students at the Kyoto University of the Arts. Formerly led by Teiji Furuhashi (1960–95), Dumb Type works in Butoh-inspired performance as well as Installation. Their highly theatrical video installations, which explore issues of sexual and cultural identity, are expressly related to their practice of dance and theater. *Lovers* (1994), a computer-controlled, five-channel laserdisk and sound installation, features five naked men and women who move from wall to wall in a dance of missed connections. Phrases appear on the walls ('Love is everywhere,' 'Don't fuck with me, fella, use your imagination'), voices murmur indistinguishably, bodies emerge from the darkness,

183. **Teiji Furuhashi**,
*Lovers*, 1994–95.
In *Lovers*, naked bodies run, jump, fall, and approach viewers in an interactive installation created under the spectre of AIDS.

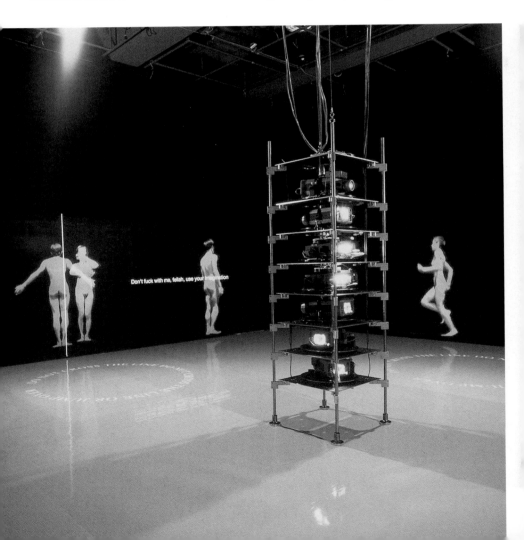

confront the viewer, then fall back into space. The shadow of AIDS, which claimed Furuhashi, hovers over this Installation.

Thanks largely to technological innovations in projection devices, video installations began to assume all sizes in the late 1980s, from Tony Oursler's minuscule projections onto small suspended ovals, to Bill Viola's and Steve McQueen's monumental full-wall presentations. Oursler (b. 1957) engages the viewer's identity directly in installations such as *Mansheshe* (1997), in which several small projections throw hybrid talking heads onto egg-shaped ovals suspended from poles. The heads, looking directly at the camera (which becomes the viewer), spout aphorisms about sexual identity, personal religious beliefs, and interpersonal relationships. Oursler's work has clear theatrical

84. **Tony Oursler**,
*Mansheshe*, 1997.
Oursler's politically charged but humorous installations remove videotaped images from the familiar site of the monitor and project them into everyday surfaces.

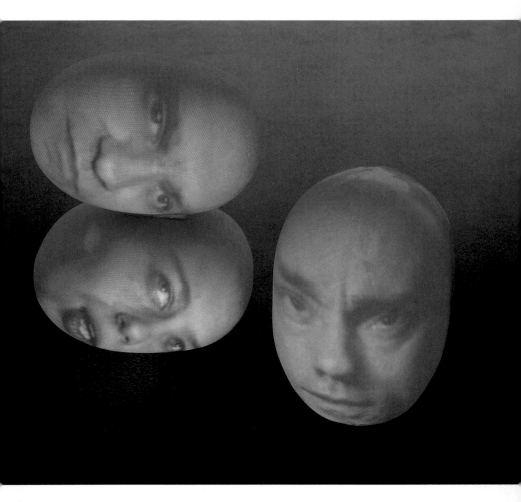

appeal, masking biting commentary in the guise of humorous, off-beat and fun projections. Formally, Oursler seeks to remove the image from the television screen and project it onto the real world.

Diverse issues of female identity are addressed by several late-century artists. US artist Amy Jenkins (b. 1966), borrowing a technique from Oursler, and before him, American media and performance artist Robert Whitman, projects images onto everyday objects like shirts or bathtubs. In *Ebb* (1996) a tub becomes a repository of bloody water which is actually projected onto its porcelain surface. A woman climbs into the tub and the blood recedes into her body, reversing the menstrual flow. One is reminded of the haunting images of Ana Mendieta who, in the late 1960s and early 1970s photographed and videotaped herself in a variety of isolated and risky situations. Palestinian-born Mona Hatoum (b. 1952) inserted a tiny camera inside her body and projected the video of her internal organs in a circular structure

185. (below) **Oursler and Kelly**, *The Poetics Project* (Barcelona version), 1997. Installation view: Patrick Painter Inc., Santa Monica, California. In *The Poetics Project*, Oursler and Kelly provide a sweeping view of 1970s culture at the point when they were emerging as artists in California.

186. (right) **Oursler and Kelly**, *The Poetics Project* (*Documenta* version), 1997. Installation view: *Documenta X*, Kassel, Germany.

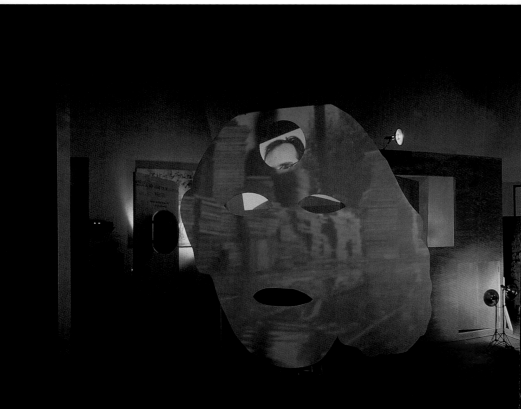

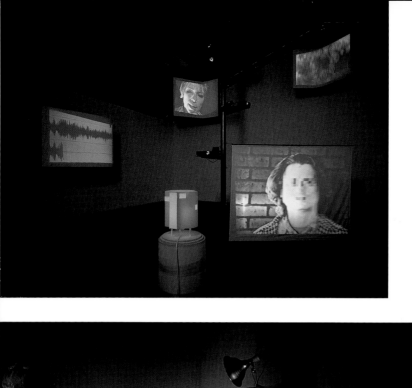

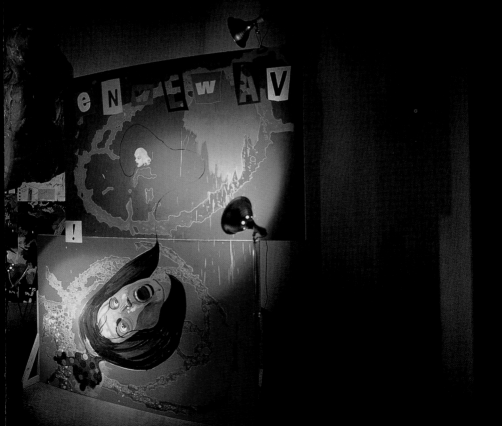

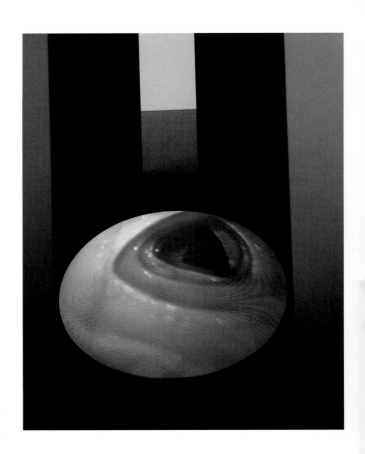

187. **Mona Hatoum**,
*Corps étranger*, 1994.

resembling an eyeball placed on the floor of a walk-in installation. Viewers are given the simulated experience of walking through the artist's reproductive system, something of an updated homage, perhaps, to Judy Chicago's *The Dinner Party* (1974–79), which featured porcelain reproductions of the female anatomy.

In her video installation *Yvonne* (1997), German artist Rosemarie Trockel (b. 1952) favored genteel appreciation for the everyday with images of children playing, fibers of cloth unwinding, and, with a hint of Diane Arbus-inspired photographs, shots of young girls skipping around the yard intercut with images of a woman covered in tarantulas. Tracey Moffatt insinuated the female gaze into the male stronghold of voyeurism in her video installation, *Heaven* (1997). Working in a casual style with a camcorder, Moffatt filmed young men undressing before they hit the waves. The footage seems unedited, a record of Moffatt's afternoon at the beach in the outdoor locker room of Australia's idealized visual commodity, the surfer.

Pipilotti Rist's installation, *Ever Is Over All* (1997), features 192-93 two large projections that meet in the corner of a wall. The artist juxtaposes slowly changing shots of long-stemmed red flowers with the movements of a glamorously dressed woman strutting down a street, humming to herself and smashing car windows. Rist's scenario, played out with fashionable attention to red color patterns, extends the feminist ideology she professed earlier in the frenetic *I'm Not the Girl Who Misses Much* (1986). Rist has contin- 1-3 ued to favor this split-screen joined at a corner technique in such installations as *Meadow Saffron or Fall Time Less* (2004), an elegiac meditation on her childhood home of St Gallen, Switzerland.

The Scottish team of Stephanie Smith and Edward Stewart confound relations between the sexes in their installations, *Intercourse* (1993) and *Sustain* (1995). Issues of domination and

88. **Rosemarie Trockel**, *vonne*, 1997.

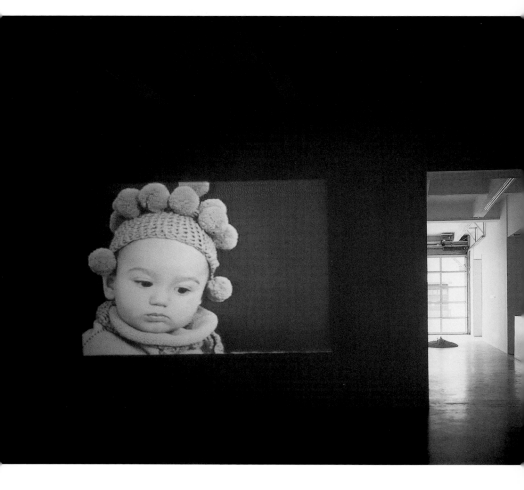

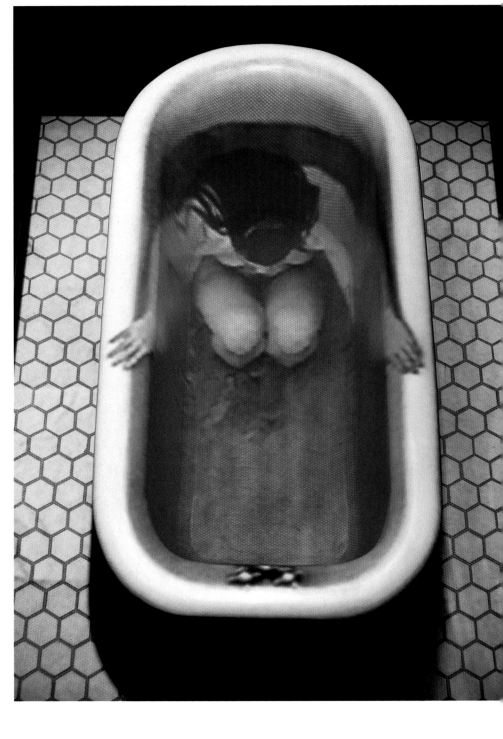

89. (left) **Amy Jenkins**,
*bb*, 1996.
porcelain tub becomes a
rojection surface in Amy Jenkin's
xploration of female identity.

90. (below) **Stephanie Smith**
nd **Edward Stewart**,
*ntercourse*, 1993.

submission, violence and desire, are explored as the couple videotape themselves caught in private rituals.

A member of the new wave of young British video artists
to emerge at the end of the 1990s (including Keith Piper, b. 1960,
and Sonia Boyce, b. 1962), Steve McQueen (b. 1966) has gone
far to create new images for the black male in his combination
video/film installations.

In full wall projections such as *Bear* (1993) during which two    194
naked men (one of whom is McQueen) engage in a boxing match,
as much a playful pas de deux as combat, and *Five Easy Pieces*
(1995), an enigmatic and fractured narrative, McQueen replaces
familiar images of the black male from sports and news accounts
with fuller, more complex characters. It is as if he were filling in
the 'empty spaces' in representations of the black male in contemporary media that American film historian Ed Guerrero speaks of:

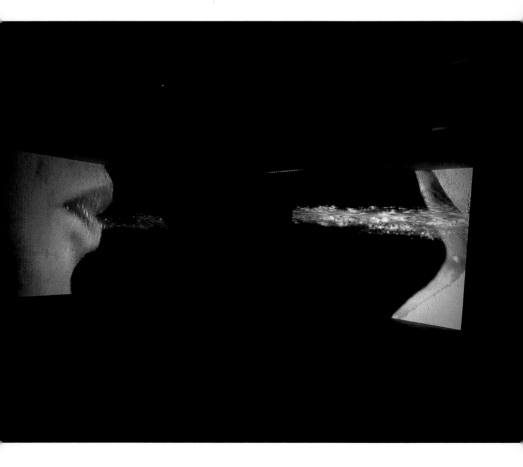

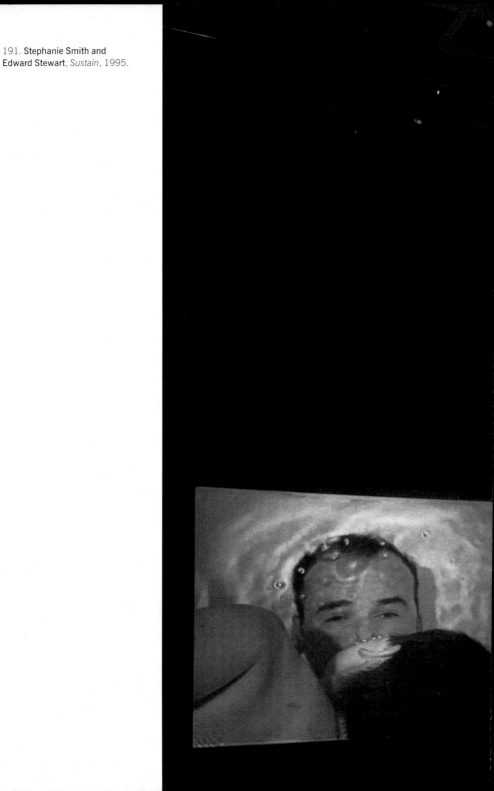

191. Stephanie Smith and
Edward Stewart, *Sustain*, 1995.

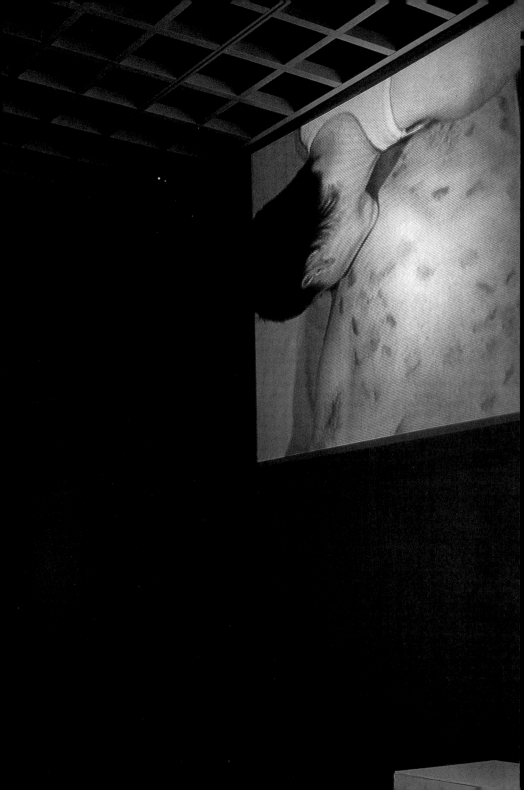

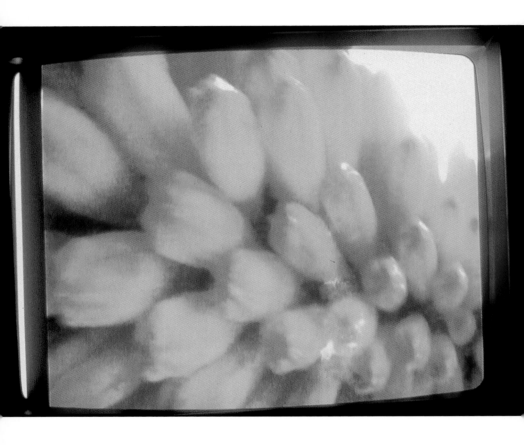

192, 193. **Pipilotti Rist**, two stills from *Ever Is Over All*, 1997.
Rist juxtaposes colorful, pastoral images from a home garden
with the casually violent gesture of a woman smashing car
windows on a clean, safe street in Switzerland.

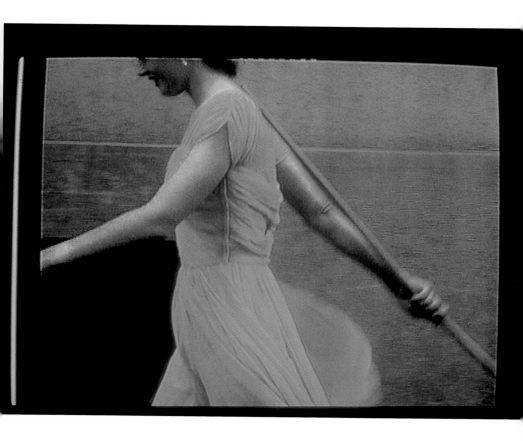

that 'nowhere zone' between the glorified athlete or pop star and the nameless thug on the late night news. McQueen creates for himself a monumental persona in *Deadpan* (1997), a four-minute film in which he appropriates a slapstick moment from a Buster Keaton film, *Steamboat Bill, Jr.* (1928), and turns it into a paean to black determination and resolve.

In the mid-1990s digital cameras became more widely available to the average user, a step some regard as the 'cinematization' of video. Accompanied by more sophisticated editing equipment, especially digital, non-linear systems like Avid, video production attained closer links to cinema. Artists like Barney represent the trend toward mimicking the large-screen viewing experience of cinema by turning to full wall or screen projections of what are essentially single-tape videos and calling this work 'installation,' as opposed to the multi-monitor or multi-object environment commonly used in installation. Barney's *Cremaster 5*, in fact, was shown in a movie theater while the 'installation' proper, consisting largely of props and scenery from the video/film combine, was exhibited in a gallery. For other artists, like Steve McQueen and Pipilotti Rist, the full wall gallery projection of one tape at a time remains the most desirable form of display because it situates the work in an art context, even though it suggests the scale of

194. **Steve McQueen**, *Bear*, 1993. McQueen's large-scale, silent projections encompass the spectator with strong, but often complicated images of the black male, usually played by the artist himself.

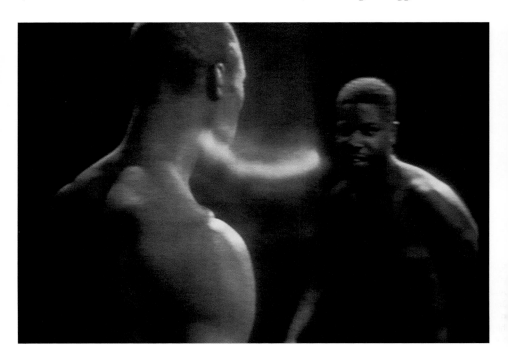

cinema. But some artists, like Canadian Conceptual artist Rodney Graham (b. 1949) are already using Cinemascope cameras for short, personal narratives that are shown as installations. Graham's lush *Vexation Island* created for his country's pavilion at the 1997 Venice Biennale, is a nine-minute retelling of the Robinson Crusoe story which Graham, in the manner of other Conceptual artists who came to prominence in the 1970s, associates with theories on violence by French philosopher Gilles Deleuze. To the well disposed art enthusiast, *Vexation Island* can be an enticing fragment, like a segment from a lengthy Pina Bausch dance or a relief from an oversized Rauschenberg canvas. raham's careful use of familiar strategies like repetition, slow motion, and shifting perspectives remove the film from the practices of normal, narrative cinema, transporting it to the company of Godard and Warhol.

Contrary to former predictions, including those from this author, video has triumphed as a medium. What was thought to be facing extinction (videotape) has been revitalized by digital technology. The lure of 'filming,' literally understood as the use of 16- or 35-millimetre film in the making of moving-image art, is no longer an issue. Filmmaking, or cinema, has become an art of video with filmmakers of all stripes using digital video, high definition video especially, as their source. Recent examples from the film world that were shot totally or largely on video and, in some, but not all cases, transferred to film for projection are: *Time Code* (2002); *Russian Ark* (2002); and George Lucas's series of 'prequels' to his enormously successful *Star Wars* series.

This historical shift provides important challenges to video artists. How does video art now distinguish itself from cinema? Some artists are clearly participating in the cinematic in their installation work (Shirin Neshat, Eija-Liisa Ahtila, Steve McQueen, Isaac Julien, to name a few). Does where artists show their work (galleries, museums versus movie houses) mark the distinction between video art and cinema? Commercial value? Intent of the artist? If artists merely mimic cinema, but in a shorter, less expensive manner, video art will have no sustainability. In his essay 'Battle of the Images' (2000), French critic Raymond Bellour states that cinema is 'under siege' from 'other image systems,' including, presumably, video games and video installations. I think video art faces similar battles, for video artists must continually differentiate themselves from the possibilities of cinema. As digital technology consumes even cinema, the digital video artist must define a space that is uniquely artful, a place where narratives, perceptions and visual expectations become disrupted.

Following pages:
95. **Rodney Graham**,
*Vexation Island*, 1997.
raham films this short narrative
n Cinemascope, further blurring
he boundaries between art and
ommercial film.

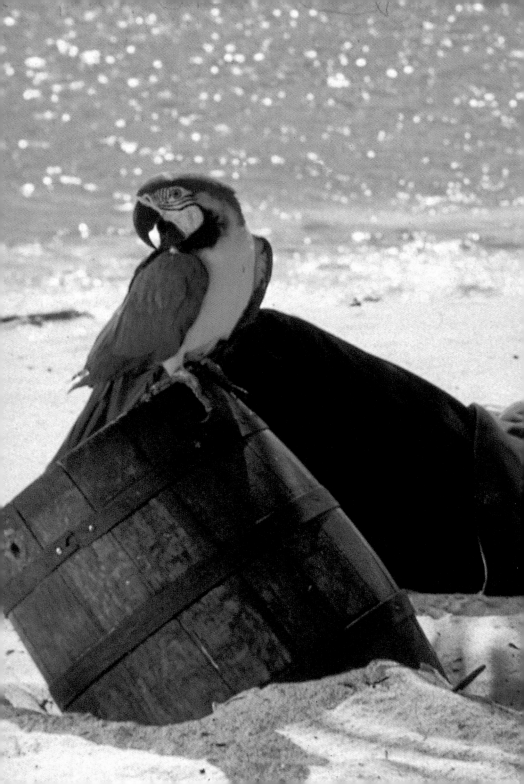

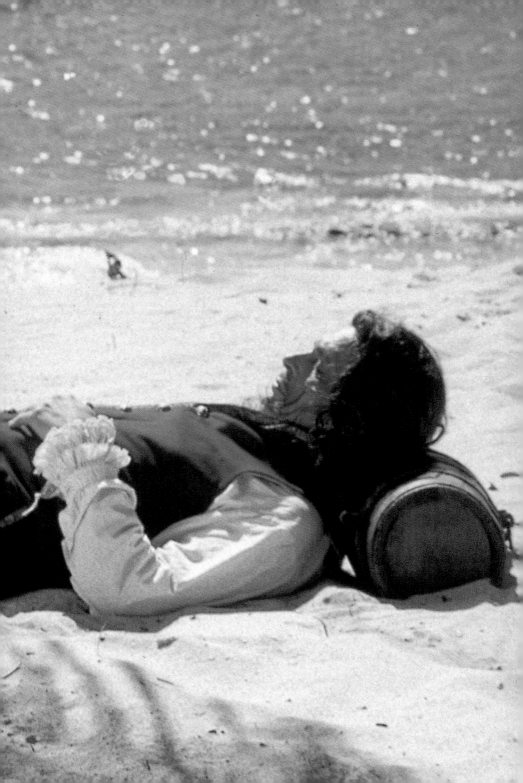

# Chapter 4:    The Digital in Art

It would be difficult to exaggerate the effect of digital technology on the production of art in the twenty-first century. From digitally altered photographs to rapid prototyped sculptures to quantum (cameraless) movies, the use of digital technology is pervasive. Even some 'traditional' painters are making preliminary drawings in their computers before heading for their easels.

Among the larger public, the youth in industrialized countries are spending more time online than watching television and families are sending their old drawers full of photos and home videos to digital processing companies and getting back DVDs edited to look like top-of-the-line documentaries. The American film critic Edward Halter has a rather dystopian view of the digital revolution: 'In a time defined by celebrity leaders, videotape memories, personal technology, electronic terrorism, multi-channel overload and digital social lives, the new generations are those for whom workfare and warfare have become downloadable games and history represents a bunch of files cluttering the desktop.'

Just as at the end of the nineteenth century when stylistic evolutions in art (codified as Classicism, Romanticism, etc.) no longer served as useful classifications of artmaking, today any description of the practice of art that refuses to make room for the technological is lacking. The alliance, often uneasy, between art and technology has come of age: the inexorable march of the world toward a digital (or computerized) culture has included art in its step. Digital art is a mechanized medium whose potential appears limitless. As American writer and curator George Fifield expresses it: 'The artist's ability to effortlessly reposition and combine images, filters, and colors, within the friction-less and gravity-free memory space of the computer, endows them with an image-making freedom never before imagined.'

Digital technology is the engine that drives computer art, internet art, digital photography and digital video, much of contemporary sound art, experimental sculpture and a host of other practices, each with its own history and relevant artists.

Walter Benjamin's essay *The Work of Art in the Age of Mechanical Reproduction*, written in 1936, remains an essential reference in any attempt to develop a language that addresses issues of art in the age of technology. For Benjamin, technology, especially that of the still and moving camera, raised issues of authorship and the very uniqueness of the art object whose 'aura' is lost in reproduction. If an image can be reproduced easily, wherein lies the art? The issue of 'reproducing' images via moving or still cameras has little to do with the radically new capabilities now of creating work that has no referent in a non-digital world; indeed, that has no referent in the three-dimensional world as we know it. 'Reproduction' is to the digital world what the hot-air balloon once was to aviation. Using digital technology artists are now able to introduce new forms of 'production,' not 'reproduction.' 'Virtual reality,' for example, one of the more mystifying outgrowths of digital technology, is not a mere translating of data into life-size images that mimic reality. It is its own reality. According to architect and critic Paul Virilio, 'We are entering a world where there won't be one, but two realities: the actual and the virtual. There is no simulation, but substitution.' Benjamin's point about reproducibility, prescient when he raised it in the late 1930s, concerns the 'aura' and uniqueness of the art object and is also related to representations of space through the use of the laws of perspective, a preoccupation of artists since the fifteenth century. 'Perspective' and 'reproducibility' are, for Benjamin, concepts related to representation of the real; but there are no longer agreed notions of 'the real.' The digital world, which goes far beyond the mere non-linearity introduced into art by Cubism, is becoming a new reality for which a new critical and aesthetic language must yet be developed.

Digital technology, for which the computer is the basic tool, embraces all areas of contemporary, technologically involved art, from films, to photography, synthesized music, CD-ROMs and much more. The new power that digital technology brings to the image renders it infinitely malleable. Formerly, visual information was static in the sense that the image, although editable in film or capable of being incorporated into other images in montage, was fixed. Once transferred to digital language in the computer every element of the image can be modified. The image becomes 'information,' in the computer, and all information can be manipulated. 'For the first time in history,' says digital media pioneer Peter Weibel, 'the image is a dynamic system.'

This chapter cannot address the overarching reach of digital technology into all art forms. It will attempt only to highlight those computer-based practices that various representative artists are using to make art that extends our definitions yet farther from the canvas toward worlds unimagined when the twentieth century

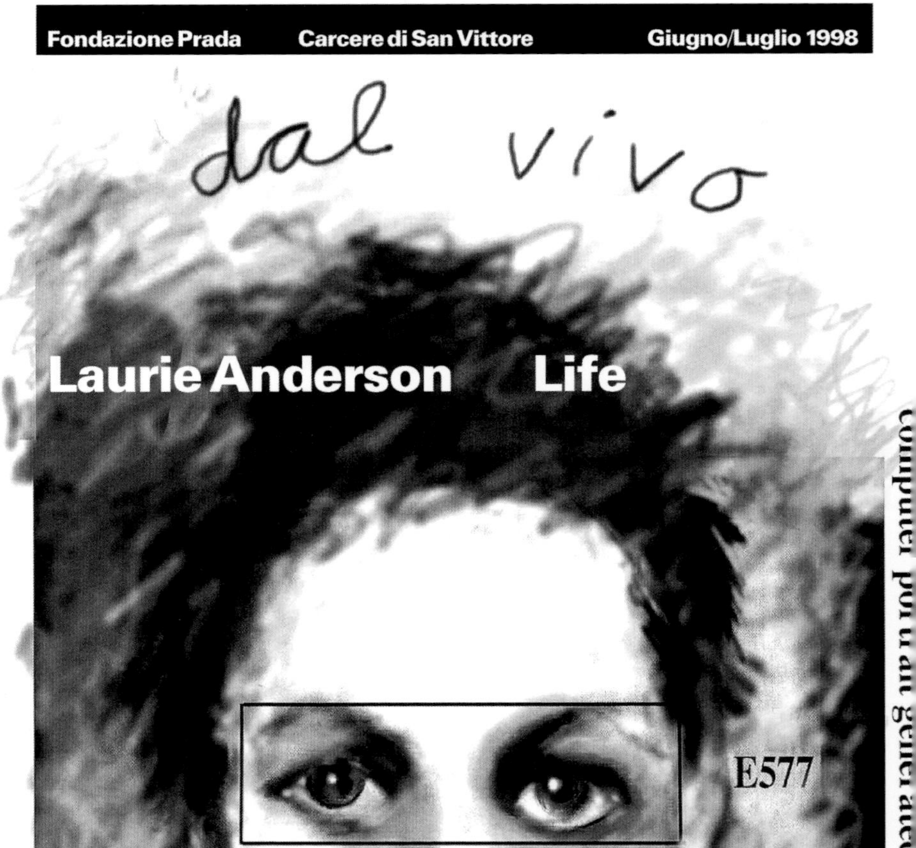

*dal vivo*

## Laurie Anderson    Life

E577

N33

Q40

computer portrait generated from verbal description

**Fondazione Prada**   20135 Milano, via Spartaco 8,   Tel. 02.54670216/0202   Fax 02.54670258

began or even when it was half over. Such is the speed with which new forms of digital art are being created that, by the time this book is published, the work discussed may seem old fashioned, its newsworthiness already faded. The days of manifestos and predictions are gone. Any declarations on 'the way things will be' are outdated by the time they are printed, or even e-mailed.

Referring to the all-digital electronic computer, which was introduced at the Moore College of Electrical Engineering in Philadelphia in 1946, US curator Charles Stainback writes:

*Some forty-five years after its introduction, this technological wonder has assumed countless roles in culture – placing itself at the center of what could be called the second technological transformation, a shift from the industrial age to the electronic era. It is the fuel from the restrictions of the analogue world to the speculative, seemingly limitless potential of an expanding digital universe.*

In art, visual literacy is no longer limited to 'the object.' It must embrace the fluid, ever-changing universe that exists inside the computer and the new world the computer facilitates: an interactive art world that can be virtual in its reality and radically interdependent in its incorporation of 'the viewer' into the completion of the work of art. When Duchamp suggested that the work of art depended on the viewer to complete the concept, little did he know that by the end of the century some works of art (such as interactive films) would literally depend on the viewer, not only to complete them, but to initiate them and give them content.

'Interactive' has emerged as the most inclusive term to describe the type of art of the digital age. Artists interact with machines (a complex interaction with an 'automated but intelligent' object) to create further interaction with viewers who either summon up the art on their own machines or manipulate it through participating in pre-programmed routines, that can themselves vary (thus far only in limited ways) according to the commands, or simply movements, of the viewer. In the Japanese group Dumb Type's interactive installation *Lovers* (1995), viewers' movements in front of a laser-operated visual system triggered pre-filmed images of actors walking toward the viewers and addressing them. Outside the museum, video games such as 'Pac-Man,' 'Battlezone,' 'Frogger,' and 'Maneater' have taught a generation of teenagers and their elders about interactive media. Aesthetic questions abound, as they did with video art, but, as with video, which is now present in every international survey of contemporary art, if artists apply their tenacity to it, art will emerge.

96. Computer-generated image used to advertise **Laurie Anderson's** *Dal Vivo* installation : Fondazione Prada, Milan. A fundamental change in the making and perceiving of images occurred with the advent of digital technology. The image could now be created from numbers (digits 1 and 2) and subjected to manipulation as never before.

## Digitally Altered Photography

The increased usage of the personal computer ushered in an age when many artists were able to take primary source material (a photograph) and manipulate it using the language of the computer. Photographs are translated into computer language via scanning, a now simple process in which a two-dimensional image is rendered into the mathematical binary (or digital) language of the computer. The primary material (the photograph) becomes malleable since it now consists solely of discrete digits.

It is interesting that, despite the abstract nature of several notable early computer art works (Noll, Whitney), the representational image made a big comeback with digitally altered art in the 1980s as artists toyed with the mechanical possibilities of computer imaging techniques. Several digitally reworked images of Leonardo's *Mona Lisa*, for example, appeared in the work of Jean-Pierre Yvaral and Lillian Schwartz. Yvaral's *Synthesized Mona Lisa* (1989), eerily similar to a Chuck Close portrait, consisted of a structural reconstitution of the famous face based on numerical analysis. Schwartz's *Mona/Leo* (1987) matches in the same frame half of Mona Lisa's face with half of Leonardo's. These artists, enamored of the capability of the computer to reactivate an overly familiar image, may be practising the 'art of appropriation' (popular in the 1980s work of Sherry Levine and others), but, by giving it a technological twist, they are attempting, in Popper's words, 'to create visual phenomena in which figuration and abstraction are no longer in opposition.' In Lera Lubin's *Memory of History Meets Memory of the Computer* (1985) the artist

197. **Lera Lubin**,
*Memory of History Meets Memory of the Computer*, 1985.

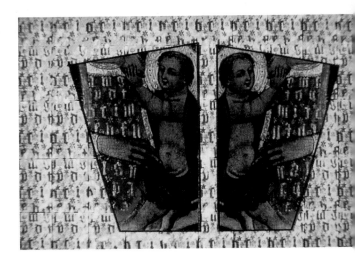

*184*

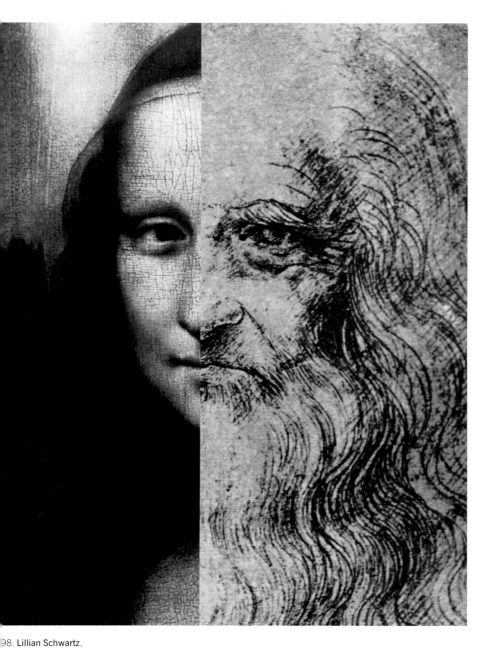

98. **Lillian Schwartz**,
*ona/Leo*, 1987.
:anning allows artists
 translate photographs
 any printed material into
e computer's digital language
ld manipulate the image.

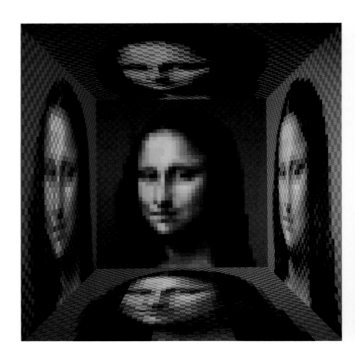

199. **Jean-Pierre Yvaral**, *Synthesized Mona Lisa*, 1989. Numerical analysis allowed for the reconstitution of Da Vinci's famous face in this digital image.

scans images from classical paintings of the Madonna and Child into her computer then reworks them to illustrate sexual intentions hidden in the paintings.

American artist Keith Cottingham (b. 1965) has relied exclusively on digital manipulations of images in all his photographic work to date. He grappled with the myths he sees behind traditional painted and photographic portraiture in his digitally constructed color photographs, *Fictitious Portraits Series* (1992). Starting with a photograph and applying the tools of digital painting and montage he creates composite images which, though appearing at first glance like normal photographs, confound the boundaries of race, gender and age. A more disturbing series of digital photographs was made by American Anthony Aziz (b. 1961) and Venezuelan-born Sammy Cucher (b. 1958) in their collaborative project, *The Dystopia Series* (1994). Critical of some technological advances in photography ('with the end of truth in photography has come a corresponding loss of trust;' they say, 'every image, every representation, is now a potential fraud') they took normal photographs of people and digitally erased their eyes and mouths, resulting in dehumanized heads.

British-born artist Victor Burgin (b. 1941) seeks affinities with the painterly tradition in his work, especially in terms of the practice of chiaroscuro (rendering light and dark to enhance a three-dimensional effect). His interest in semiotics and psychoanalysis has also been evident in his photography since 1971. He turned to digitizing images in the 1990s in works such as *Angelus Novus (Street Photography)*, 1995, a triptych of digital prints in which a central image of a woman (a photograph taken by the artist in 1980) is re-worked in terms of its light and dark contrasts and then flanked by two manipulated photographs of bombs dropping from planes in the Second World War.

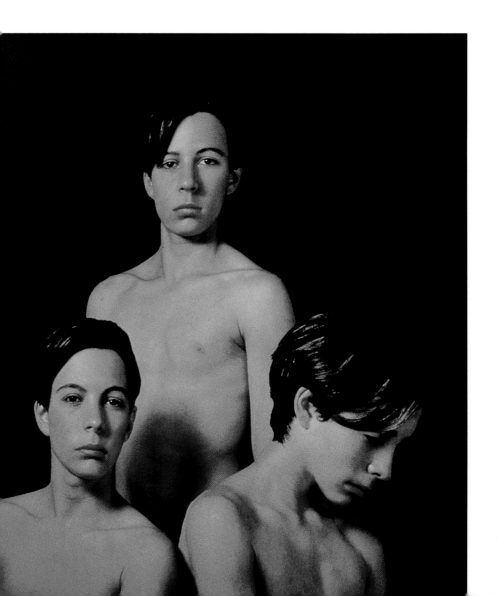

American artist Chip Lord (b. 1944) made an elaborate series of digitized prints called *Awakening from the Twentieth Century* (1994–95) in which he seamlessly combines, within the computer, images of a fish vendor and motor scooters with advertising on them in Japan, and, in Mexico, a priest at a local festival and a man selling shoes on a street corner, all in an attempt to portray a worldwide view of people 'left behind by the communication revolution.'

Artists often refer to their use of the computer to 'modify' their photographs, that is, altering their original photograph digitally to represent a different reality. Japanese-born Mariko Mori photographs herself in costumes she designs to suggest surreal creatures. In *Birth of a Star* (1995), after digitally manipulating her image, she appears as a plastic doll/pop star, looking both gruesome and mysterious.

Canadian artist Jeff Wall (b. 1946) is representative of photographic artists who use digital technology to expand the visual possibilities of their work. He uses the computer to make montages that 'couldn't be made otherwise,' he says. In *A Sudden Gust of Wind* (1993), for example, he creates what looks like a freeze-frame of papers and objects flying in the air in a gust of wind.

Wall sometimes refers to his photography as 'cinematography,' because his methods used to gain the picture he wants involve many of the same elements as the motion picture, including staging performers in very precise ways and lighting the scene very specifically. His final product also bears comparisons to digital motion picture editing. For *Dawn* (2001), a ten-foot-wide

201. (below) **Chip Lord**, Central Market, Los Angeles, December, 2006/Sony Electronics, 3300 Zanker Road, San Jose, California, August, 1994 from the series *Awakening from the Twentieth Century*, 1994–95.
Taking a cue from the film *Blade Runner*, Chip Lord digitally combines images from around the world in scenarios depicting a future that 'recognizes the existence of the past and the present as components of cultural continuity.'

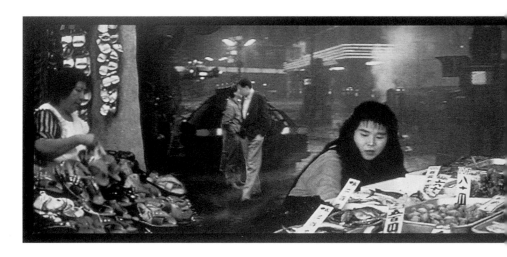

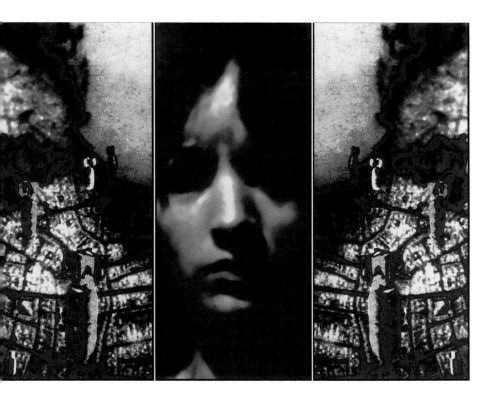

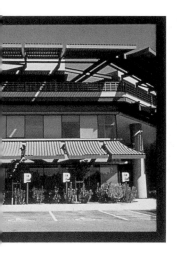

202. (above) **Victor Burgin**,
*Angelus Novus (Street
Photography)*, 1995.
In this digital photograph triptych,
Burgin wants us to see an 'angel'
looking outward from the center,
flanked by 'wings' on either side.
Actually the young girl's face,
excerpted from a photo taken
by the artist years before, sits
between aerial views of Second
World War bombing raids.

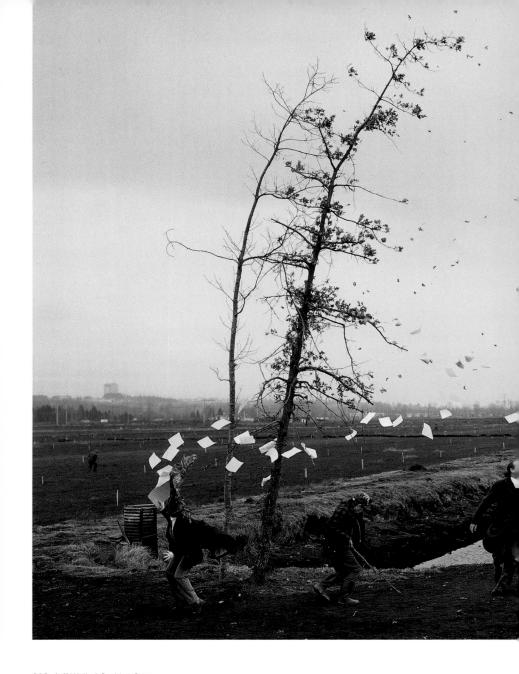

203. **Jeff Wall**, *A Sudden Gust
of Wind (after Hokusai)*, 1993.
With digital technology artists can
create fictional narratives that bear
little relationship to traditional,
chemically processed photographs.

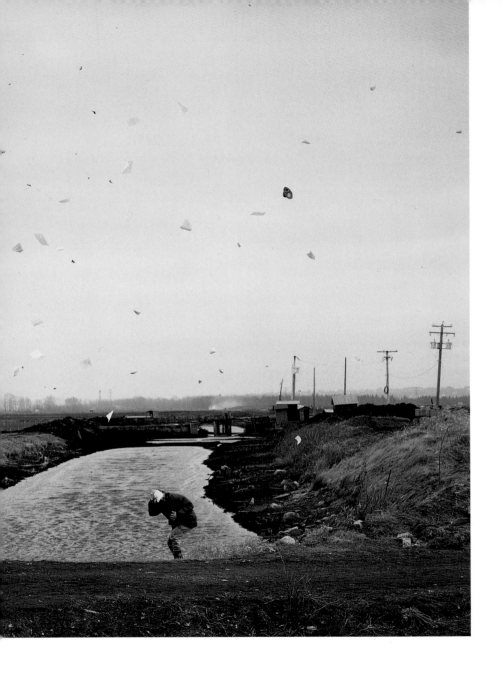

photograph, he digitally combined eight separate images of a street light at different times in order to get just the right look. He uses the computer extensively to create what are essentially montage photographs, though the montage is not visible to the naked eye.

The German artist Andreas Gurksy (b. 1955), who has achieved notoriety for his enormous interior photographs, uses subtle digital manipulations to achieve the outsize complexity of works such as *Chicago Board of Trade II* (1999), which contains an impossibly large number of floor traders or *Siemens, Karlsruhe* (1991), which also features an excessive number of laborers working at machines. Even the legendary London-based art couple Gilbert and George (Gilbert was born in Italy in 1943, George in England in 1942) have launched into digital re-processing with a vengeance. Their 2004 exhibition *Perversive Pictures* featured

204. **Jeff Wall**, *Boys Cutting through a Hedge, Vancouver*, 2003.
Jeff Wall uses digital technology to service his conceptual notions of the photograph as 'experience.' He works and re-works images, inserting different shots into a given scene in order to provide a comprehensive experience for his viewers, but not one based on documentary evidence. In this photo he reconstructs a scene he witnessed while making another work several years before.

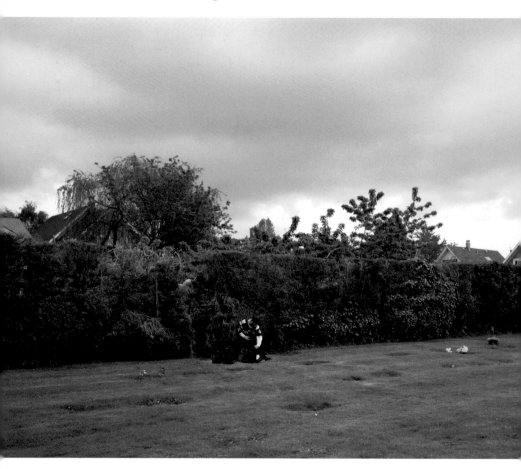

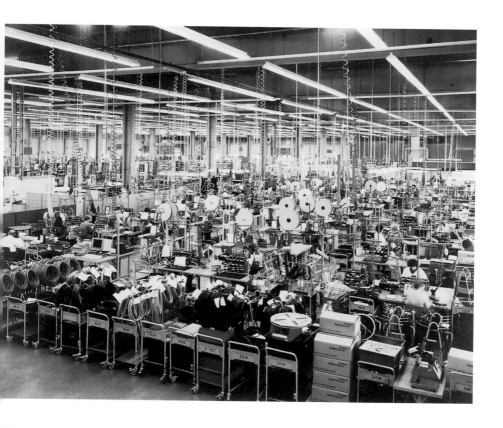

205. **Andreas Gursky**, *Siemens, Karlsruhe*, 1991.

galleries of manipulated photos often based on hip-hop culture, including the kaleidoscopic *Cool*.

206

As in any technology-driven medium, the most dynamic work occurs when the technology catches up with the visions of the artists, or, conversely, artists catch up with the technology. In painting or sculpture, it is the concepts and uses of materials that change in the art. With technology-based art, the medium itself radically changes when the technology changes. The excitement that Muybridge felt in being able to capture movement with his 'chronophotography' is now replaced by an enthusiasm for altering reality, for making the real illusory. For some critics, computer-based art lacks the depth of interest they associate with, for example, abstract painting. They find it boring, or like holography, too superficial in its trickery. American photography critic A. D. Coleman, reacting to much of what he saw at Montage 93, the International Festival of the Image, held in Rochester, New York in 1993, said 'mostly it's bells and whistles and buttons to push: everything here hums and clanks and flickers and turns on and off.'

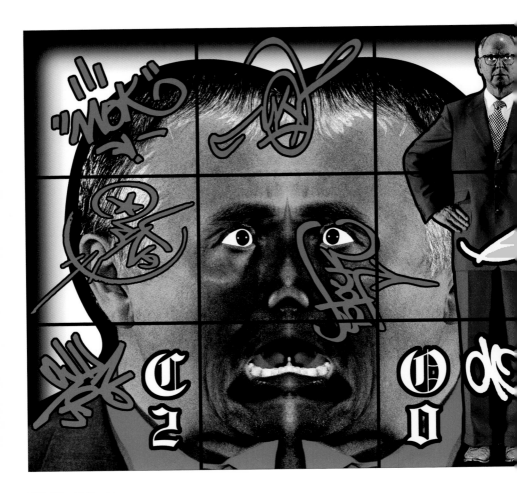

206. **Gilbert & George**,
*Cool*, 2004.

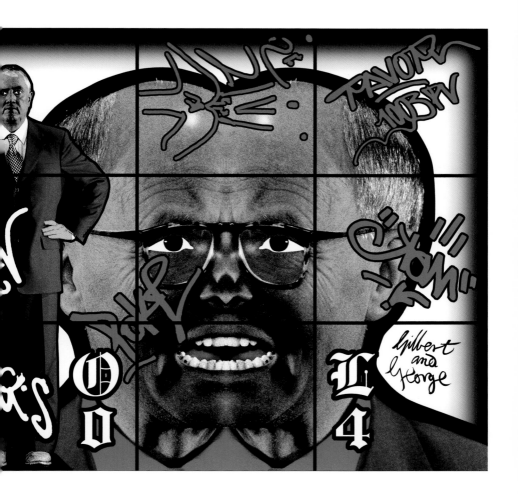

## The Digital Cinematic

Movies were, arguably, the dominant art form of the last century, global in reach, both popular and defiantly avant-garde, supercilious and memorably profound. Humans, it would appear, delight in the illusions of moving or still pictures that animate their own experience of living. All the better if those images were filmed in 35 millimetre, so lush and romantic is its texture.

The 'grand' story of twentieth-century cinema as told through the lens of masters such as Sergei Eisenstein, David Lean, and Ingmar Bergman is over. Cinema has become an art of video (not Video Art, for that has its own history as an art medium), and as such, it is a digital art, a new-media art. Directors (Jean-Luc Godard, Steven Spielberg) have become new-media artists. Not that they have any choice. Digital video now permeates filmic art. Digital technology, some fear, will forever alter even the mainstream movie machine as actors, locations, scenery, even cameras are replaced with computer-generated images, as was the case with director Robert Zemeckis's 2004 film, *The Polar Express*. Media artist and author Lev Manovich summarized the current and future state of digital cinema rather baldly in his 1995 essay, 'What Is Digital Cinema?': 'Live action footage now…functions as raw material for further compositing, animating, and morphing.'

207. (below) **Shirin Neshat**, *Fervor*, 2000.

208, 209. (right) **Shirin Neshat**, *Rapture*, 1999. Filmic artist Shirin Neshat is representative of installation artists whose urge is clearly toward the cinematic. Her lushly filmed installations, which can be both single and multi-screen, are usually shot on 16mm film, then transferred to DVD or laser disc for projection. Her striking narratives, shot in Morocco, address issues of identity and sexual repression in her native Iran.

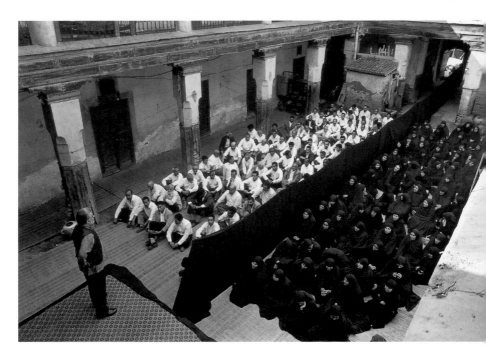

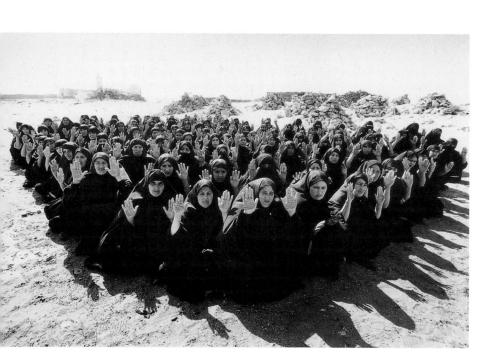

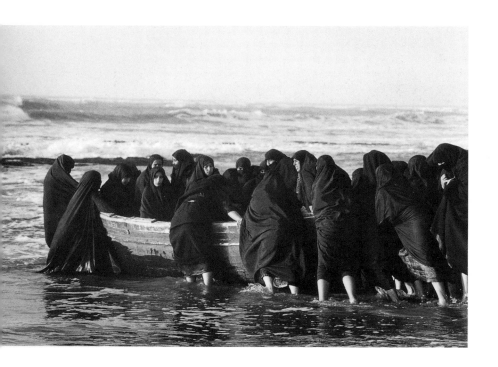

197

The 'new art cinema' is comprised of installations that are multi-screen, panoramic, dome-projected, multi-user, nonlocal (i.e. on-line). Multi-screen and multi-image projections, familiar since the 1960s, are reaching an apotheosis with the cinematic installations of artists such as Isaac Julien (b. 1960), Eija-Liisa Ahtila (b. 1959), Pierre Huyghe (b. 1962), Doug Aitken, among many others.

The British artist Isaac Julien began making short narrative films and documentaries in 1983 while still in art school. His 'drama/documentary,' as he called it, *Looking for Langston* (1989), brought him wide exposure on the film-festival circuit. In 1996 he made the first of the multi-screen film installations with which he is most identified. *Trussed* was a double projection of a ten-minute black and white 16-millimetre film about two young males (one black, one white) engaging in a sadomasochistic drama. Issues of racial and sexual identity mingle with an elegiac sense of loss in a time of AIDS. Languorous tracking shots, overhead views, dramatic lighting, makeup and costumes all contribute to an unmistakable cinematic effect.

Later works, including *The Long Road to Mazatlán* (1999), *Paradise Omeros* (2003), and *Baltimore* (2004), all utilize multiple screens and feature lush colors in a filmed environment of cinematic sophistication. Julien's broad palette embraces not only issues of

210. **Isaac Julien**,
*Baltimore*, 2003.

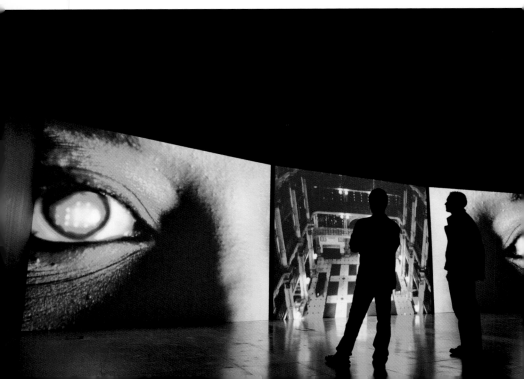

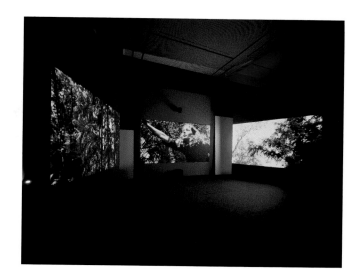

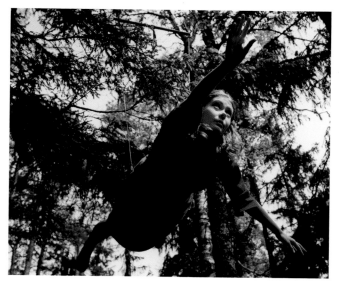

racial and class identity, but also the history and theory of film as well as painting, choreography, and the psychology of memory.

Multi-screen projections are also central to the work of the Finnish-born artist Eija-Liisa Ahtila, who began her career as a film and television director. Her interests in transforming complicated cinematic narratives into divided screens reflects her subjects' psyches, which are often tormented by deep psychological conflict. In *The House* (2002), a three-screen projection, a solitary woman imagines herself flying through the trees.

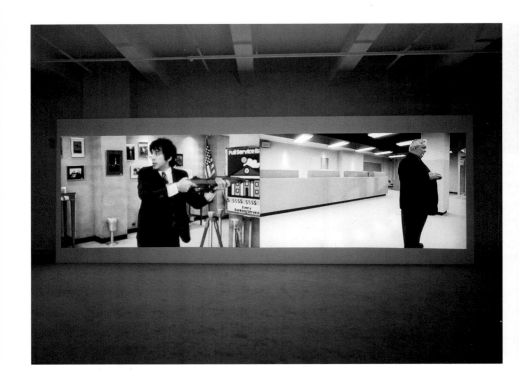

213. **Pierre Huyghe**,
*The Third Memory*, 1999.

The Frenchman Pierre Huyghe, known, too, for his sculpture and conceptual art, has used cinema as a basis for several installations, including *Remake* (1995), a re-staging of Alfred Hitchcock's 1953 film, *Rear Window*; and *The Third Memory* (1999), a re-imagining of Sidney Lumet's *Dog Day Afternoon* (1975). In each case, Huyghe hired amateur actors to do scenes from the original film, not with an intention of mimicking the earlier work, but for the purpose of exposing the mechanisms of cinema (saying lines, as opposed to 'acting,' for example). This 'distancing' from the original provides a new reality to the experience of watching a scene. In a 1999 interview for the exhibition *Cinema Cinema* at the Stedelijk Van Abbemuseum, Eindhoven, Huyghe said, 'The actors first see their lines a few hours before shooting starts....It's precisely their problems, hesitations, silences and so on that I record in real time.' Huyghe's digital videos utilize cinematic techniques (dolly shots, tracking), but not toward narrative ends. He disrupts the narrative tension of films in order to create a new relationship between the viewer and the action. In this sense, his work shares affinities with Douglas Gordon's *24–Hour Psycho* (1993), but Huyghe's methods and goals are quite different. While Gordon uses the original footage in his installations, Huyghe

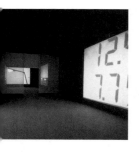

14. (above) **Doug Aitken**, *ectric Earth*, 1999.

15. (below right) **Michal Rovner**, *ore*, 2003.

16. (below) **Michal Rovner**, *me Left*, 2003.

reworks the original with a new 'collective' of actors whose interactions in real time are more important to him than the narrative content of the film. Nonetheless, his point of departure remains cinema.

Doug Aitken has progressed from multi-screen projections to multi-screen environments. Working with both 16-millimetre film and digital video his camera has moved from the sorry island of Montserrat (*eraser*, 1997), decimated by a volcano in 1996, to the streets of Los Angeles where a young loner moves in the shadows during a long night alone (*electric earth*, 1999). In the latter, a maze of scrims becomes projection surfaces for his solitary wanderings.

The work of Israeli video artist and photographer, Michal Rovner (b. 1957) is the product of painstaking digital editing that whittles away recognizable individual traits from whatever living object she is filming. In the hundreds of small, silent, simply clad people she populates her videos with she seems to be breathing the spirits of Beckett and Giacometti. Her singular artfulness is also infused with a political sensibility stemming from her lifelong experiences with conflict in her native Middle East.

*Time left* (2003), is a monumental wall-to-wall video installation of row after row of silhouetted figures marching in the hundreds of

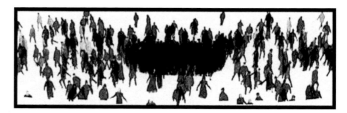

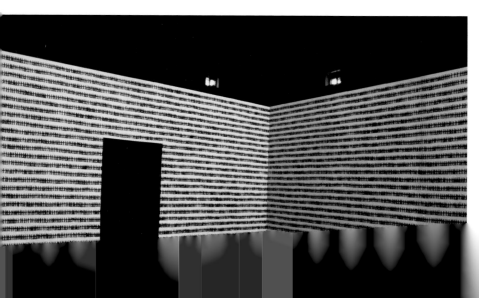

thousands toward an unnamed end, accompanied by droning electronic music. Associations with condemned prisoners or survivors of an apocalyptic event, or simply pilgrims walking of their own accord toward an anticipated religious revelation, are apparent. Or none of these. The installation can and does mean many things.

An astonishing series of work from an exhibition entitled *In Stone* (2004), featured digital video projections of similar silhouetted figures marching across large slabs of stone. The slowly moving figures appeared to be passing through the pages of ancient scrolls, trying to communicate with us from an ancient time. For Rovner, digital editing is a tool used to suit her own vision. She makes of these tools fine materials like the smoothest of marble or the supplest of paints.

The American artist Paul Pfeiffer (b. 1966) has also mastered certain post-production digital editing techniques to accomplish his sophisticated examinations of identity and social structures. In *JOHN 3:16* (2000), the artist digitized more than five thousand individual frames of a basketball shot and repositioned them to highlight the fetishization of the ball among black males, thus rendering a sort of elegy for the black male sportsplayer. So, too, in *Fragment of a Crucifixion (After Francis Bacon)* (1999), he edited video footage of another basketball game and isolated the figure of a player after making a 'slam-dunk' shot. Pfeiffer edited out all

217, 218. **Eve Sussman**, *89 Seconds at Alcazar*, 2004. Shot on High Definition Video, this 12-minute loop imagines the activities of the same people in the Spanish royal court featured in Velasquez's painting, *Las Meninas*. The Velasquez is known for its prescient photographic quality. Sussman's work, rich in cinematographic detail, is itself a subjective documentary on one of art history's best-known paintings.

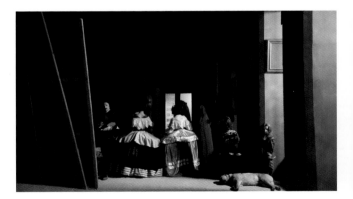

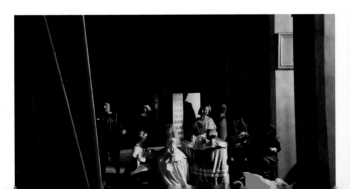

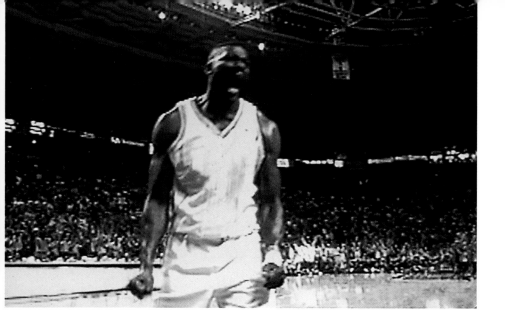

219. **Paul Pfeiffer**, *Fragment of a Crucifixion (After Francis Bacon)*, 1999.

the other players and all the commercial logos from the original footage. The player appears at once angry and ecstatic as the crowd around him roars their approval, much like the Romans of old cheering for the gladiators as they faced the lions.

*Computer Art*

As is the case with many advancements in technology and art, digital art has its roots not so much in academies of art as in the marketplace, in this case in military defense systems. The Cold War between the West and the now defunct Communist bloc energized rapid advances in technology during the 1950s and 1960s, especially in the research and development of computerized intelligence. The world's first digital computer, the ENIAC (Electronic Numerical Integrator and Computer, about the size of a large garage), had been introduced at the University of Pennsylvania in 1946; and in 1951 the first commercially available electronic computer (UNIVAC), able to handle numerical and textual information, was patented. Research centers, often supported by governments, fostered intense experimental investigations in computer technology, some of which involved music and art. Because many of these investigators were first scientists, with non-vocational interests in art, the aesthetic standards of so-called early computer art are questionable.

The American A. Michael Noll, often mentioned as one of the first 'digital artists,' along with Germans Frieder Nake and Georg

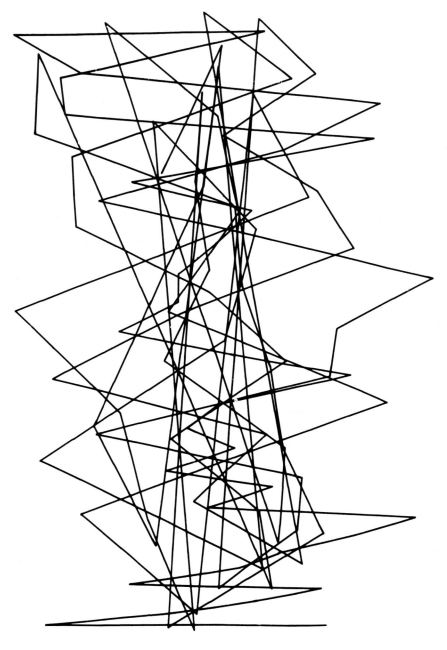

GAUSSIAN–QUADRATIC (1963)
BY  A. MICHAEL NOLL

Nees, is a case in point. As a young researcher at Bell Laboratories in New Jersey, where he worked on telephone transmission quality, he began producing abstract, computer-generated images, such as *Gaussian Quadratic* (1963), which he found suggestive of Picasso's Cubism. In 1965, New York's Howard Wise Gallery, in what was thought to be the first exhibition devoted to computer art (actually Nake and Nees had shown publicly a few months before at Galerie Niedlich in Stuttgart), presented *Computer-Generated Pictures*, which included several works by Noll and his colleague Bela Julesz. The exhibition's title came about because not everyone involved considered what they were doing with computer images to be art. Several of Noll's early works were based on paintings by others, including Mondrian. Noll himself pointed to the aesthetic problem of early computer art: 'The computer has only been used to copy aesthetic effects,' he wrote in 1970, 'easily obtained with the use of conventional media…The use of computers in the arts has yet to produce anything approaching entirely new aesthetic experiences.'

While the desire for 'an entirely new aesthetic experience' may be an overly utopian aim, Noll voiced a concern that endured for the first couple of decades of computer art. In fact, it is only at the end of the 1990s that the aesthetic bar has been raised in this art form. Frank Popper, in his widely researched *Art of the Electronic Age* (1993), considers very few examples of computer art prior to the mid-1980s worthy of mention. Reminiscent of their Constructivist forebears (e.g., sculptors Alexander Archipenko and Naum Gabo), who looked to the machine as their partner in art, early computer artists seemed drawn to mechanical or futuristic imagery, as if the art of the machine had to bear some resemblance to the machine itself. While this may be natural, the art can have a certain sameness to it as the geometric forms of much early computer art testify.

One of the difficulties in both the development and assessment of computer art is that artists who were either well known or were soon to become so did not take to this form in their own artwork. Unlike video art, whose early practitioners included Bruce Nauman, Richard Serra, and John Baldessari, computer art can claim no such well-known artists. This is due, in part, to the anti-technology sentiment among counter-culturalists and artists in the mid-1960s and 1970s. Various ecological and anti-nuclear groups were protesting at governmental experiments in nuclear energy and technology, which may have overshadowed artistic experimentation with computer technology. Also, there was no easy-to-use computer comparable to the Sony Portapak video or the hand-held camera, which were affordable

220. **Michael Noll**, *Gaussian Quadratic*, 1963. Early computer art often resembled geometric abstractions.

alternatives to expensive, commercial film equipment. The personal computer did not start appearing on the average desk until the 1980s.

In common with Michael Noll, several other early practitioners of computer art were associated with research institutions, especially Bell Laboratories in the US. Experimental filmmaker Stan Vanderbeek and artist Lillian Schwartz worked there with engineer Kenneth Knowlton, producing what are now considered seminal works of computer art. Vanderbeek's 1964 *Poem Fields*, a rapid-fire film of digitally generated abstract images, and Schwartz's 1970 film *Pixillation*, also composed of programmed abstract images, are two examples. Even earlier, filmmaker John Whitney had developed a mechanical analogue computer which produced his *Catalog* (1961). A short film consisting of computer-

221–24. **Lillian Schwartz**, *Pixillation*, 1970.

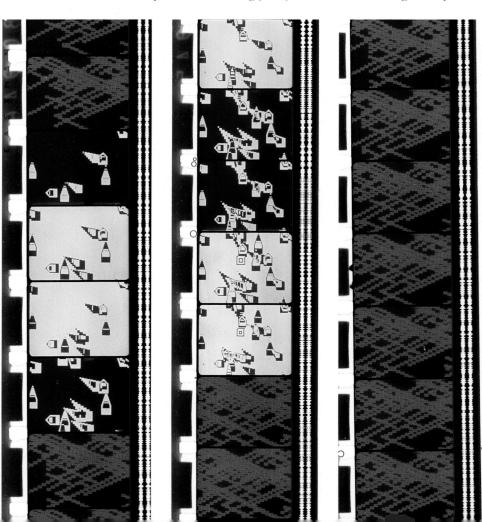

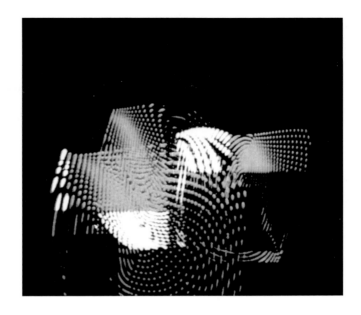

produced abstract images, *Catalog* was created using outdated military computing equipment.

In addition to filming abstract images, some early computer artists attempted to re-invent the animated image so familiar to moviegoers from Disney films. Animation always had its so-called high-art practitioners. American Charles Csuri's 1967 animated film *Hummingbird*, made in collaboration with computer programmer James Schaffer, showed an image of the bird dissolving, then becoming reconstituted, all accomplished through a computer program. Animation has continued to play an important role in computer art. As artists like South African William Kentridge (b. 1955) have demonstrated in video and film, animation can be the locus for extraordinary formal and contextual experimentation. French artist Michaël Gaumnitz created a series of personal animations on the computer between 1985 and 1989 entitled *Sketches, Portraits, and Homages*. Utilizing the easily available techniques of pasting, erasing, displacement, and multiplication the artist developed an 'electronic palette' with which he improvised on themes related to personal memory.

Innovative use of technology by artists, also evident in the early days of video art, has led to significant advances in the technology itself. In the mid-1970s artists Manfred Mohr, John Dunn, Dan Sandin, and Woody Vasulka developed software for the creation of two- and three-dimensional imaging. Composers Herbert

226

227

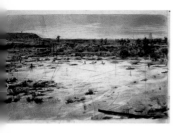

226. **William Kentridge**,
*Untitled (drawing for Journey to the Moon)*, 2004.
William Kentridge uses the medium of animation to create piercing films and videos about the cruelties of apartheid in South Africa. Starting with charcoal or pastels he shoots with 16mm film and transfers to video for projection. His animations are seamless flights of fantasy grounded in the real, nightmarish experiences of his countrymen.

Brun and Lejaren Hiller devised compositional tools for the computer that anticipated the keyboard synthesizers now used by all mainstream musicians.

Vera Molnar, considered a pioneer in computer art, translated a Minimalist sensibility to computer images, in intricate, highly controlled works on the computer, such as *Parcours* (1976), which looks at first like a series of hasty line drawings. She uses the computer to expand her repertoire into an avant-garde that makes 'the accidental or random subversive in order to create an aesthetic shock and to rupture the systematic and the symmetrical.'

Although other innovations occurred in computer art through the mid to late 1970s it is generally agreed that computer art languished after the first burst of energy in the early 1970s. In the 1980s when computers became more affordable and accessible they began to be used by a wide spectrum of artists, including those whose primary work was in other media. In her book *Digital Visions: Computers and Art*, American writer and freelance curator Cynthia Goodman, while emphasizing the work of several of the artists already mentioned here, also includes work by David Hockney, Jennifer Bartlett, Keith Haring, and Andy Warhol, each of whom had used the computer in some way in the development of art. This is not to suggest that any new medium need be validated by referencing artists already established in other media.

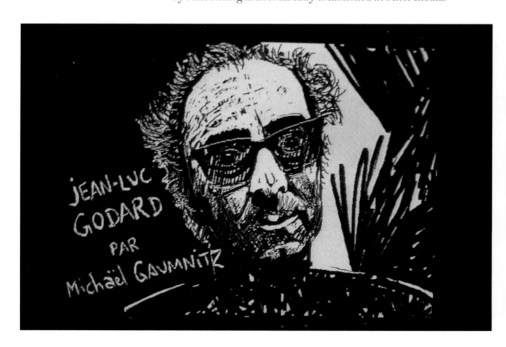

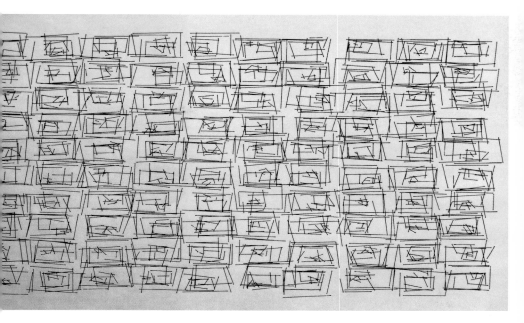

The increased availability of personal computers in the 1980s brought with it a burgeoning of computer based art, which includes a broad range of computer graphics, animation, digitized images, cybernetic sculptures, laser shows, kinetic and telecommunication events and all manner of interactive art that require the involvement of the viewer/participant. Notable are the programmed light installations of German-born innovator Otto Piene (b. 1928) and [233] the outdoor laser art performance sculptures of American artists Norman Ballard (b. 1950) and Joy Wulke (b. 1948). [232]

Abstraction is still very much alive in computer art. Edward Zajec, much like a choreographer, has created computer images that unfold to the rhythms of a musical score by composer Giampaolo Coral. The result, *Chromas* (1984–87), is a melange of abstract images, dominant in blue, that curve, point and circle in response to the musical score. French artist Miguel Chevalier, who cites Mondrian, Warhol, and Nam June Paik as influences, creates sequentially ordered images that sometimes look like the insides of a massive telephone wiring system. His *Anthropometry* [234] (1990) is an intricately layered series of lines mixed with colors that suggest a map of a digital universe. Other artists create what might be called hyper-real computer images that derive from fantasy or nature. William Latham's *The Evolution of Form* (1990), [229–31] which he refers to as a 'computer sculpture,' is a series of complex

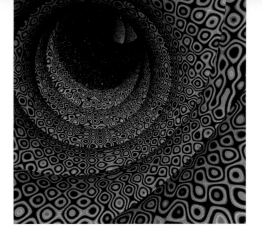

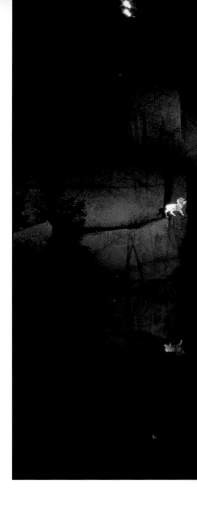

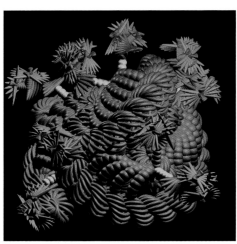

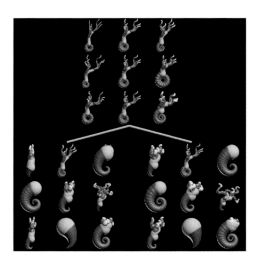

229–31. (left) **William Latham,** *The Evolution of Form,* 1990. Latham was among the first to create 'genetically' alive forms that resemble living organisms, though their mutations only occur inside the computer.

232. (above) **Norman Ballard** and **Joy Wulke,** *Visualization of Time/Quarry Sundial,* 1995. In this outdoor performance, lasers are mechanically 'choreographed' to interact with natural elements and sculpture.

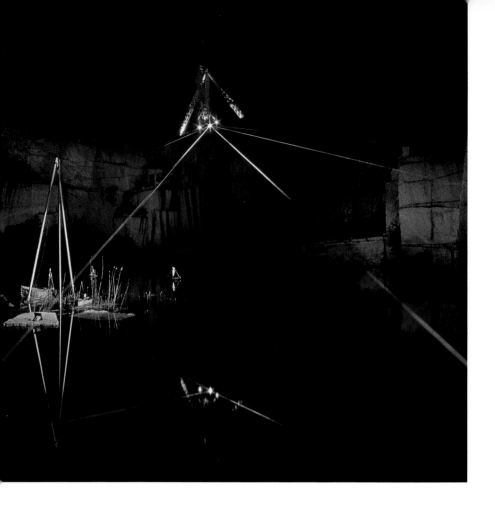

forms, resembling hybrid sea shells. He has been inspired by
Surrealist painters Salvador Dalí and Yves Tanguy in his quest for
forms that can be manipulated, reshaped (or 'carved,' in virtual
sculpture) within the computer.

In her book *Digital Art* (2003), curator and media historian
Christiane Paul distinguishes between art that uses digital
technology 'as a tool for the creation of traditional art objects –
photography, print, sculpture, or music – and art that employs
these technologies as its very own medium.' Today, 'computer art,'
strictly speaking, has little meaning since most artists using digital technology, use computers. The computer is most often the
intermediary between the artist and the realization of the artist's
idea, rather than a medium in itself.

233. **Otto Piene**, *Olympic Rainbow*, 1972.
Light (including lasers) is controlled and manipulated by computers, as it once was by the artist on canvas.

234. **Miguel Chevalier**, *Anthropometry*, 1990.
The graphically composed lines in this computer image suggest the endless wiring needed for computers worldwide to function.

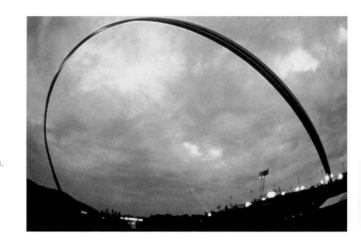

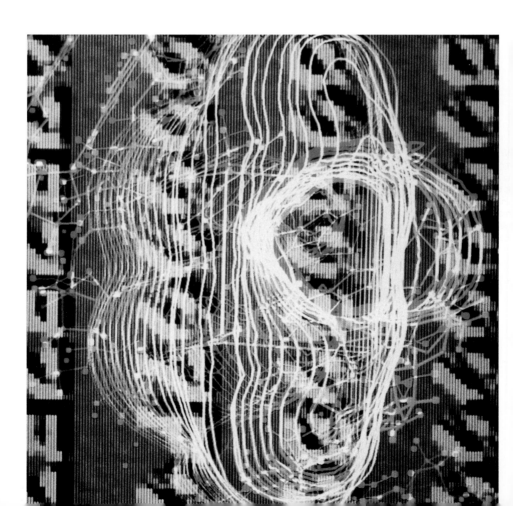

## Interactive Art: The Internet

It is axiomatic in our time that technology changes rapidly; so, too, the art that utilizes it. CD-ROMs, DVDs, video games, computer games, robotics, and many forms of advanced entertainments involve the active participation of the user, or consumer. Interactivity, art that requires viewer participation to be complete, has emerged as a new medium. The immediate danger here is that such interaction can degenerate into mere pastimes or diversions. A high-tech event or game, while possibly containing artful components, is not art as we have defined it here. The value of interactivity as art is in its exploration of multiple points of view, without fear of the challenges of non-linearity or unusual modes of perception. To this extent, the new medium, if we may call it that, extends both modernist and post-modern agendas of radically transforming how art is made and experienced.

In his 1999 essay, 'On the History of Artistic Work with Telecommunications Media,' Timothy Druckrey discusses a prototype of what we now call 'interactive art' held at the Centre Georges Pompidou in 1985. In an exhibition called *Les Immateriaux* (*The Immaterials*), several noted French artists and intellectuals (including Daniel Buren, Jacques Derrida, Jean-François Lyotard) were connected by computers (before e-mail) and engaged in a collaborative writing project from their own residences, which could be witnessed in real time in the museum on another computer. Druckrey notes that the reason such art practices (including also telephone concerts, fax performances and satellite conferences) have largely escaped historical notice is that 'they left no traces behind when finished.'

Art developed specifically for the Web is such a recent phenomenon that the Guggenheim Museum in New York, recognized

35. **John Simon**,
*very Icon*, 1997.
he historically revered 'grid'
as become a favored starting
oint for several computer artists.
'mon uses it as a locus for a
ever-ending succession
° calculated visual tricks.

**Given**:
An icon described by a 32 X 32 grid.

**Allowed**:
Any element of the grid to be colored black or white.

**Shown**:
Every icon.

Owner:          John F. Simon, Jr.
Edition Number:   Artist's Proof
Starting Time:   January 14, 1997, 21:00:00

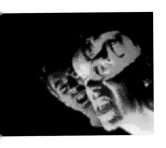

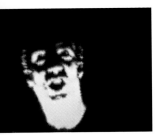

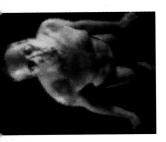

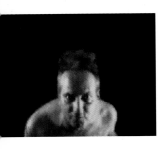

for its involvement with new media, launched its first artist project for the Web only in the summer of 1998 with New York artist Shu Lea Cheang's *BRANDON,* an exploration of gender and cultural issues. While other institutions, especially Ars Electronica in Linz, Austria, and The Center for Art and Media in Karlsruhe, Germany, had presented Web projects in conjunction with their international festivals since the mid-1990s, it is useful to keep in mind that the Worldwide Web (www) was launched only in 1989. Designed by English computer scientist Timothy Berners-Lee, it was originally intended to aid international communication among physicists working for the European Laboratory for Particle Physics. Prior to then, similar networks were used exclusively by government institutions and research universities involved in military projects.

Internet artists, while growing in sophistication all the time, often incorporate images that have been developed outside the computer and then fed into it by a scanner or digital video or other imaging equipment. Some artists, however, either on their own or with commissions from museums and art centers, are developing work that truly engages the computer as a medium. Prominent among them is American John F. Simon, Jr. (b. 1963), whose *Every Icon* (1997, *www.numeral.com/everyicon.html*) addresses computer language directly in a conceptual scheme that seems to take 'time art' to its limits. He created a 32-by-32 square grid containing 1,024 smaller squares within it. These tiny squares change constantly between light and dark in endlessly differing combinations, one line at a time. The top line alone has 4.3 billion variations, which would take sixteen months to display on a continuously operating computer. The second line would take six billion years, and so on. Looking on screen like a kinetic Josef Albers or Agnes Martin, Simon's 'art game,' in which he invites the viewer to watch the grid as it lightens and darkens, can never be completed, but it goes far toward visualizing a notion of infinity. Simon's *Unfolding Object* (2002) is an interactive computer work featuring what looks at first like a box in a field of color. The object changes shape and color as users click within and around it. New flaps open and spread out, according to users' manipulations; colors evolve hourly. The object does indeed appear to unfold *ad infinitum* (*www.numeral.com*).

Simon assisted other conceptually oriented artists, Jenny Holzer, Lawrence Weiner, and the team of Kolmar and Melamid, in the design of their art on the web. Holzer placed a series of provocative statements online in *Please Change Beliefs* (1998). Each phrase ('loving animals is a substitute activity,' 'murder has its sexual side') could be highlighted and another phrase would appear. Each screen page stated at the bottom 'Please Change Beliefs.' Echoing his own work in other media, Lawrence Weiner, like Holzer, posted pithy statements that also could be highlighted, yielding other statements, meant to illustrate his engagement with 'reality' and 'dreamscapes.' The Russian-born team of Kolmar and Melamid created *The Most Wanted Paintings* (1997), which began with an online survey of people from many different nations that asked what they like to see in a painting and what they didn't like. Based on those people's expressed preferences artists then made paintings that were exhibited online. A thread of intentional banality ran through each of these works on the Web.

The Dia Center in New York sponsors an ongoing project of artist commissions for the Web. Its first, *Fantastic Prayers*, commissioned in 1995 from the American collaborative team of writer Constance DeJong, video artist Tony Oursler and musician Stephen Vitiello, is a labyrinth of fragmented texts, sounds, and images centered around an imagined land of Arcadia, whose 'residents are unaware of locations and times' until a mysterious voice invades

40–43. (below, clockwise from top left) **Cheryl Donegan**, *Studio Visit*, 1997. Donegan invites visitors to her website to come inside her studio where she engages in offbeat encounters with the tools of her craft, amounting to a postmodern digital 'studio visit.'

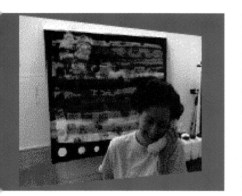
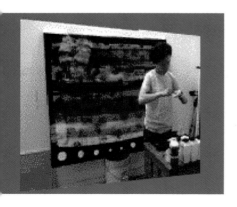
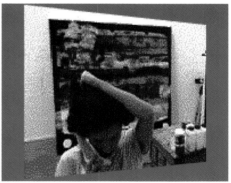
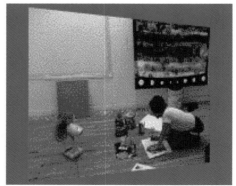

their serenity. Upon entering this seemingly endlessly navigable site (www.diacenter.org), one finds a maze of connections that range from Oursler's disembodied mouths spouting phrases ('some of it I liked') to a tract on the Tibetan Book of the Dead, all of them accessible by a mere click of the mouse. After repeated clicks, one's starting point appears lost forever as free association replaces any sense of linear narrative.

At the same site is American video artist Cheryl Donegan's *Studio Visit* (1997), a virtual studio of ideas, web paintings, video, and graphic displays. Donegan captures here the same sense of artful playfulness that characterizes her single-channel videos. Here the artist places herself, clad in a shower cap and covered in strands of videotape, within large swirls of primary colors. Images are intercut with one another (they don't 'morph' into one another as in films) as the visitor clicks on and on. The artist's studio is also the subject of Allen Ruppersberg's *The New Five Foot Shelf* (2004), an obsessively complicated collection of books based on the fifty-volume Harvard Classics series of world learning, but personalized by the artist. Visitors to the site (*www.diacenter.org*) can open the books and also take a pictorial tour of the walls of the artist's studio.

Humor plays a big role in many internet art projects. Clever manipulations of data, texts, phrases and images often contribute to wry commentaries on politics, art and every imaginable subject. One such work at *www.obsolete.com/artwork* reacts to the pervasive use of Walter Benjamin's essay on art in the mechanical age. Entitled *Walter Benjamin: The Work of Art in the Age of Mechanical Reproduction* (1998), the site consists of words and numbers flashing so fast on the screen that the viewer is unable to read them. The anonymous artist or artists who created the work add the following explanatory note at the bottom of the computer screen: 'a translation meant for readers who do not understand the original.' They evidently believe that the speed of reproducibility has accelerated so much since Benjamin that even his words, when reproduced, have little meaning.

The group called ®TMARK, founded in the US in 1993, is an activist, web-based collective that targets large corporations. According to one of its founders, it 'supports the sabotage (informative alteration) of corporate products, from dolls and children's learning tools to electronic action games, by channeling funds from investors to workers for specific projects.' They are self-described 'serious pranksters.' Visitors to their website can request sponsorship for a particular, usually subversive, but not physically dangerous, activity. One of their most noted (and notorious) projects involved the internet toy manufacturer eToys and the art group 'etoy.' The David and Goliath tale, described on *rtmark.com*, involved hundreds of supporters who rallied in favor of etoy through the on-line efforts of ®TMARK.

Why, one might ask, is this considered art? The actions of groups like ®TMARK, Electronic Disturbance Theater and others recall the protestations, both artistic and political, of Fluxus artists, Situationists, Viennese Actionists and a wide array of individuals and groups from the 1960s and 1970s. Art, to these practitioners, can often take the form of 'interventions.' The artfulness of these actions may simply be based on the fact that the artists involved declared them so. While the suspicion that these actions are outside the realm of art is understandable, there is little doubt that new definitions of art have emerged since the mid-1960s. The new face of art includes Performance and the multiple manifestations of minimalism, conceptualism, earth art and whatever else artists turn their attention to.

Perhaps the work of American activist and artist Mark Napier (b. 1961), who keeps some of his involvements anonymous, can help facilitate appreciation for the vitality of the artistic imagination in internet art. His website, *www.potatoland.com*, has programs such as *the shredder* and *digital landfill*, which are exasperatingly clever deconstructions of web-life. Users who visit the site experience the disintegration of images and data as they innocently navigate Napier's wicked environment.

Easily accessible as art is American artist Matt Mullican's (b. 1951) evolving site, *www.centreimage.ch/mullican*, which features 'pictograms,' as he calls them, colorful computer drawings that morph and complexify as visitors click on them. British artist Jake

245

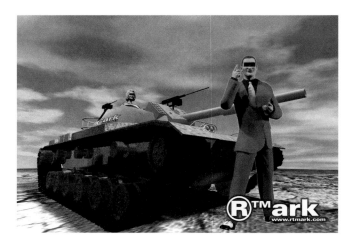

245. (below) **Matt Mullican**, image from website piece *Up to 625* produced for *documenta x*, 1998.

246. (right) **Jake Tilson**, selection of screens from website *The Cooker*, 1994–99 *(http://www.thecooker.com)*. Tilson, who has used all manner of found objects in his work in the past, has taken this sensibility to the computer where he combines images from his world travels into an interactive experience for his website visitors. For example, they can 'order' breakfast in a number of restaurants worldwide and hear the sounds in that restaurant as they sit in front of their computer.

Tilson, who has had a longstanding fascination with the technical aspects of art production and reproduction, uses the Web for his image-laden encounters with randomness and fragmentation. His site (*www.thecooker.com*), an ongoing project begun in 1994, contains a dizzying array of playful associations contained in nine different Web art projects. *Macro Meal* (1994) allows the visit to tour the globe 'ordering' breakfast, lunch, and dinner from scores of countries, accompanied by video images of a typical restaurant and sounds that might be heard within it.

It is clear that graphic design plays an integral role in art developing on the web. Blurring boundaries between art and craft, computer graphic artists, expert in lettering, layout, and multi-dimensional imaging, assist visual artists from other media in adapting to the computer. American artist Peter Halley's (b. 1953) project *Exploding Cell* (1997, archived at *www.moma.org*) consists of nine squares that 'explode' with a kaleidoscopic array of colors.

Reading, as is often noted, has re-emerged as an integral part of the interactive art experience. The computer and the Internet are, at least at this moment, dependent on words and require reading skills that popular visual media, especially television, do not. German artist Frank Fietzek addresses the ambiguities of learning to read in his *The Blackboard* (1993). Fietzek placed a monitor

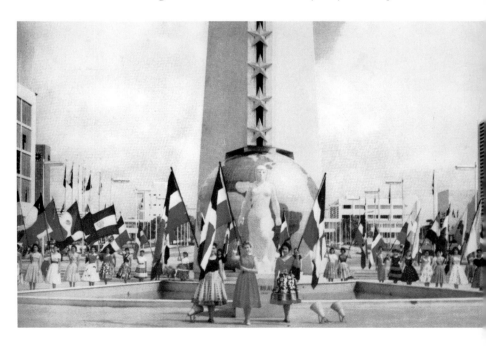

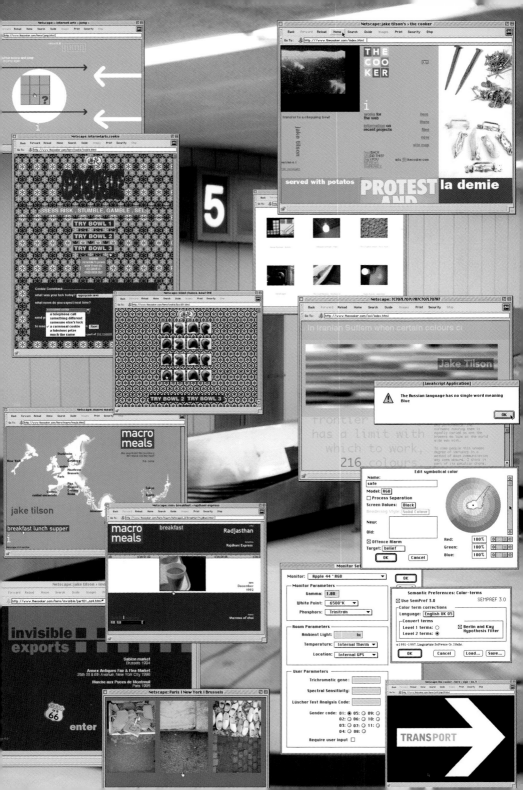

on rails affixed to a blackboard. The viewer can move the monitor around the surface of the blackboard as words make an appearance on the monitor. The words disappear into the dark space of the video, which, for the viewer, according to critic and curator Rudolf Frieling, is comparable to 'the immateriality of the lonely reader surfing the Internet.' 'Are we still reading,' he asks, 'or are we looking at images that appear and vanish before we have had the time to grasp their potential meaning? Our eyes are continuously scanning the surrounding world for hidden information and clues to a better understanding of its chaotic surface.' Frieling's existentialist view of the experience of interacting with the Internet, including the art one finds on it, addresses the radical impermanence of interactivity. Once it is engaged, the machine, in effect, forces compliance with its structural demand to 'keep moving.' One cannot remain static with the interactive Web screen. It will simply shut down once the Web carrier decides the user has been inactive too long. Whatever was on the screen disappears into an unknown darkness. The only way to avoid the forced closure is to keep clicking on more hyperlinks and risk forgetting where one started in the first place.

Live performances are also taking place on the Web where space and time are not separated by geographical distance. A collection of artists from Canada, Australia, Hawaii, Austria, Germany, and Argentina participated in *Oudeis*, an updated version of the Odyssey, during the 1997 Ars Electronica Festival in Linz, Austria. Linked by the Web, performers in each of these countries contributed aspects of the overall presentation. New York's Franklin Furnace, founded by Martha Wilson, and for decades a place for experimental performance, closed its doors in 1997 and converted itself into a virtual performance place that presents new forms of performance at specific times on the Web only.

Two American artists calling themselves MTAA filmed a droll take on Sam Hsieh's 1978 performance in which he 'imprisoned' himself in a room for a year. MTAA (*www.mteww.com*) filmed themselves in two matching rooms (obvious stage sets with simple wooden beds and desks). They, too, go about daily tasks, but, unlike Hsieh, they do it in front of what looks like a live video camera and invite viewers to watch them for a year. If one so chose, one could watch them for a year, thanks to editing magic. The artists are not actually performing for that length of time; they only filmed a few actual hours of tape and then seamlessly multiplied the footage, stretching the viewing time to 31,536,000 seconds. Kevin (b. 1967) and Jennifer (b. 1968) McCoy created their own type of media performance by digitally cataloging

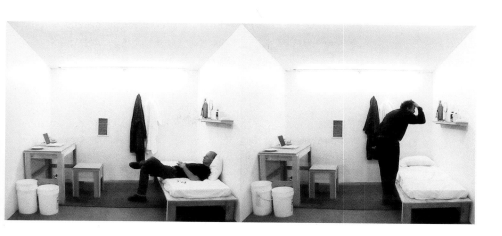

247. **MTAA**, *1 Year Performance Video*, 2004.

every scene from the 1980s television show *Starsky and Hutch* and making them available on a series of computer screens in their installation *Every Shot, Every Episode* (2001). Viewers could choose rapid-fire re-plays of the entire show. Part fetish, part deconstruction, the work was at once playful and terrifying, mimicking as it did the consuming nature of commercial television.

Another dominant material in internet art consists of databases, or what Lev Manovich might call 'information as aesthetics.' Numerous artists, including W. Bradford Paley and internet pioneers Joan Hemskeerk, Dirk Paesman (a.k.a. 'jodi') and Vuk Cosic, among many others, have manipulated imported data and internal computer data to often dizzying effects. In their artworks, time is a primary material: time compressed, elongated, twisted, manipulated. Paley's *TextArc* (2002, *www.textarc.com*), for example, places the complete text of *Alice in Wonderland* on one page of a site designed to look like the map of a new galaxy.

It bears repeating that internet art, as diverse and intricate as it has become, is still in its early stages, like the Worldwide Web itself. At this writing, the art world at large has done little to encourage the future of art on the net. One of the first online art services to foster this young art form, 'äda web,' went out of business, its archive being donated to the Walker Art Center in Minneapolis, which in turn in 2003 relinquished its net-art initiatives. Video art might be viewed as having had a similar, start/stop beginning, but actually video artists were admitted access to museums and galleries in much greater number early on than net artists. This was largely true because artists noted for other practices such as Richard Serra, Vito Acconci, and Bruce Nauman also turned to video as an extension of their art, and, in the case of

Acconci and Nauman, used video extensively. Nonetheless, it did take video art about twenty years (1965–85) to assume high visibility in international exhibitions.

Net art has a fundamentally different trajectory, housed as it is in one of the most democratic, in the broadest sense, inventions in the history of technology: the internet. Though much can (and should) be made of the discrepancies between those who do and those who don't have access to the net because of economic constraints, the net itself is an extraordinarily open and fluid enterprise, at least to date. This may be a good thing for the masses; it is not a good thing in terms of the marketability of net art. In the interconnected art system of galleries, collectors, and museums, art that is freely accessible is not desirable art. Net art is devising its own system of circulation and respectability. Many artists (John F. Simon and W. Bradford Paley among them) sell aspects of their net art on their websites. For others, galleries and museums, considered outposts of a pre-net-historic time, are not their goal anyway.

### Interactive Art: Installation and Cinema

Beyond the 'clicking' and 'surfing' activities of the Web, which are, indeed, forms of interaction with computer technology, several contemporary artists have created works, often on a large scale, that are truly participatory. The entry of 'interactivity' onto the art scene has caused critics (as well as lexicographers) to revise what they call people who enjoy such art: museumgoers or viewers have become participants, players and users. Duchamp's dictum that viewers complete the work of art has taken on a new, more active meaning. There is no art in this arena without the public. The most comprehensive survey of this new art to date was organized by Jeffrey Shaw and Peter Weibel at ZKM, Center for Art and Media, Karlsruhe in 2002. *Future Cinema: The Cinematic Imaginary after Film* was a broad overview of major works in interactive, digital art.

Several examples of viewer participation with the machine have existed in the canon of contemporary art since the last century – Duchamp's *Rotary Glass Plates (Precision Optics)* made with Man Ray, 1920, require the viewer to turn on the optical machine and stand one meter away. Fluxus events and 1960s Happenings involved audience participation, but the new interactive art is not controlled by the artist in the way, say, Kaprow's *Eighteen Happenings in 6 Parts* (1959) was with his strict instructions for the participants. Interactive artists like Americans Ken Feingold, Perry Hoberman, Lynn Hershman-Leeson, Karl Sims, Jeffrey

248. **Marcel Duchamp**,
*Rotary Glass Plates (Precision Optics [in motion])*, 1920.
Duchamp's rotating device, an early example of 'interactive art.' The viewer becomes an active participant in the art.

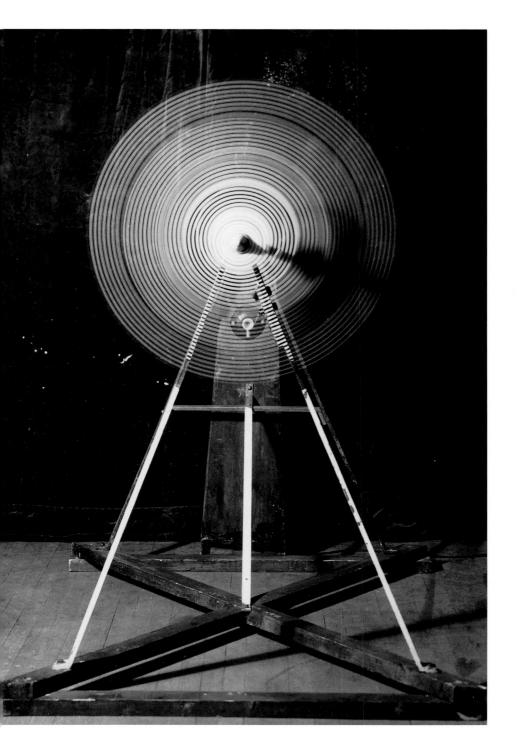

Shaw, Grahame Weinbren, the Japanese Masaki Fujihata, the Germans Bernd Lintermann and Torsten Belschner, to name a few, positively encourage viewers to create their own narratives or associations with their interactive works. In fact, they are designed with this purpose in mind. Granted, the content available for choice currently remains in the hands of the artist, but what participants do with this content has numerous variations. The conceptual rigor (if also playful) of a Fluxus event (e.g. Mieko Shiomi's *Mirror*, 1963, which requires the performer to 'stand on the sandy beach with your back to the sea. Hold a mirror in front of your face and look into it. Step back to the sea and enter the water') is replaced with a wealth of possibilities limited only by the amount of time the participant has to engage the work. Critically, interactivity introduces a new task for those who would try to evaluate it. Timothy Druckrey states it bluntly: 'If images are to become increasingly experiential, then a theory of representation must be evolved to account for the transaction provoked by participation.'

Issues of representation are evident in the work of American artist Bill Seaman and Polish artist Tamas Waliczky. Seaman attempts in his work to create technological links to art-historical forms like the triptych, creating for the viewer/participant poetic experiences akin to the viewing of paintings, but in an interactive way. *Passage Set/One Pulls Pivots at the Tip of the Tongue* (1995) is an interactive installation, presented as a triptych, in which three projections allow the viewer to press on 'hotspots,' or highlighted texts, that yield further texts and images, resulting in a spatial poem that, in Seaman's words, reflect the layering or collision of psychological spaces. Instead of simply layering images in random fashion, Seaman's installation allows for a sequential reading, much like viewing a painting or reading a poem. Waliczky plays with perspective in his 1994 installation *The Way*. As viewers move closer to a projection screen placed at the end of a long corridor, images on the screen, prompted by the viewers' movements, recede, reversing the normal experience of perspective.

Interactivity also provides for artists concerned with social issues the opportunity to involve viewers in very heightened ways. American artist Paul Garrin's *White Devil* (1993) places viewers in the midst of an imagined 'neighborhood.' As the viewers pass through the gallery space surveillance cameras track their movements and vicious dogs appear on video monitors to scare them away. Lynn Hershman-Leeson, whose project *Lorna* (1979–83) was the first interactive video-disk, creates interactive artworks

249–51. **Bill Seaman**,
three screens from *Passage
Set/One Pulls Pivots at the Tip
of the Tongue*, 1995.
In this interactive installation,
visitors press 'hot spots,' areas
highlighted on screen, that call
up further images in an ongoing
unfurling of fragmented images
and texts.

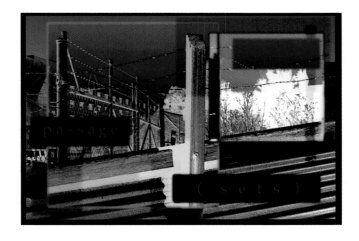

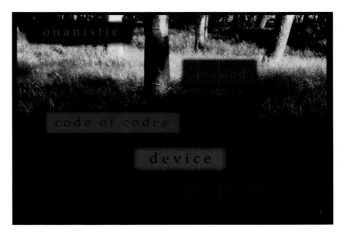

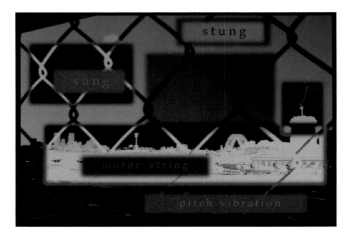

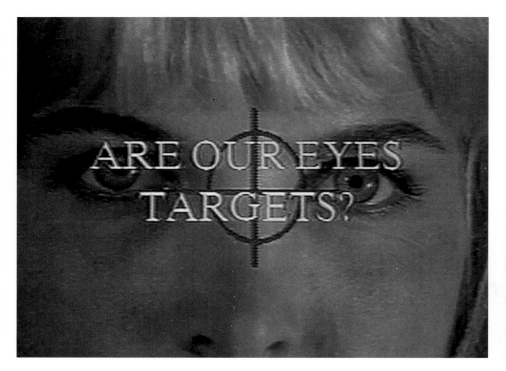

252. **Lynn Hershman-Leeson**, *Room of One's Own: Slightly Behind the Scenes*, 1990–93. For Hershman-Leeson, digital technologies 'are the landscape of the present. Digital techniques further enhance the believability of manipulated images, even when they are bizarre and unquestionably inauthentic.'

that address feminist issues in a very direct way. In *Room of One's Own: Slightly Behind the Scenes* (1992) she created a 'peep show' in which the very act of looking into her vertical installation sets off a series of images related to the depiction (often eroticized) of women in the media. The viewer becomes a 'voyeur' as his or her gaze activates images related to a bed, or telephone, or piece of clothing, all of which are stored on video-disk.

In American artist Ken Feingold's interactive installation *Childhood/Hot and Cold Wars (The Appearance of Nature)*, 1993, a globe sits on a formica table which is wrapped around a grandfather clock. The face of the clock, however, is also a screen upon which video images are projected from within the clock when the viewer rotates the globe. The same viewer can control the flow of images (hundreds of them, from the banal to the horrifying, culled from TV images from the 1950s and 1960s). In Feingold's words: 'The viewer-participant interacts with the work's circuitry and computer programs, controlling the speed and direction of a video-laserdisk player, the movement of the hands of the clock, and the playback of digitized audio.'

It is apparent from these examples, each of which rely on pre-recorded video footage, that the video installation has become

256

255

253, 254. **Ken Feingold**,
*Childhood/Hot and Cold
Wars (The Appearance
of Nature)*, 1993.
Feingold considers the viewer
a participant. In this interactive
installation, by touching the globe
on the table, the viewer initiates
a flood of images representative
of 1950s and 1960s culture,
projected from within the clock.

dynamic, reducing the degree of separation between artist and viewer. Authorship, however, has not disappeared. The artist has now become a facilitator of the art experience with the interactive artwork becoming, in a sense, an extension of education, a hands-on type of creative learning.

Some artists, however, are adamant about challenging authorship. Karl Sims, a Massachusetts Institute of Technology graduate of biotechnology, has devoted several years to developing a computer-based graphic art that recalls Darwin's natural selection theory.

In two complex interactive installations, *Genetic Images* (1993), shown first at the Centre Georges Pompidou in Paris, and *Galápagos*

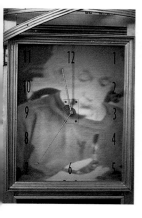

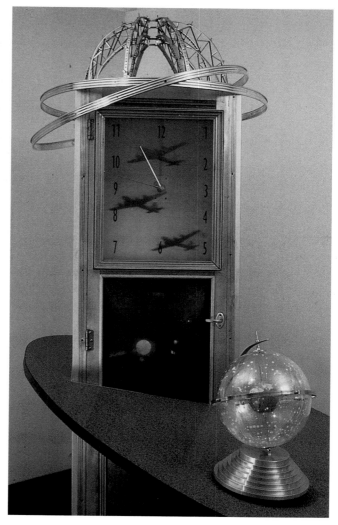

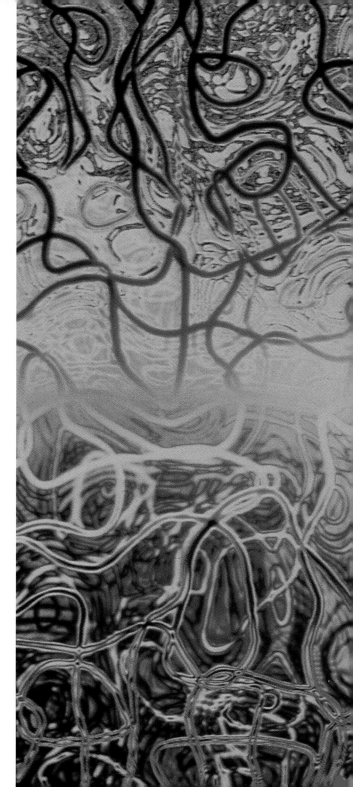

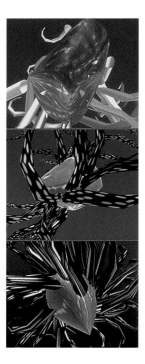

255. (above) **Karl Sims**,
*Galápagos*, 1995.
Inspired by Darwin's theory
of natural selection, Sims
has created a system whereby
'genetic' organisms seem
to develop within their own
environment inside the computer.
The viewer chooses one from a
display of simple pictures, and
then random changes in color,
texture, shape, and other
parameters occur, resulting in
another 'generation' of creatures.

256. (right) **Karl Sims**,
*Genetic Images*, 1993.

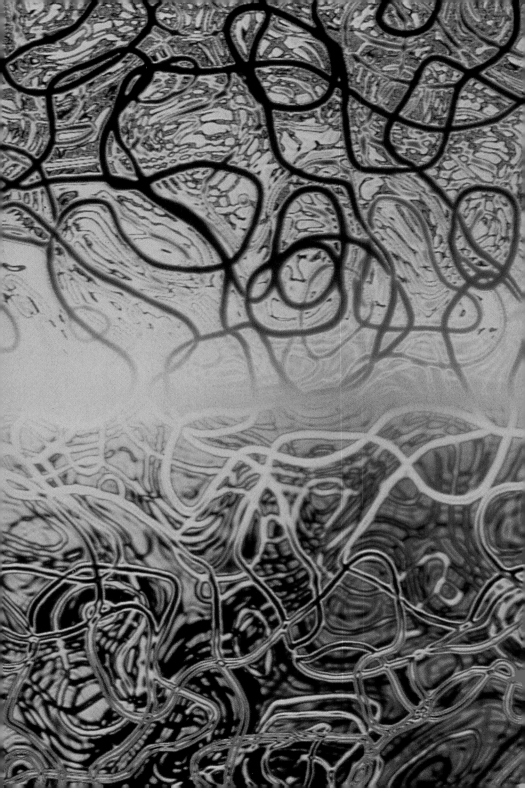

(1995), which is on permanent exhibition at the Inter-communication Center in Tokyo, Sims allows viewers to create their own 'artificial life forms' that 'grow' inside the computer in a rapid simulation of Darwinian principles. In *Galápagos*, twelve monitors with a computer-generated three-dimensional 'creature' visible on each are arranged in a semi-circle, with a footpad attached to each monitor. The viewer chooses a monitor, steps on the pad, and all the other screens go blank. Random mutations of the chosen creature appear on the monitor and continue transforming into new generations of genetic images.

Brazilian artist Eduardo Kac (b. 1962) has been creating digital works that refer to the natural and futuristic (robotic) world for several years, such as *Time Capsule* (1997), a project that utilized, among other things, a microchip implant, a live television broadcast, a webcast, and interactive telerobotic webscanning of the implant. *Darker Than Night* (1999), which involved humans, robots and bats, took place in a bat cave in Rotterdam. In *Uirapuru* (1996–99), Kac manufactured a 'flying fish' wired with audio and video, which streamed live footage on the web. When people interacted with the image on the web, the fish would start to 'sing' live in the gallery in Tokyo where it was suspended.

Interactive cinema using original as opposed to appropriated imagery is immensely complex and costly. Among its principal practitioners are American artists Toni Dove and Grahame Weinbren. With the films of both these artists stories proceed only with the participation of viewers. In Dove's *Sally or the Bubble Burst* (2002), viewer/participants meet Spectropia, the subject of an earlier installation. The year is 2099 and no historical records exist; they have been disallowed. Spectropia enters a three-dimensional world in which she can access former times. Here she finds herself in the Depression years of the 1930s. Viewers can now interact with a character of the time, dancer Sally Reed, whose famous 'bubble dance' can be re-choreographed by viewers.

In his 1995 essay, 'Another Dip into the Ocean of Streams of Story,' Weinbren, also a writer and theorist, said, 'We compress, excerpt, exclude, and reorganize when we tell stories about ourselves. If the interactive cinema is a more faithful rendering of reality, it is precisely because it can bypass...criteria of narrative structure.' In works such as *The Erl King* (1983–85), *Sonata* (1991/93), *Frames* (1999), and *Tunnel* (2000), Weinbren and his collaborators presented installations in which the movements of viewers triggered pre-filmed footage that comprised a moving-image collage.

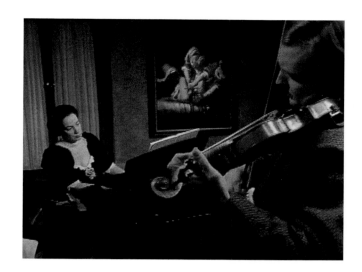

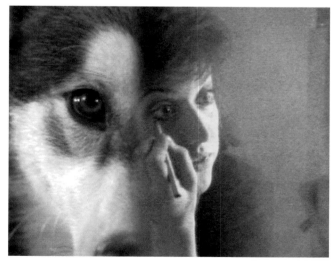

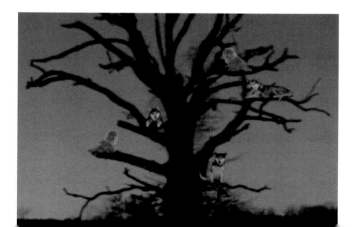

57–59. Grahame Weinbren, three stills from *Sonata*, 1991/93. By pointing at the screen at any time the viewer is able to reconstruct the narrative of Sonata and see alternate views of the same situation. For Weinbren, this is a new form of cinema, an interactive cinema that involves 'a moment-by-moment collaboration between the viewer and filmmaker.'

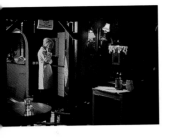

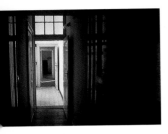

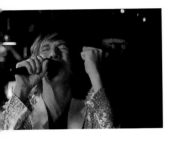

Weinbren is important not only because he is incisive about the non-linear reality of everyday life (a notion honored by the avant-garde at least since Bergson) but because he can articulate this idea with his superior gifts as a cinematographer. Weinbren's work is worthy because he wields a camera so well. This is important to emphasize because interactivity is only a device based on filmed images, directions, programs, diagrams, etc. Though traceable through apparatuses from handheld video in the late 1960s and 1970s to the digital technology of today, artistic advancement depends on the talent and craft of individual artists.

*Sonata* (1991–93), a labyrinthine experiment, enables the viewer, by touching infra-red sensors on the monitor, to explore layers of filmed images that interweave characters from a Tolstoy short story ('The Kreutzer Sonata'), a psychological case study by Freud ('Wolf Man') and the biblical story of Judith and Holofernes as depicted in paintings from the fifteenth century to the present. The viewer can loop back to any of the other stories as one is being played out and create a narrative. Seated in an open steel cube with a single monitor and a large steel container holding the machinery, the viewer, in Weinbren's words, participates 'in a moment-by-moment collaboration with the filmmaker...which enables a portrayal of the same events from different points of view.'

While interactive cinema may seem to presage a new experience of 'movie-going' (for both art aficionados as well as regular filmgoers), it is a practice that references, indeed is based on and comprised

260–62. (above) **Janet Cardiff** and **George Bures Miller**, *The Berlin Files*, 2003. Janet Cardiff and George Bures Miller are video and sound artists whose works, like Bruce Nauman's and Michael Snow's before them, challenge common audiovisual perceptions. Intense attention to sound makes the viewer feel immersed in their installations. *Berlin Files* is a non-linear montage of videotaped scenes presented with surround sound that suggests mystery and fear.

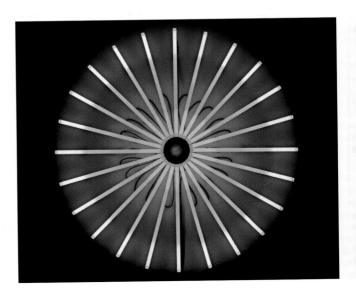

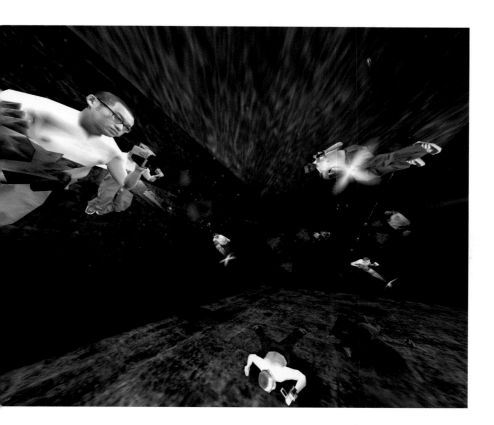

of, cinema. But what about camera-less, screenless image experiences such as the computer-generated virtual realities in Mark Napier's *The Waiting Room* (2002), or the synthesized images from human brains (BIOS team's *Bidirectional Input/Output System*, 2002), to name a few, neither of which involves a moving or still camera. Virtual reality isn't cinema. It may at this point depend on photography for content, but, in essence, it inaugurates another level of human perception that has far-reaching consequences for art and life.

### Virtual Reality

In Virtual Reality (VR), the still passive aspect of watching a screen is replaced by total immersion into a world whose reality exists contemporaneously with one's own. In a sense, everything one sees on a computer is part of the 'virtual' universe. Images and texts only exist in a wired world that appears and disappears with electronic switches. The term 'Virtual Reality' refers to a three-dimensional experience in which a 'user', with the help of head-mounted displays, data gloves, or body suits (containing fiber-optic cabling), experiences a simulated world that appears to respond to the user's movements.

Australian-born Jeffrey Shaw, of the Center for Art and Media in Karlsruhe, Germany, hints at what a Virtual Reality system might be like using a computer graphic 3D animation system, in his interactive installation *The Legible City* (ongoing since 1990). A bicycle is placed in the midst of three large projection screens, and, as the viewer pedals, he or she takes a ride through a virtual recreation of Manhattan, Amsterdam, or Karlsruhe. Streets, corners, signs, buildings, words, all large and multidimensional, appear and dissolve with the rapidity of the pedal movements. *The Legible City* is only a teaser for what is to come in Virtual Reality. Currently, the experience is based on pre-recorded video images powered by very strong computers, but in the future, virtual interactions will take place in real time as people, raised with a familiarity with 'virtual' space, engage their Virtual Reality 'tools' with the ease with which we now turn on our television sets or use our telephones.

While the most striking breakthroughs in VR are currently taking place in medical technology (virtual surgery in which an off-site physician is 'conducting' the procedure), VR is only slowly infiltrating art, largely due to the hefty costs involved. Keep in mind, however, that virtual realities are increasing exponentially everyday on the internet. As more and more people invent new and increasingly fantastical alternative personalities online (in chat rooms, for example), the 'virtual' is actually blending with the so-called real.

Dan Sandin, co-director with Tom DeFanti of the Electronic Visualization Laboratory at the University of Illinois at Chicago, has been developing video-computer tools since the early 1970s (his Analogue Image Processor was a well-known example). It is at the university that Sandin, DeFanti, and Carolina Cruz-Neira began creating *The Cave* in the late 1980s. A cubic room, three meters square, *The Cave*, first exhibited in 1992, is a virtual environment, consisting of stereographic computer graphics which react interactively to the actions of the 'user,' who is equipped with stereo glasses which make it possible to see the other 'playmates' (Sandin's word) in *The Cave*. Stereo projection of thirty images per second in real time are thrown on all the walls of the space as the user manipulates a 'wand' (a type of 3D mouse) programmed to jump-start the images. This total immersion makes the user feel as if in a newly created space and time. In *The Cave* all perspectives are calculated from the point of view of the user, mediated through the stereo glasses. Sandin's project has spawned a research network called CAVERN which supports collaboration in design and training in VR.

Maurice Benayoun's *So.So.So. Somebody, Somewhere, Sometime* (2002), is an immersive installation in which users with VR binoculars enter an environment of panoramic spheres that display images of people engaging in a variety of activities at a particular time (7:47 a.m.). As users focus on one element (a person, an object) different scenarios unfold, with the user, in a sense, creating a new reality based on the pre-existing one.

'Reflecting interests in 'the body,' so prevalent in the art of the last fifty years, Diane Gromola, a former art director at Apple Computer, created *Dancing with the Virtual Dervish: Virtual Bodies*, a VR environment she began developing in the early 1990s. Working with a choreographer and a computer scientist, Gromola constructed the environment from computer-based visualizations of her own body which she manipulated and animated to represent symbolically continual decay and reformation. As she describes it,

*the virtual body is overwritten with texts, meditations on pain, Eros and Thanatos. Each organ contains another surreal, virtual world. Wearing a head-mounted stereoscopic video display, users feel immersed within the body and interact with it. Such interactions include 'touching' the text, which then changes, or 'flying' into an organ – say, a heart – to find another surreal world. Three dimensional sound helps users locate themselves in surreal virtual spaces.*

265. **Diane Gromala**, *Dancing with the Virtual Dervish: Virtual Bodies*, 1996.
In this experiment in Virtual Reality, users feel as if they are entering actual human organs, like the heart or the stomach. Architect and cultural critic Paul Virilio warns: 'The day when virtual reality becomes more powerful than reality will be the day of the big accident. Mankind never experienced such an extraordinary accident.'

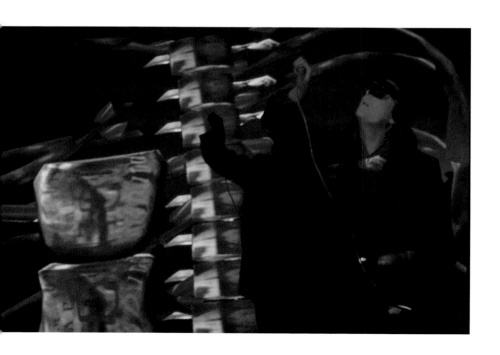

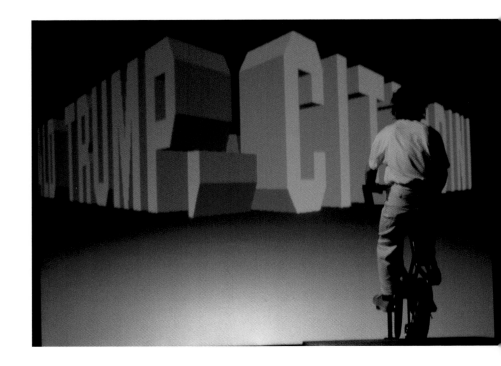

266. **Jeffrey Shaw**,
*The Legible City*, 1989–91.
In this interactive work,
the visitor is able to ride a
stationary bicycle through
a simulated representation
of a city that is constituted
by computer-generated
three-dimensional letters
forming words and sentences
along the sides of the streets.

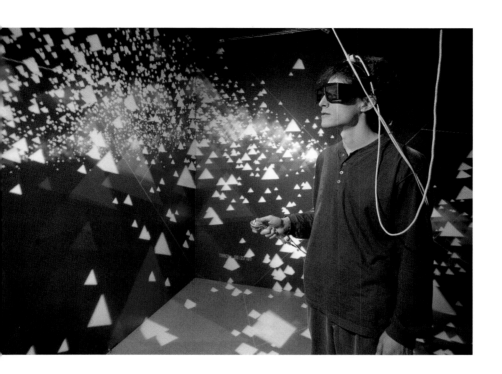

267. **Dan Sandin**, *The Cave*
'Virtual Reality Theater'
Prototyped: Electronic
Visualization Laboratory,
University of Illinois,
Chicago, 1991; publicly
showcased: SIGGRAPH 92,
Chicago, 1992).
Virtual Reality, accessed
through dark stereo glasses,
allows users to feel as if they
were in a totally different
universe. For Paul Virilio,
'We are entering a world
where there won't be one
but two realities: the actual
and the virtual.'

Since most VR environments are being created in universities and other research centers, they tend to have an educational or applied flavor. As the equipment becomes more accessible to artists, the content might be shaped more toward artistic ends.

Many more examples of digital art (in sound and music particularly, but also 3D sculpture produced on copying machines) could be mentioned. Regardless of when or whether traditional art venues like museums or galleries accept the intangible presence of interactive digital art, an irrefutable change has occurred in the experiencing of art (to say nothing of its creation). Interactivity is a new form of visual experience. In fact, it is a new form of experiencing art that extends beyond the visual to the tactile. Viewers are essential, active participants in this art. No longer mere viewers, they are now users. We have come a long way from the passive viewing of the *Mona Lisa*, for example, which hangs behind a bulletproof shield and can be seen only from a distance. As more and more artists of quality turn to the digital world (and they will, for who can resist having their work seen by millions of people with the click of a mouse without waiting for the 'approval' of the gallery and museum system?) a reconfiguring of the meaning of art, of aesthetics, of artists' relationships to dealers and institutions, indeed, of artists' relationships with any kind of market, will occur. We end here with digital art and Virtual Reality because they are the newest, and to that extent, most foreign manifestations of art in our present world. It is probable that these technologies as used in art will prove to be as ephemeral as the *camera obscura* or the stereoscopes of the nineteenth century. The digital future defies our current abilities to describe it. And so we ask what lies beyond the digital, beyond the virtual? What will we call 'new media' at the end of the twenty-first century?

In his 2002 essay, *The Time Will Come When...*, Australian media-curator and theorist Ross Gibson suggests that artists of the future 'won't be fabricating objects so much as experiences – they will offer us intensely "moving" immersion in (or perhaps beyond) the objective world...People will partake of this new art in order to *be* differently in themselves.' One supposes entertainment will take this shape as well, offering alternative reality experiences to replace the thriller rides and IMAX movies of today. Art will need to do something else. It will need to do what it has always done: invite us to transcend, transform and change the way we inhabit the world.

We began this overview of new media by a brief glance back to the fertile experiments on the canvas by Braque and Picasso; the photographic innovations of Marey and Muybridge; and the radical conceptual gestures of Marcel Duchamp. Two of Duchamp's friends, Gianfranco Baruchello and Henry Martin, wrote after his death,

*Filling things with an atmosphere absolutely overcharged with meaning is what he was always up to doing, and that, after all, is what modern art is all about. You take just about anything at all and fill it with all the meaning you can give it, all the entirely personal and entirely arbitrary meanings it can possibly hold, all the mystery, all the enigma it can hold. That's one of the most fundamental lessons Duchamp had to teach us.*

For some this has meant the death of art; for others, it has heralded vast beginnings.

With advancements in art and technology beginning more than fifty years ago, the Duchampian revolution, pervasive in all forms of contemporary art, achieves some historical closure. The advent of digital art, an art so beyond materiality that discussions of the 'object,' much less the canvas, seem hopelessly dated, inaugurates a new era in which traditional art-historical terms, even Duchampian ones, and methods of evaluation no longer apply. Spaceless, timeless, imageless experiences have entered the domain of art. Interactivity and immersive artistic environments, let alone whatever lies beyond such virtual realities, are dictating a new discourse.

In *About Looking* (1980), John Berger asked, 'What served in place of the photograph, before the camera's invention? The expected answer is the engraving, the drawing, the painting. The more revealing answer might be: memory. What photographs do out there in space was previously done with reflection.' What, we might now ask, will be the content of memory if we can no longer distinguish simulated events and experiences from 'real' ones? Life as we have known it, including the memories that our lives have formed, will be forever changed as the 'virtual' and the 'real' become increasingly indistinguishable. Perhaps memories and dreams will become one.

# Select Bibliography

## Introduction

Abel, Manuela (ed.), *Jeffrey Shaw: A User's Manual* (Karlsruhe 1997)

Bergson, Henri, *Matter and Memory*, N. M. Paul and W. S. Palmer, translators (New York 1988)

Braun, Marta, *Picturing Time* (Chicago 1992)

Danto, Arthur, *After the End of Art* (Princeton 1997)

Hulten, Pontus *Marcel Duchamp* (Milan 1993)

James, David, *Allegories of Cinema* (Princeton 1989)

Jenkins, Janet (ed.), *In the Spirit of Fluxus* (Minneapolis, Walker Art Center 1993)

Kaufman, Stanley, *Living Images* (New York 1973)

Kilchesty, Albert, *Big As Life: An American History of 8mm Films* (San Francisco 1998)

Lovejoy, Margaret, *Art and Artists in the Age of Electronic Media* (Ann Arbor 1989)

Parkinson, David, *History of Film* (London 1995)

Sitney, P. Adams, *Visionary Film: The American Avant-Garde 1943–1978* (New York 1974)

Youngblood, Gene, *Expanded Cinema* (New York 1970)

## Chapter 1: Media and Performance

*Avalanche* magazine, Winter 1971, Winter 1972

Birringer, Johannes, *Media and Performance: Along the Border* (Baltimore 1998)

Debord, Guy, 'The Society of the Spectacle', 1967

Fogle, Douglas, *The Last Picture Show: Artists Using Photography 1960–1982* (Minneapolis, Walker Art Center 2003)

Goldberg, Roselee, *Performance Art* (London 1988)

Goldstein, Ann (ed.), *A Minimal Future? Art as Object 1958–1968* (Los Angeles 2004)

Hershman-Neeson, Lynn, *Clicking In: Hot Links To a Digital Culture* (Washington 1966)

Hopps, Walter and Susan Davidson, *Robert Rauschenberg: A Retrospective* (New York, Guggenheim Museum 1997)

Jameson, Fredric, *Postmodernism in Consumer Society*, in Hal Foster (ed.), *The Anti-Aesthetic* (Washington 1983)

Kirby, Michael, *The Art of Time* (New York 1969)

McLuhan, Marshall, *The Medium Is the Message: An Inventory of Effects* (New York 1967)

Rush, Michael, *Still Moving: Video Art in the Scholl Collection* (Baltimore 2003)

Schimmel, Paul, *Out of Actions: Between Performance and the Object 1949–1979* (Los Angeles 1998)

Simon, Joan (ed.), *Bruce Nauman* (Minneapolis 1994)

Simon, Joan, interview with Joan Jonas, *Art In America*, July 1995

## Chapter 2: Video Art

Goldstein, Ann and Anne Rorimer, *Reconsidering the Object of Art* (Los Angeles 1995)

Hill, Christine, *Surveying the First Decade: Video Art and Alternative Media in the United States*, exhibition notes, San Francisco Museum of Modern Art, October 23–November 23 1997

Hall, Doug and Sally Jo Fifer (eds), *Illuminating Video* (New York 1990)

Iles, Chrissie, *Into the Light: The Projected Image in Amnerican Art 1964–1977* (New York, Whitney Museum of American Art 2001)

Popper, Frank, *Art of the Electronic Age* (London 1993)

Renov, Michael and Erika Suderburg (eds), *Resolutions: Contemporary Video Practices* (Minneapolis 1996)

Sichel, Berta, *Monocanal* (Madrid, Museo Nacional Centro de Arte Reina Sofía 2002)

Third Biennale de Lyon, 1995 (CD-ROM)

Van Assche, Christine (ed.), *Vidéo et après* (Paris, Centre Georges Pompidou 1992)

Zippay, Lori (ed.), *Electronic Arts Intermix: Video* (New York 1991)

## Chapter 3: Video Installation Art

*Art Journal*, vol. 4, no. 54, Winter 1995

de Oliveira, Nicolas, Nicola Oxley, Michael Petry, *Installation Art* (London 1994)

Herzogenrath, Wulf, *Nam Jun Paik: Video Work 1963–88* (London 1988)

Levin, Thomas, Ursula Frohne and Peter Weibel (eds), *CTRL SPACE: Rhetorics of Surveillance from Bentham to Big Brother* (Karlsruhe, Center for Art and Media 2001)

O'Doherty, Brian, *Inside the White Cube: The Ideology of the Gallery Space* (Santa Monica and San Francisco 1976, 198)

Quasha, George and Charles Stein, 'Liminal Performance', *PAJ*, no. 58, January, 1998

Rush, Michael, *Video Art* (London 2003)

Whitney Museum, *Bill Viola* (New York 1997)

## Chapter 4: The Digital in Art

Baruchello, Gianfranco and Henry Martin, *Why Duchamp* (New York 1985)

Berger, John, *About Looking* (New York 1980)

Coleman, A. D., *The Digital Evolution* (New York 1988)

Druckrey, Timothy (ed.), *Electronic Culture* (New York 1996)

Druckrey, Timothy (ed.), *Iterations: The New Image* (Massachusetts 1993)

Fifield, George, 'The Digital Atelier', *Art New England*, October/November 1997

Goodman, Cynthia, *Digital Visions: Computers and Art*, 1987

Greene, Rachel, *Internet Art* (London 2004)

Hayward, Philip (ed.), *Culture, Technology, and Creativity in the Late Twentieth Century* (London 1990)

*Leonardo*, vol. 31, issue 5, October 1998

Negroponte, Nicholas, *Being Digital* (New York 1995)

Noll, A. Michael, 'The Beginnings of Computer Art in the United States: A Memoir', *Leonardo*, September 199

Paul, Christiane, *Digital Art* (London 2003)

Shaw, Jeffrey and Peter Weibel, *Future Cinema: The Cinematic Imaginary After Film* (Karlsruhe, Center for Art and Media 2003)

Sommerer, Christa and Laurent Mignonneau, *Art @ Science* (New York 1998)

# List of Illustrations

**56** Performance at the Brooklyn Academy of Music, New York. Photo © Edward Grazda 1999
**57** December, 1977, PS1, Long Island City, New York. Courtesy of the artist
**58** Animation: Kleiser-Walczak. Courtesy IPA. BAM Press, New York
**59** Photo: courtesy of the artist
**60** 23:50 mins, black and white and colour. Courtesy of Electronic Arts Intermix, New York
**61, 62** 13:38 mins, colour, sound. Courtesy of Electronic Arts Intermix, New York
**63** 23:55 mins, colour, sound. Courtesy of Electronic Arts Intermix, New York
**64, 65** 13:38 mins, colour, sound. Courtesy of Electronic Arts Intermix, New York
**66–68** Photo © Paula Court
**69** Next Wave. Courtesy BAM, New York
**70** Photo: Dan Rest. Courtesy BAM, New York
**71** Photo: Stephanie Berger © 1999, copyright belongs to Stephanie Berger. All rights reserved
**72** Performance as part of 1992 Next Wave Fest. Photo: Alastair Muir. Courtesy BAM, New York
**73** Photo © Gilles Abegg
**74** Barbara Chan, Dawn Saito. Performance at La Mama, NYC. Projections Jan Hartley. Photo: Brendan Bannon. Courtesy Ping Chong Productions, NYC
**75** Video still, single-channel video. Production/ performance by Kristin Lucas. Photo: courtesy of the artist. © the artist, 1997
**76** Photo courtesy of John Arnone
**77** Photo: Silvia Taccani
**78** Photo: Joan Marcus
**79** Digital C-Print photographs, museum board, foam core and polystyrene, 182.9 × 101.6 × 101.6 (72 × 40 × 40) with vitrine. Courtesy Max Protetch Gallery
**80** Still. © The artists 2004
**81** Courtesy of the Advertising Archives, London
**82** 1 in. reel-to-reel videotape, black and white with sound, 60 mins. © 2005 The Andy Warhol Museum, Pittsburgh, PA, a museum of the Carnegie Institute. All Rights Reserved. © The Andy Warhol Foundation for the Visual Arts, Inc./ ARS, NY and DACS, London 2005
**83** 1 in. reel-to-reel videotape, black and white with sound, 30 mins. © 2005 The Andy Warhol Museum, Pittsburgh, PA, a museum of the Carnegie Institute. All Rights Reserved. © The Andy Warhol Foundation for the Visual Arts, Inc./ ARS, NY and DACS, London 2005

**84** 61:28 mins, black and white with sound. Courtesy of Electronic Arts Intermix, New York
**85** Ink and tomato on paper, 404 × 36 (159 × 14³⁄₁₆). Museum Wiesbaden, Germany. Courtesy of Museum Wiesbaden, Germany and the artist
**86** Photo: Maytick, Cologne, Germany and the artist
**87** Photo: George Maciunas. Courtesy of George Maciunas/The Gilbert and Lila Silverman Fluxus Collection, Detroit and the artist
**88** Museum of Modern Art Ludwig Foundation, Vienna (formerly Collection Hahn). Courtesy of the Museum of Modern Art Ludwig Foundation, Vienna and the artist
**89** TV sets behind canvas in a wooden box, 200 × 300 × 50 (79 × 118 × 20). © DACS 2005. Photo: J. F. Melzian, Berlin. Courtesy Fine Art Rafael Vostell, Berlin
**90** Courtesy of Electronic Arts Intermix, New York. © Douglas Davis/ DACS, London/VAGA, New York 2005
**91–93** Courtesy of Electronic Arts Intermix, New York. © Douglas Davis/DACS, London/VAGA, New York 2005
**94** Video still, 26:49 mins, colour and sound. Courtesy of Electronic Arts Intermix, New York
**95** Video still, 11:55 mins, colour with sound. Courtesy of Electronic Arts Intermix, New York
**96** Video still, 25 mins, colour with sound. © ARS, New York and DACS, London 2005
**97** Video still, 27:37 mins, colour with sound. Courtesy of Electronic Arts Intermix, New York
**98, 99** Photo courtesy of Bengt Modin
**100** Video still, 18:40 mins, black and white with sound. Courtesy of Electronic Arts Intermix, New York
**101** Video still, 2:03 mins, colour with sound. Courtesy of Electronic Arts Intermix, New York and the artist
**102–104** Video still, 10:17 mins, colour. Courtesy of Electronic Arts Intermix, New York
**105** Video still, 33:15 mins, black and white with sound. Courtesy of Electronic Arts Intermix, New York
**106** Courtesy Pat Hearn Gallery, New York. Copyright © 1976, Babette Mangolte, all rights of reproduction reserved
**107** Performance at Musée Galleria, Paris. Beatrice Helligers. Courtesy Pat Hearn Gallery, New York
**108** Video still, 2:39 mins. Courtesy Pat Hearn Gallery, New York

**109** Courtesy Ronald Feldman Fine Arts, New York. Copyright the Estate of Hannah Wilke
**110** Video still, colour, stereo, 5:50. Courtesy of the artist and Electronic Arts Intermix, New York. © 1978/79
**111, 112** Video stills. Courtesy of Electronic Arts Intermix, New York
**113** Video still. 23:42 mins, black and white with sound. Courtesy of Electronic Arts Intermix, New York
**114–16** Videotape, 60 mins, black and white with sound. © ARS, New York and DACS, London 2005. Photo courtesy of Video Data Bank, Chicago
**117** © ARS, New York and DACS, London 2005. Photo courtesy of Video Data Bank, Chicago
**118** Video still, 18:35 mins, black and white and colour with sound. Courtesy of Electronic Arts Intermix, New York
**119** Video still, 27 mins, black and white with sound. Courtesy of Electronic Arts Intermix, New York. © ARS, New York and DACS, London 2005
**120** Video still, 3:39 mins. Courtesy of Electronic Arts Intermix, New York
**121, 122** Video still, 28:43 mins, colour with sound. Courtesy of Electronic Arts Intermix, New York
**123** Video still, 12:45 mins, colour with sound. Courtesy of Electronic Arts Intermix, New York
**124** Colour music device. From the archives of Institute Promotei, Kazan, Tatarstan, Russia
**125–27** © DACS 2005
**128** Video still, 89 mins, colour with sound. Courtesy of Electronic Arts Intermix, New York
**129** Video still, 2:49 mins, colour with sound. Courtesy of Electronic Arts Intermix, New York
**130** Video still. Photo courtesy of Video Data Bank, Chicago
**131** Video still, 11 mins, black and white and colour with sound. Courtesy of Electronic ArtsIntermix, New York
**132** Courtesy of the artist
**133** Courtesy Maureen Paley/Interim Art, London
**134–36** DVD, 9 mins. Courtesy of the artist
**137** Silent double DVD projection onto single translucent screen, dimensions variable. Courtesy Gagosian Gallery, London and New York
**138** Video. Courtesy Mariko Mori and Deitch Projects
**139** Installation view. Continental US – c. 765 × 1632 × 204 (180 × 384 × 48). Alaska – c. 255 × 471.3 × 85 (60 × 84 × 20). Hawaii – c. 306 × 306 × 63.8 (72 × 72 × 15). Courtesy the artist and Holly Solomon Gallery, New York

**40** Part of Nam June Paik's 'video catalogue' produced for the national touring exhibition *The Electronic Superhighway: Nam June Paik in the 90s*, which premiered at The Museum of Art in Fort Lauderdale, Florida in 1994. Courtesy the artist and Electronic Arts Intermix, New York
**41** Video still, 42 mins. Courtesy of Electronic Arts Intermix, New York
**42** Video installation, TV with stained er plywood. Courtesy of Frederieke Taylor/TZ'Art, New York
**43** Wallboard and wood, 243.8 × 609.6 × 50.8 (96 × 240 × 20). Solomon R. Guggenheim Museum, New York. Panza Collection, Gift, 1992. © The Solomon R. Guggenheim Museum, New York (FN 92.4162). © ARS, New York and DACS, London 2005
**44** Videotape, 60 mins, black and white with sound. © ARS, New York and DACS, London 2005
**45** Video Installation. Photo: Kay Hines. Courtesy of the artist
**46** Photo courtesy of the artist
**47–49** Two channel video installation. Courtesy of the artist
**50** Mixed media video installation, dimensions variable. Courtesy Andrea Rosen Gallery, New York. © Julia Scher
**51** Mixed media surveillance installation, dimensions variable. Courtesy Andrea Rosen Gallery, New York. © Julia Scher
**52** Video still. Courtesy of Electronic Arts Intermix, New York
**53** Multi-channel installation. Videotape, 44:35 mins, black and white. Courtesy of Electronic Arts Intermix, New York
**54** Multi-channel video installation: photo panel (3 sections), gelatin silver print. Variable dimensions. San Francisco Museum of Modern Art. Accessions Committee Fund: gift of Collectors Forum, Doris and Donald G. Fisher, Evelyn and Walter Haas, Jr., Byron R. Meyer, and Norman and Norah Stone. © 1982–93. Photo: Ben Blackwell 1993. Courtesy of the artist
**55** 25 channel video wall, colour, silent, two live closed-circuit cameras, SEG with pre-set luma key, satellite receiver, custom designed light wall. Encasement: steel and black spandrel glass. 732 × 610 × 112 (288 × 240 × 44). Photo: Dara Birnbaum © 1989. Courtesy of the artist and Rena Bransten Gallery, San Francisco
**56** Video installation, Venice Biennale, 1997. Courtesy of the artist
**57, 58** Mixed media installation with video projection, computer detritus, small motors, sound. Photo courtesy of Judith Barry

**159** Video installation. Courtesy of the artist and Matt's Gallery, London
**160** Single screen video installation with sound. Dimensions variable. The British School at Rome. Photo: Mimmo Capone. Courtesy of the artist and Matt's Gallery, London
**161** © ADAGP, Paris and DACS, London 2005. Photo: Laurent Lecat. Courtesy Jack Tilton Gallery, New York
**162** Video installation. Photo: Javier Campano. Courtesy of Museo Nacional Centro de Arte Reina Sofía. © DACS 2005
**163** Four 1 in. master videotapes, four colour-corrected D2 masters, 28 laserdiscs, 1 in. master videotape (for the single-monitor installation – French and English language versions), Magno 'draw' disc, 16 mm film internegative, two 1 in. master videotapes (for the single monitor installation – German and Spanish language versions). Collection Walker Art Center, Minneapolis. Justin Smith Purchase Fund, 1995. Courtesy Sean Kelly Gallery, New York. Copyright Chantal Ackerman & Lieurac Productions, 1998
**164–66** Video stills. Venice Biennale, Venice, Italy 1997. Courtesy Sean Kelly Gallery, New York. © DACS 2005
**167** Video projection (2 screens), dimensions variable. Courtesy Lisson Gallery, London
**168** © Canal Street Communications, New York
**169** Video 18:28 mins, colour with sound. Courtesy of Electronic Arts Intermix, New York
**170, 171** Installation for the 1997 Venice Biennale, 16 mins, colour with sound. Courtesy of Electronic Arts Intermix, New York
**172** Video/sound installation. Edition 1, Collection of the Bohen Foundation, promised gift in honour of Richard E. Oldenburg to the Museum of Modern Art, New York. Edition 2, Museum for Contemporary Art, Zentrum für Kunst und Medientechnologie, Karlsruhe. Photo: Charles Duprat. Courtesy of the artist
**173, 174** Video/sound installation. Edition 1: The Chaplaincy to the Arts and Recreation in North East England. Edition 2: Collection of the Bohen Foundation, promised gift to the Solomon R. Guggenheim Museum, New York. Edition 3: Albright-Knox Art Gallery, Buffalo, New York. Photo: Kira Perov. Courtesy of the artist
**175** Video/sound installation. Edition 1: The Bohen Foundation, promised gift to the Solomon R. Guggenheim Museum,

New York. Edition 2: Pamela and Richard Kramlich, San Francisco. Edition 3: Dallas Museum of Art, Texas. Photo: Kira Perov. Courtesy of the artist
**176** Video/sound installation. Museum für Moderne Kunst, Frankfurt-am-Main, Germany. Photo: Kira Perov. Courtesy of the artist
**177** Courtesy of the artist and Donald Young Gallery, Seattle
**178** Installation view, Lennon Weinberg Gallery, New York, March– April 1995. Courtesy of Lennon, Weinberg Gallery, New York. Photo: David Allison
**179** Video installation: two videotapes, colour, sound, 18:30 mins; seven monitors, varying from 12–21 inches; synchronous starter. Whitney Museum of American Art, New York. Purchased with funds from the Louis and Bessie Adler Foundation, Inc., Seymour M. Klein, President, and Mrs Rudolph B. Schulhof. Courtesy of Electronic Arts Intermix, New York
**180** Installation view of the exhibition *Dislocations*. The Museum of Modern Art, New York. October 16, 1991 through January 7, 1992. Photograph © 1998 The Museum of Modern Art, New York
**181** Prosthetic plastic clipboard and clamps, latex foam, cibachrome prints. 71.1 × 26.7 × 6.4 (28 × 10½ × 2½). Photo: Larry Lame. Courtesy Barbara Gladstone Gallery, New York
**182** © 1997 Matthew Barney. Photo: Michael James O'Brien. Courtesy Barbara Gladstone, Gallery, New York
**183** Computer controlled, five channel laserdisc and sound installation. Co-produced with Canon ARTLAB, Tokyo. © Canon ARTLAB
**184** Ceramic, glass, video player, videocassette, CPJ-200 video projector, sound. *c.* 27.9 × 17.8 × 20.3 (11 × 7 × 8) each. Courtesy the artist and Metro Pictures, New York
**185** Installation view: Patrick Painter Inc., Santa Monica, CA. Photo: Fredrik Nilsen. Courtesy of the artists and Patrick Painter Inc., Santa Monica
**186** Installation view: Documenta X, Kassel, Germany. Photo: Werner Maschmann. Courtesy of the artists and Patrick Painter Inc., Santa Monica
**187** Video installation with cylindrical wooden structure, video projector, amplifier, four speakers. 350 × 300 × 300 (138 × 118 × 118). Courtesy of the artist. Photo: Philippe Migeat
**188** Video and 10 pieces of clothing in suitcase. 12 minute video on 90 minute loop. Edition of 2. Installation View. Photo: David Regen. Courtesy Barbara Gladstone Gallery, New York. © DACS 2005

189 Mixed media video installation (top view, detail). Video projection on miniature ceramic tub, tiled pedestal, metal supports, audio. Sculpture dimensions 35.6 × 50.8 × 66 (14 × 20 × 26). Photo: Erma Estwick. Courtesy of Anna Kustera Gallery, New York, New York. © Amy Jenkins 1996
190, 191 Video installation. Photo: Smith/ Stewart
192, 193 Courtesy of the artist and Luhring Augustine, New York
194 16 mm film/video transfer (still). © the artist. Courtesy Anthony Reynolds Gallery, London and Marian Goodman Gallery, Paris/New York
195 Laserdisk video loop projection. Laserdisk player, AC-3 Amplifier, 5 speakers, 1 subwoofer, 156 × 366 (62 × 144) Pearlescent Dasnap screen, Barco projector 701 S HQ. Installation dimensions: 200 × 400 × 550 (79 × 158 × 217). Edition of 4. Exhibited: Venice Biennale, Canadian Pavilion, 15 June–4 November 1997. Courtesy Lisson Gallery, London
196 Courtesy of the artist and Fondazione Prada, Milan
197 Mixed media installation with video projection of digitally altered images. Courtesy of the artist
198 © 1987 Computer Creations Corporation. All rights reserved. Reprinted by permission
199 © ADAGP, Paris and DACS, London
200 Digitally constructed photograph, 156.2 × 135.3 (62 × 53). Courtesy Ronald Feldman Fine Arts, New York
201 Iris print from digital file/type C print from colour negative. Courtesy of the artist
202 Triptych of 3 digital prints, 213.4 × 91.5 (84 × 36) each. Total dimensions: 213.4 × 274.5 (84 × 108). Courtesy of the artist
203 Transparency in a light box. Image 229 × 377 (90 × 148). Tate Gallery, London. Courtesy of the artist
204 Transparency in aluminium light box, 222.8 × 278.7 × 26.3 (87¾ × 109¾ × 10⅜). Courtesy Marian Goodman Gallery, New York
205 C-Print, 175.5 × 205.5 (69⅛ × 80⅞). © Courtesy: Monika Sprueth Galerie, Köln/VG Bild-Kunst, Bonn and DACS, London 2005

206 Photograph, 189 × 450 (74⅜ × 177⅛). Courtesy Sonnabend Gallery, New York
207 Production still. Courtesy Gladstone Gallery, New York. Photo Larry Barns. © 2000 Shirin Neshat
208 Production still. Courtesy Gladstone Gallery, New York. Photo Larry Barns. © 1999 Shirin Neshat
209 Gelatin silver print, 111.8 × 173.4 (44 × 68¼). Courtesy Gladstone Gallery, New York. © 1999 Shirin Neshat
210 Courtesy the artist and Metro Pictures
211, 212 14 mins, DVD installation for 3 projections with sound. © Crystal Eye Ltd, Helsinki
213 Double projection, beta digital, video on monitor, 9 mins 46 seconds. Courtesy Marian Goodman Gallery, New York. Photo John Berens, New York
214 Installation with 8 laserdiscs. Courtesy 303 Gallery, New York; Galerie Eva Presenhuber, Zurich and Victoria Miro Gallery, London
215 Still of video projection. Courtesy the artist
216 Installation at Venice Biennale. Courtesy the artist
217 Still, digital C-Print, 61 × 91.4 (24 × 36). Courtesy Roebling Hall
218 Still, digital C-Print, 61 × 91.4 (24 × 36). Courtesy Roebling Hall
219 CD-Rom, projector and mounting arm, dimensions variable. Courtesy the artist and The Project, New York and Los Angeles
220 Computer Graphics. © A. Michael Noll 1965
221–24 AT&T. Reprinted by permission. Collection of the Museum of Modern Art, New York
225 Computer generated images. Courtesy of the European Media Art Festival Archives, Osnabruck
226 Charcoal on paper. Courtesy William Kentridge
227 © ADAGP, Paris and DACS, London. Photo courtesy of the artist
228 Computer graphics. Courtesy Galerie Emilia Suciu, Ettlingen
229–31 © William Latham
232 Outdoor laser sculpture. Photo: T Charles Erickson
233 Light installation at the closing ceremony of the XX Olympiad, Munich 9.11.72. Photo: Wolf Huber. Courtesy of the artist

234 © ADAGP, Paris and DACS, London 2005
235 Computer generated image. Courtesy of the artist
236–39 Copyright Tony Oursler, Constance DeJong, and Stephen Vitiell Courtesy Dia Center for the Arts (www.diacenter.org)
240–43 Copyright Cheryl Donegan. Courtesy Dia Center for the Arts (www.diacenter.org)
244 Digital illustration. Courtesy ®Tmark/Creative Commons
245 Courtesy of the artist
246 Courtesy of the artist
247 Website with Flash video
248 Motorized optical device: five painted glass plates (braced with wood and metal) turning on a metal axle; largest blade, set vertically 166.3 (64) high; at base 120.6 × 184.1 (48 × 73); glass plate 99 × 14 (39 × 6). Yale University Art Gallery, New Haven, Connecticut. Gift of the Société Anonyme. © ADAGP, Paris and DACS, London 2005
249–51 Photos by Will Newell
252 Interactive installation with computer programming in collaboration with Sara Roberts. Courtesy of the artist
253, 254 Interactive sculpture: Videodisks, computers, aluminium, wood, plastic, circuitry. © Ken Feingold 1993
255 © 1997 Karl Sims
256 © 1993 Karl Sims
257–59 Installation construction designed by Laura Kurgan with James Cathcart. Actors in the slides are Ken Taylor and Nicole Farmer with musicians Peter Winograd and Marian Hahn. Courtesy of the artist
260–62 Mixed media, dimensions variable. Courtesy of the artist and Luhring Augustine, New York
263 LED tubes, transformers, diameter 274.3 (108). Courtesy Sandra Gering Gallery, New York
264 Installation, PC, CRT display, 3D glasses, fish tank and water with live fish. Courtesy the artist
265 Gromala © 1996
266 Interactive computer/video installation. © Jeffrey Shaw
267 Image courtesy of the Electronic Visualization laboratory, University of Illinois at Chicago

# ndex